THE CRASH
OF THE
MILLENNIUM

THE CRASH
OF THE
MILLENNIUM

SURVIVING THE COMING
INFLATIONARY DEPRESSION

RAVI BATRA

Harmony Books
New York

This publication is designed to provide accurate and authoritative information in regard to the subject matter covered. It is published with the understanding that the publisher and author are not engaged in rendering legal accounting or other professional service. If legal advice or other professional advice, including financial, is required, the services of a competent professional person should be sought.—*From a Declaration of Principles, jointly adopted by a Committee of the American Bar Association and a Committee of Publishers*

Published by Harmony Books, 201 East 50th Street, New York, New York 10022. Member of the Crown Publishing Group.

Random House, Inc. New York, Toronto, London, Sydney, Auckland
www.randomhouse.com

HARMONY Books is a registered trademark and Harmony Books colophon is a trademark of Random House, Inc.

Printed in the United States of America

Library of Congress Cataloging-in-Publication Data
Batra, Raveendra N.
The crash of the millennium: surviving the coming inflationary depression / Ravi Batra. — 1st ed.
Includes index.
1. Investments—United States.   2. Finance, Personal—United States.
3. Business cycles—United States.   4. Economic forecasting—United States.   I. Title.
HG4910.B276   1999
338.5'42—dc21   99-29467

ISBN 0-609-60512-7

10   9   8   7   6   5   4   3   2   1

FIRST EDITION

To my wife and my pal, Sunita

Hang tough in adversity,
for tomorrow will surely
come a glorious age of
joy, peace, and prosperity.

CONTENTS

ACKNOWLEDGMENTS

In completing this project I gratefully acknowledge help from the group of seven—Peter Guzzardi (without whose assistance and initiative this work might still be in incubation), Indro Dasgupta, Thor Thorgeirsson, Bernie Ingasson, Dina Siciliano, Spencer Mcgowan, and, above all, my dear wife, Sunita.

RAVI BATRA
May 1, 1999

1

INTRODUCTION: A TORNADO
ON THE HORIZON

January is normally a placid month of the year in the southern part of the United States. The average temperature is just right, a balmy 64° F. City parks are filled at the weekend with revelers, screaming children, and their doting parents. But January 1999 turned out to be deadly, the single worst month on record for tornado disasters. The month was barely half over when more than a hundred twisters ripped across the quiet plains of Texas, Oklahoma, Louisiana, Tennessee, Florida, Georgia, Mississippi, and Alabama, killing scores of people, uprooting trees and power lines, and anything else that had the gall to be in the way. Business and property damage climbed into the billions.

Was nature's fury a premonition or just a passing wave? I believe there are much bigger tornadoes on the horizon, not of the weather but of financial mayhem. They are not the twisters of wind, water, and lightning but of share price crashes, inflation, and job losses. They are out there if anyone has the binoculars to see them, and they are fast headed our way. From my calculations, they will be here by the fall of 1999, at the latest by the millennium.

Ever since the early 1980s, stock prices, with temporary hitches, have been sizzling in the United States, building the biggest speculative bubble in history. Some people call it the market of the millennium; others compare it with eating your cake and having it too. Whatever you call it, the bubble is about to burst. Millions of

Americans, including some journalists and computer experts, are worried about the perils of the so-called millennium bug; I submit we have more to worry from the millennium bubble, whose explosion would be heard around the world, even where computers have yet to make a dent. The market of the millennium is about to slip into the crash of the millennium, possibly a few months before the Y2K bug gets a chance to contribute to the damage. Here is why.

Free enterprise functions smoothly only if the twin forces of demand and supply operate without constraints; this means that high competition prevails among firms so that wages rise in sync with productivity. Wages are the main source of demand, and labor productivity the main source of supply. If salaries lag behind productivity, as they have all over the planet due to the prominence of monopolies, the supply-demand balance can be maintained only through artificial means; eventually, artificial props give in, and demand falls short of supply, leading to production cutbacks, layoffs, and a recession. As wages trail productivity, profits and hence share markets jump. When the demand gap comes to the surface, stock prices drop, business and consumer confidence wanes, and a recession becomes inevitable.

At this point, nations may resort to deficit budgets, monetary expansion, or foreign loans, and the problem may be postponed without instituting fundamental reforms that free the supply side from the constraints of monopoly capitalism. Eventually, bigger trouble follows, because share markets go into a frenzy, only to plummet when the demand gap returns with a vengeance. If a country has borrowed freely from abroad, its currency crashes, and both inflation and layoffs follow.

The long-term cure lies in restoring the balance between supply and demand rather than in short-term palliatives that create debt, strengthen the supply side, and relatively weaken demand. One proper policy, for instance, is to encourage high competition among industries and discourage mergers between large and solvent companies. But the whole world has been doing just the opposite at least since 1990, and now an economic disaster of an inflationary depression is simply inevitable.

Is there a way out? Not in the short term. But if we follow plain sense and introduce fundamental economic reforms to build a truly free enterprise system, then the crisis could be limited to just three years. However, if we resort to the usual artifacts of creating more government debt, monetary expansion, or both, then I am afraid the coming calamity could outlast the new decade, and we still would have to change our course eventually. This is my worst nightmare and is the more likely of the two scenarios. In other words, we have to prepare for the worst, and I can offer you some simple and commonsense advice about protecting your assets in case the horror becomes a reality.

THEME OF THE BOOK

Thus the moral running through my work is plain and simple. When a country postpones its economic ills through massive borrowing from abroad, at first share markets and the economy roar, but then a bigger calamity of an inflationary depression follows.

I have written a number of books forecasting the future of the world economy and society; some forecasts have been optimistic, some pessimistic, although most associate me with Cassandra-like predictions. I am also the one suggesting that, following our manifold catastrophes, the world will witness its first golden age. For the 1980s, too, my predictions were overly optimistic to many, as I wrote that oil prices, inflation, and interest rates would sharply fall, even as share prices skyrocket, culminating in a great depression in 1990. Fortunately, the United States and the rest of the world only had a recession that year, but, unfortunately, they prevented a depression not through fundamental economic reforms but through mammoth inflows of foreign capital, especially from Japan.

That misguided policy is about to produce bleaker results. I have usually maintained that the coming depression would be deflationary or accompanied with price stability. However, now I believe that, for the first time in history, the U.S. depression will be inflationary, at least at the start. The reason is that under crony or monopoly capitalism that today reigns the world, including the United States, when a country postpones its ills through massive loans from other countries there is first a giant speculative bubble; then the bubble bursts, the currency collapses, and a lethal combination of inflation and depression erupts. The evidence for this hypothesis comes from recent crises enveloping the Asian Tigers, Mexico, Russia, and Latin

America. All these regions borrowed huge sums from abroad in the late eighties and the nineties to finance their prosperity and trade deficits. For a while they enjoyed lofty growth or a stock market binge or both, only to see their currencies plummet since July 1997, when the Thai baht collapsed.

The currency depreciation spawned share price crashes, high unemployment, as well as inflation. And the rare phenomenon of an inflationary depression followed. Thailand has seen its gross domestic product (GDP) fall by 10 percent, along with an equal rise in prices. This is a country that routinely used to grow at the rate of 8 percent per year. What happened to its paradise? Foreign debt devoured it. Conditions are no better in South Korea, the Philippines, and Malaysia, while Indonesia is the worst hit among the Tigers. Russia is in even worse shape than the troubled nations of Asia. Mexico, Brazil, Venezuela, and Argentina are beginning to limp again. What do all these countries have in common? They all have crony capitalism, suffered a slump in 1990, and kept the recession from turning into a depression by borrowing vast sums from abroad.

The United States is now in the same position. In fact, it is a giant version of Thailand. The United States also suffers from crony capitalism, albeit of a different variety, has borrowed generously from the rest of the world since 1990, and created false prosperity for Americans. Its share markets have already seen a crash, in August 1998, something, if I may be permitted to say so, I had predicted to the month in my 1997 work, *Stock Market Crashes of 1998 and 1999: The Asian Crisis and Your Future.*

Bigger crashes are about to come; then the dollar will collapse, culminating in an inflationary depression. From my calculations, this scenario will start unfolding toward the end of 1999 and then stretch into the next century. Unless fundamental economic reforms are introduced, inflation and unemployment could stay high for years to come.

PLAN OF THE BOOK

I have raised and answered a number of questions that puzzle an investor today. First, why has America so far escaped the financial meltdown afflicting many of its trading partners? Is the U.S. economy sound enough to withstand the trouble brewing in foreign lands? Second, what propels share markets; why do they zoom at times while stagnating at others? Third, should we be concerned about the mushrooming debt among U.S. consumers, corporations, and speculators? Fourth, what are the likely consequences of the millennium bug that daily captures headlines and is expected to strike computers globally in 2000? Fifth, how can we defend ourselves from the coming financial tornadoes? Finally, how do we fundamentally reform our economy so as to avoid or ease the travails plaguing nearly half the world today—the Tigers, Eastern Europe, Japan, India, and Latin America?

The book has a total of twelve chapters, in which you will discover the historical background behind the current and the potential crisis. The second chapter gets right into the nitty-gritty, highlighting the special significance of the year 1999 itself. It shows that ever since 1929, the last year of a decade has produced a nightmare somewhere on earth, with global and toxic consequences. The next chapter updates the cycle of inflation I explored in my 1985 publication, *The Great Depression of 1990,* because this cycle has been very helpful in the precision of my forecasting record, which is examined in chapter 4. There I list thirty-three predictions that I have made since 1978, starting with my first work on history, *The Downfall of Capitalism and Communism.* Although most of these forecasts were denounced as far-fetched, you will notice that two turned out to be *partially* or totally wrong. For example, communism, as I predicted, has vanished before your very eyes, but in 1990 there was only a global recession, not a depression. Yet some forces were unleashed that year to generate trends that have now brought us to the verge of economic devastation.

The next two chapters examine the role of supply and demand in any society and show how critical it is that wages keep up with productivity to generate a sound economy creating high-paying jobs for all. The economic ramifications of the millennial computer virus are explored in chapter 7. Following this, the focus of the work shifts to the causes and consequences of the millennial bubble. The future is discussed next. Then comes the critical chapter on self-defense against the coming catastrophe, followed by two chapters that outline necessary economic reforms.

Despite the current milieu of doom and gloom in Asia and the potential of a cataclysm in the United States, the future is very bright for us all, because cataclysms always seed new systems, and since every new system has excelled the old, the world is invariably heading toward its first golden age. In the past, glorious interludes have appeared in different nations at different times, but not in the entire world at the same time. Yet in the near future, following a short-lived economic turmoil, we will be the first generation to create a global golden age. Nothing great is born without strife, hardship, and sacrifice. Ours will be a struggle worthwhile, bestowing an enduring legacy of joy and prosperity to our children and grandchildren.

2

THE LAST YEAR OF A DECADE

Thre is a well-known, but terribly overused, Chinese maxim that best describes the state of the world today: May you live in interesting times. Some call it a curse, because interesting times may not be pleasant but are always harbingers of things to come. Often they represent a break from the past—good at times, bad at others. However, over the great span of human history, they have usually heralded a new age with the good outweighing the bad, culminating in an enhanced life for all.

Events unfolding on the planet since November 1989, when the Berlin Wall fell, would certainly place us among such times. One startling episode after another has kept us edgy and electrified during the nineties. Global events have become so absorbing and unpredictable that there are now three twenty-four-hour news channels, CNN, MSNBC, and Fox, and all are profitable, enjoying record viewer ratings. In fact, all through 1998 the world was riveted by a single episode, the Clinton-Lewinsky melodrama, which climaxed in the impeachment of the president of the United States. For the first time in the American chronicle, against all odds and expectations, the House of Representatives launched a process whereby a twice-elected president could be removed from office. Something similar had happened in 1868 when Andrew Johnson was impeached, but he had not been elected head of the republic. He had been the country's vice president in 1865 and became chief of state when Abraham Lincoln was assassinated. In 1974 Richard Nixon resigned rather than face the prospect of certain removal. So William Jefferson Clinton became the first popularly elected president to earn the dubious distinction of impeachment.

Major events usually occur once in a generation, great ones once in half a century, epochal ones once in a hundred years, and earth-shaking ones once over several centuries. Such is the dictum of history. But the 1990s belie this dictum. In just the first two years of this decade, the world was repeatedly astonished.

The decade began with the collapse of the once invincible Tokyo Stock Exchange, as the Nikkei index started to sink from the first trading day of 1990. Then came Kuwait's invasion by the Iraqi dictator Saddam Hussein, followed a year later by his humiliation in the unprecedented Gulf War in which great powers of the planet were largely united against a tiny force. In the same year, an aborted coup triggered the fall of Soviet communism and its empire. And let's not forget the unification of West and East Germany in October 1990, an event that partly ignited the Soviet coup by fanning communist anxieties. Each of these episodes was unprecedented at the time it occurred, and all except the Tokyo crash were sparked by the collapse of the Berlin Wall.

Why were so many events of such significance crammed into the first two years of the 1990s? This is the type of question we tackle in the pages to come. Ever since the 1920s, history has unfolded in such a way that the last year of each decade ends up generating at least one epochal event, setting the agenda for the next decade or several decades. Throughout recorded history, major events have been few and far between, but the twentieth century has already witnessed dozens of them. The busy calendar of the nineties may reflect the culmination of an eventful century as well as the millennium.

It may be that the earth has become a global village with several systems but one civilization, so when any system is torn apart, we all hear its direct or indirect echoes. In the past, for instance, the fall of the Roman empire, an epochal event, had little impact on India and China, but a similar episode today, such as the collapse of the Soviet empire, reverberated across the globe. The French Revolution of 1789 caused few ripples in Japan, but the German unification of 1990 had planetary economic consequences. Thus an event such as the fall of the Berlin Wall might not have unleashed a flurry of other events, had the globe not been interlinked through a vast network of communications.

The twentieth century reveals that ever since 1929, the year that triggered the worst economic depression, the last year of each decade has generated one terrible episode with worldwide repercussions. To be sure, some of these years also had a salutary side, but for the most part they sparked events with devastating consequences. Set in motion several years before, the crises were rarely anticipated, always taking society by surprise.

This is not to say that major episodes of this century have occurred only in the last year of a decade, nor that such years triggered only nightmares, but history remembers them mostly for the destitution they created. This seems to be an eerie historical pattern of our time. It is as if nature or providence has been trying to tell us something in advance of coming events.

1929: THE YEAR OF THE GREAT DEPRESSION

Let's begin with 1929, the first year of the unprecedented depression. The decade known as the Roaring Twenties began with a sharp recession coupled with inflation, creating great agony for Americans, but the misery lasted only a year. By the end of 1921, a promising industrial and financial boom had set in. Investment, employment, productivity, profits, and the GDP all expanded briskly, while the stock market broke record after record. Taxes were cut repeatedly, as the government budget remained in perennial surplus, and by the middle of 1929, the country was at full employment with no inflation. This was, in modern jargon, a Goldilocks economy, the best in a generation. So when the sky-high share prices crashed in October 1929, almost everyone, especially the government, pundits, and economists, was caught napping in paradise. This was not supposed to happen, not in a supposedly free-market economy.

What erupted in 1929 set in motion the events of the next decade. Stock markets crashed all over the world. Product prices collapsed, and so did many industries. In the United States, unemployment soared, but real wages (the purchasing power of salaries) of those lucky enough to be employed actually went up. In Britain and France, by contrast, real wages plummeted, but joblessness remained well under control.[1] Germany, however, suffered the worst of both worlds—high unemployment combined with shriveling paychecks.

Initially, the depression plagued the entire planet, democracies as well as dictatorships. It didn't even spare Latin America and the developing countries, which excelled in farming and had largely avoided the industrial excesses of the Roaring Twenties in the United States. Through international commerce and investment, however, the well-being of agrarian nations was linked to the advanced economies, and when the latter fell into an abyss, the poor became even poorer. Some farm exporters, severely indebted to the industrial countries, had to default on their loans. Others were on the verge of starvation, as their export prices sank to rock bottom. Thus the stock market crash of 1929 triggered the collapse of the world economy, generating untold suffering around the globe.

Four years after the crash, nearly one out of five Americans had no job; millions were underemployed, with skeletal incomes. Thousands of college graduates drove taxicabs or operated elevators. Russia, where jobs were plentiful, looked like paradise to some people. An average of three hundred Americans per day applied for a job at Armtorg, the Russian Trading Company, even though this meant a move to the Soviet Union. No U.S. profession was secure. Engineers, doctors, accountants, executives, and scientists all worried about losing their jobs. In large metropolitan cities such as New York and Boston, breadlines and soup kitchens for the unemployed were common. Such was the destitution and hopelessness that lingered not for a few months but for years and years.[2]

The first installment of the depression lasted until 1933, when joblessness began to dip and share prices recuperated somewhat, inducing the authorities to cut back on government spending. As a result, the depression made a terrible comeback. Even at the end of the 1930s, the U.S. unemployment rate was as high as 15 percent, compared with only 3 percent in 1929. What had begun in October 1929 relentlessly continued for the entire decade. Not only was the cataclysm very deep, it also seemed endless to its hapless victims.

1939: THE YEAR OF THE SECOND WORLD WAR

The free world had tried everything to escape the clutches of poverty inflicted by the depression, but failed, whereas the Nazis, fascists, and communists had made sensible adjustments to restore a semblance of prosperity. Through deficit budgets, military buildup, and money supply expansion, they had managed to combat unemployment. However, emergency or not, such measures were anathema to ideologues in the free world. Trapped in their dogmas, the democracies were unable to recover from the economic cataclysm. Such was the paradox in the late 1930s. Germany under Hitler, Italy under Mussolini, Russia under Stalin, and Japan under a militarized regime were prosperous but autocratic, whereas Britain, France, and the United States were democratic but destitute. Germany and Italy sizzled with booming factories, but markets for their products were under the colonial control of their neighbors. A collision between the opposing political ideologies was therefore inevitable.

Hitler and Mussolini were the products of the decade of depression. They rose to power by promising jobs and steady income to the people in return for their civil rights and freedoms. Hitler began to invade the neighboring nations as early as 1936, but Britain and France didn't cross swords with him until September 1939. That was the first year of the Second World War, a culmination of a long chain of events in Germany, Italy, Russia, and Japan. Eventually, the conflict entangled the entire world.

Historians speculate that if Britain and France had reacted strongly to even one of Hitler's recurrent provocations, such as his occupation of Rhineland in 1936 or his march into Austria in 1938, perhaps the global conflict would have been nipped in the bud. The terrible war could have been avoided or ended quickly, because the German dictator was not yet confident enough to challenge the combined might of his neighbors, who huffed and puffed but essentially did nothing. They weren't suspicious even when Hitler and Mussolini met each other in Rome or when Germany occupied Sudetenland and practically annihilated Czechoslovakia.

The two sides, democracy versus fascism, championed such opposing philosophies that a long and barbaric conflict between them was unavoidable, and, providence, it seems, delayed open warfare until 1939. In fact, the conflagration could have also erupted in 1937, when Japan attacked China, but did not. Once the global war started in the last year of the 1930s, then in keeping with the historical pattern we have observed, it would go on to shape the events of the entire next decade. The conflict itself was over by 1945, but its aftershocks rumbled until the end of the forties and, in some cases, thereafter. Germany, Japan, and Italy were vanquished and ruined, while the European powers among the allies—Britain, France, the United States, Canada, and Australia—even though victorious, were in shambles. Russia, which had later joined the allies owing to Hitler's treachery, had also won, but like others in Europe, lay crippled. Strangely enough, there indeed was a salubrious side to the conflagration. The depression had ended in Canada, America, Australia, and even the Third World.

Joblessness in America had given way to a shortage of labor; employment, wages, productivity, and profits had already surpassed the 1929 levels. Thanks to the war, but no thanks to prevailing ideas that condoned monopolies, the economy was booming again, and the United States had emerged an overwhelmingly predominant economy in the world.

As soon as the war came to an end, localized conflicts erupted among the imperialists and their colonies. The French, the Dutch, and the Portuguese fought pitched battles against nationalists on three continents—Asia, South America, and Africa. Warfare continued with uncontrolled butchery and ferocity. As two historians, Edward Burns and Philip Ralph, pinpoint in *World Civilizations,* "These were among the bloodiest and most destructive of all the outbursts of savagery that marked the period after World War II. Several eclipsed the savagery of the war itself and did much to brand our own age as one of the most barbarous in history."[3] It was a decade during which millions of Jews and soldiers were slaughtered, a period when America discovered the atomic bomb and dropped it twice on Japan. As usual, some good things also developed. Many colonies such as India, Pakistan, and Indonesia gained independence, inspiring other subject nations to follow suit. Nazism and fascism were perhaps exterminated forever.

Thus the mayhem and butchery that had erupted in September 1939 bedeviled the world for the whole decade. The agenda for the forties had actually been foreshadowed by the last year of the previous decade.

1949: THE YEAR OF THE DRAGON

This time the last year of the decade saw not just one but many significant events that were to convulse the world over the next ten years or more. Perhaps the most dramatic moment took place in China, which is symbolized by a dragon.

Even before World War II broke out, Japan had invaded China in 1937 and occupied the key cities of Peking and Shanghai. China's president at that time was Chiang Kai-shek, who retreated and transferred his capital to the far western city of Chungking. The Japanese advance was actually stopped by Chinese communists under the dynamic leadership of a warrior named Mao Tse-tung, whose guerillas had earlier fought their own corrupt government. Now they attacked and constantly harassed the foreign foe. When the global war broke out in 1939, Japan's forces in China were bogged down. After driving the Japanese out, Mao took control of the northern part of his country. At the end of the war in 1945, U.S. forces helped Chiang return to the major cities, but much of the countryside was held by the communists.

The chief U.S. goal in China was to establish a democratic and, if possible, honest regime under a coalition of the communists and the nationalists. The effort succeeded, but only for two years, because in 1947 the Chinese civil war resumed on a wider scale. Siding with the nationalists, the United States offered military advisers and financial assistance, but the inept and decadent forces of Chiang were no match for the battle-tested and ever-growing army of the communists. In October 1949 Mao established the People's Republic of China, and in December Chiang beat a hasty retreat to the nearby island of Formosa, or Taiwan, with his remaining forces.

This was a stunning reversal for the United States and its global prestige. Americans were astonished to find that even though their country had emerged as the unchallenged power after the Second World War, it could not rescue its Chinese ally from a ragtag army. The communist triumph in 1949, setting the U.S. political agenda for the entire next decade, carried on the historical pattern since 1929.

Among other things, it foreshadowed a continued loss of American prestige to communism over at least the next ten years.

The postwar period witnessed a gradual decline of the old colonial powers such as Britain and France. At the same time the Soviet Union emerged with a large empire. Poland, Hungary, Czechoslovakia, Romania, Bulgaria, and Yugoslavia were either aligned with Russia or under its direct control. Germany was divided into four zones, each under the occupation of the major allies—America, Britain, France, and Russia. Colonialism was clearly on the wane; in its place a new phenomenon had emerged—spheres of influence, which culminated in the cold war between the Soviets and the Americans. This was the great irony of the world war. Democracies had won, but autocracy was not dead. Nazism and fascism had given way to communist dictatorships.

Russia and America were at completely opposite ends of the ideological spectrum. One was authoritarian, the other democratic; one believed in state monopolies in the name of proletarian welfare, the other in private monopolies in the name of free enterprise; in one the accused was held guilty until proven innocent, whereas in the other the accused could even keep silent and remain innocent until proven guilty. Competition between the two to expand their orbit of influence was then inevitable. So when China became a Marxist state in 1949, it was seen as a triumph of the Soviet bloc, and became an event that rippled across American politics. "Increasingly significant victories of Mao-Tse-tung's Red Army in China," write historians Norman Graebner, G. Fite, and P. White, "shook the American people emotionally and politically as had few other issues in the country's history."[4]

An ambitious and unscrupulous senator from Wisconsin, Joseph McCarthy, moved quickly to take advantage of the resulting climate of fear and frenzy. He instigated a witch hunt of anyone sympathetic to Marxism inside the United States. Thousands of American communists and their supporters faced the risk of job loss, ostracism, and even jail. No one seemed safe from the senator's wrath, which held sway for four long years until 1954, when finally McCarthyism fell into disrepute, and the senator himself was censured by the Senate.

Soon after the fall of Chiang Kai-shek, the Sino-Soviet Pact of February 1950 confirmed the worst fears of official Washington. The administration feared that China would use its millions of soldiers to further Soviet designs of global expansion, especially in the Far East or Indochina, later known as Vietnam, where nationalist insurgency against France had continued to simmer, creating fertile prospects for Marxist revolution. The U.S. government hastily committed itself to the support of the French, providing assistance in the form of money and weapons.

However, Vietnam was only one of Washington's headaches. Another trouble spot was Korea, divided into northern and southern parts. The U.S. government saw North Korea as another surrogate of the Soviet Union, and its suspicions were confirmed when the North invaded the South with a well-equipped army in June 1950. Ill-prepared southern troops retreated and were quickly cornered in the southwestern part of the Korean peninsula. Fearful of another reversal at the hands of communists, President Harry Truman ordered air strikes, and when they failed he sent American troops into battle under the command of General Douglas MacArthur.

Under the general's daring assaults, the North retreated and the South was quickly liberated. But having decided to unite both the North and the South, MacArthur pushed his forces close to the Chinese border. That is when China stepped into the conflict, sending an army of four hundred thousand soldiers to face a mere twenty thousand American and South Korean troops and inflicting what to that time was the worst defeat in American history. The resulting slaughter was followed by military stalemate, with neither side able to make much headway.

The Truman administration, reluctant to go to war with China, agreed to hold peace talks in July 1951, fully a year after the start of the hostilities. While negotiations dragged on, thousands of American soldiers continued to perish in an orgy of attrition. Finally, General Dwight D. Eisenhower, elected U.S. president in 1952, threatened a full-scale war, leading to an armistice agreement in July 1953.

Another theater of contest between the communists and Americans, as mentioned earlier, was Indochina. By 1950 a general named Ho Chi Minh had emerged as the unchallenged Marxist leader of nationalist resurgence in Vietnam, and his guerillas began to inflict heavy casualties on the French. The U.S. government, sensing another Soviet-inspired plot for global expansion, convinced the French to continue the fight even at hopeless odds. America helped with money and material, but the communists continued to gain ground. The warring parties had a final showdown at the famous battle of Dien Bien Phu, where, with the help of Chinese soldiers, the Vietnamese inflicted a punishing defeat on French forces. France surrendered and convened a peace conference in Geneva, cosponsored by Britain and the Soviet Union.

Ho Chi Minh agreed to withdraw his forces to North Vietnam in anticipation of elections in South Vietnam within two years. Because of his popularity as a nationalist hero, he was sure of a victory at the ballot box. However, soon after the agreement, the United States set up a puppet government in South Vietnam under Ngo Dinh Diem, and the election was never held. In this way the United States stepped into a quagmire that would convulse the entire nation throughout the coming decade.

During this time, U.S. prestige had suffered repeated reverses at the hands of Chinese communists. Starting from the last year of the previous decade, Mao's actions influenced American politics at home and military policy abroad. In keeping with the historical pattern I propose, the triumph of communism in China would shape the world's agenda for the entire upcoming decade. U.S. presidents would come and go, but Mao would be there to pester them all.

The Chinese Revolution was not the only setback for the United States in 1949. There were a few more that also figured prominently in the world of the fifties. Russia tested its first atomic bomb, bringing it to superpower status almost overnight, which served to further hamstring American foreign policy. The North American Treaty Organization (NATO) was also born in 1949, ostensibly to contain communism. So were West and East Germany. All these were episodes that would strongly impact global activities in the future, although none so much as the Chinese Revolution. And they all occurred in 1949.

The Russian development of the big bomb crucially affected the cold war and the shape of things to come. Let me note again for clarity that my claim is not that all major events after 1928 occurred in the last year of a decade, but those that did had a lasting and often tumultuous impact worldwide.

1959: AMERICA'S HEADACHES BEGIN

What else could possibly generate global havoc after all that had happened in the thirties, forties, and fifties? How about the Cuban Revolution of 1959? This time the setting is a small island ninety miles off the coast of Florida. Cuba is an unlikely place to play a major role in world affairs, but in 1959 and throughout the next decade, almost single-handedly it galvanized the planet. Its leader, Fidel Castro, did in Latin America what Mao had done in China. Both overthrew their corrupt regimes and established communist dictatorships in direct defiance of the government of the United States.

On New Year's Day in 1959, Castro drove the autocratic President Fulgencio Batista out of the country and seized power. Although the Batista government had been in disarray for several years, it still came as a shock to Americans that a communist revolution had succeeded in their own backyard. In 1958 the United States had indeed withdrawn its support from the president but was not prepared to accept a Marxist regime right in the neighborhood. As had happened in China in the last year of the previous decade, the end of the corrupt regime in Cuba came with astonishing swiftness.

Louis A. Perez, a historian, writes on the first page of his preface: "It happened quite suddenly, and so quickly, all quite improbably: a revolution overthrew a repressive regime. . . . Cuba had been transformed into the first Marxist-Leninist state in the Western Hemisphere and the first New World nation to align itself totally and unabashedly with the Soviet Union—all this occurring ninety miles from the United States, in a region traditionally secure as a North American sphere of influence, in a country historically secure as a North American client state."[5]

The Cuban earthquake sent powerful aftershocks across the shore into the North American continent. Not only did it stun the United States, it also reverberated into Canada and Mexico. By summer, Castro had confiscated American-owned businesses and launched a Soviet-style program of agricultural reform. In retaliation, President Eisenhower placed an economic embargo on Cuba, whereupon Castro turned to the Soviet Union for economic assistance and diplomatic support.

In November 1960 John F. Kennedy was elected U.S. president, and it didn't take him long to slip into the Cuban quagmire via the well known Bay of Pigs fiasco. The rebel army, organized by the CIA in April 1961, was wiped out by Castro's forces. This was the first test of Kennedy's policy of instigating wars of liberation overseas along the Soviet lines, and it had a very poor beginning. It portended more conflicts, such as the Vietnam War, that would meet the same fate as the failure at the Bay of Pigs, but with vastly greater losses.

A year later, Cuba featured in a global crisis that brought the planet to the brink of a nuclear war. Ever since the start of the cold war, the United States and the Soviet Union had tacitly agreed not to interfere with each other's sphere of influence. In October 1962 President Kennedy learned that Cuba, just a stone's throw away in terms of air power, was building sites for Russian offensive missiles. Alarmed at what he considered the Soviet outrage, Kennedy imposed a naval blockade of the island to intercede any Russian ships bringing in weapons. Tensions ran high as a Soviet submarine gingerly approached the American fleet, but the crisis was averted in the eleventh hour when the United States promised not to attack Cuba and the Russian ships reversed course. The Cuban missile crisis brought the world to the verge of nuclear war and had a profound effect on both superpowers. It led to a dramatic increase in defense spending in both nations.

Despite its failure in Cuba, Kennedy continued to support wars of liberation from communist regimes as long as they did not intrude upon the Soviet hemisphere. This policy found full-fledged expression in Vietnam, where the regime of Ngo Dinh Diem came into increasing conflict with the guerrillas of Ho Chi Minh. By September 1963, two months before Kennedy's assassination, sixteen thousand American troops and military advisers were in South Vietnam, and the battle had just begun, with a lot more to come.

Ultimately, Vietnam turned into a U.S. nightmare that at its peak trapped more than half a million soldiers with over fifty thousand casualties. The carnage polarized the nation and created a climate of bitterness as never before since the Civil War, exactly a century before. All this tumult was triggered by a revolution in a tiny island ninety miles off the coast of Florida, but occurring as it did in the last year of the previous decade, it portended convulsions that would rock the nation for the entire next decade. It was not until 1969, when Richard Nixon became president, that America's Vietnam policy underwent a dramatic reversal, and a withdrawal of American troops began.

The Vietnam tragedy, however, presents only one side of the 1960s. The decade had its glorious side as well. For one thing, the period witnessed the longest run of prosperity in U.S. history, lasting from 1960 all the way to 1969. For another, racism, a virulent American cancer, began to retreat. Interestingly, the impetus for both these trends came from events that had unfolded in 1959.

That year federal budget deficit was $12.8 billion, the largest peacetime shortfall in the U.S. chronicle. Its main purpose was to combat a recession. Ideologically, Eisenhower had always believed in balancing the budget, but such policy had not worked in the 1953–54 slump. Thus in the recession of 1957–58, combating joblessness took precedence over the imperative of low inflation. So it was that fiscal expansion and the attendant federal deficit were first approved by a Republican president. These two developments were largely responsible for the prosperity of the 1960s. One spawned the culture of budgetary red ink, the other the use of fiscal policy to fight unemployment. Until then deficits had been scarce, mostly tolerated for purposes of defense. But once started, they became a regular habit in the 1960s, reaching the decade's peak in 1968 at $25 billion. The federal deficit would continue for many decades, rising to unprecedented heights in the 1980s and the early 1990s.

The sixties also produced landmark civil rights legislation that slowly though significantly improved the lifestyle of African Americans. Until then U.S. minorities had faced overt discrimination. Such practices were at their most toxic in the South, but even in the North, African Americans encountered racism and abject poverty. Modern racism began when Europeans colonized other continents and spread the dogmas that people of color, black as well as brown, were inferior to whites. It took two forms: individual and institutional racism. The first manifested itself in openly prejudicial ideas, mores, and practices by individuals against ethnic minorities, and the second in the form of laws that overtly or covertly discriminated against nonwhites.

Before the 1960s racism permeated every nook and cranny of

American society. Blacks, Hispanics, and other minorities faced discrimination in housing, schooling, and employment, suffering police torment, lower wages, menial jobs, long working hours, and judicial persecution. During the 1950s, millions of blacks moved out of the rural south and into the urban north, giving rise to large voting blocs in big cities, where they exerted political pressure to outlaw the most blatant of social and legal inequities. Black ferment under the leadership of the Reverend Martin Luther King Jr. also underscored the unfairness of such institutions. In 1956 the United States Supreme Court outlawed bus segregation. Another success against discrimination came when the courts moved to create integrated schools in an unlikely place, Little Rock, Arkansas. Their intent, however, was thwarted by the state governor, who chose to shut down classes rather than have blacks and whites study together. Only in 1959 did another court ruling succeed in opening the Little Rock schools with plans for gradual integration.

What began as a trickle in 1959 turned into a torrent of unprecedented civil rights legislation in the 1960s. The Civil Rights Act of 1964, reinforced by another bill the next year, was one of the most momentous pieces of legislation in the American chronicle. It outlawed discrimination in hiring and firing on the basis of race, color, religion, sex, or nationality. No longer could businesses or public places such as bus stations, hotels, and clubs treat the people unequally. The U.S. attorney general was authorized to sue apartment complexes, museums, parks, and schools to desegregate them. Indeed, the 1964 ban against discrimination was a crowning achievement of the American people.

The 1960s are best known for the Vietnam War, the length and depth of growing affluence, potent civil rights legislation, and the birth of liberalism. It is interesting that the first three had their impetus in 1959, the last year of the previous decade.

1969: THE START OF INFLATION

Are we in for another revolution? Not really. This time a tumult occurs on the economic front, something reminiscent of 1929 leading into the debacle of the thirties. The year 1969 was a benchmark year in financial developments. It is well known that the stock market crash at the end of the twenties erupted into the Great Depression over the next decade. What is less well known is that the roaring inflation of the 1970s had its origin in 1969.

The 1960s began with nary a hint of price increases. From 1960 to 1965, the consumer price index (CPI) rose at less than a 2 percent annual rate; after 1965, however, the rate accelerated and the December to December price rise was 4.7 percent in 1968, cresting at 6.2 percent the next year. There was no longer any doubt that inflation had made a strong comeback, reviving itself from the war decade of the 1940s.

If our hypothesis is correct, then some events of the last year of the 1960s would plant a seed for things to come, and indeed the coming decade would be rocked by ever growing price increases. The 1969 inflation rate was still in single digits, but in the 1970s it soared to double-digit levels, lasting well into the decade. At the same time, the whole world suffered from escalating prices. As in previous cases, when something bedeviled the United States in the last year of a decade, it convulsed the entire planet for the next ten years or more. Inflation roared over all the continents, and in some countries generated high unemployment or hyperinflation. What sparked it all and made it linger, we shall explore in chapters 3 and 7. For now let's note that the last year of the 1960s forewarned us about the major events of the 1970s.

1979: THE YEAR OF HOPE AND TURMOIL

In 1969 there was only one development, that would have global repercussions in the near future, but in 1979 there were three. One of them, of course, was yet another bloody revolution, this time in Iran, the second the Soviet invasion of Afghanistan, and the third a sea change in U.S. economic policy.

The reasons behind the Iranian revolution were the same as those behind Cuba's and China's—official graft and decadence. As usual, the U.S. government patronized the country's dictatorship, this time in the person of Mohammad Reza Pahlavi, the shah of Iran. And as always, the power elite enriched themselves with the help of state legislation and bureaucracy. However, this time there was also another element spurring popular resentment—the unabashed import of Western culture abhorred by the priesthood, the Ayatollahs. The inflationary seventies were the last straw for Iranians, who became increasingly destitute while the shah's relatives and friends frolicked in luxury.

In January 1979 an exiled priest named Ayatollah Ruhollah Khomeini, with the tacit support of disaffected army officers, overthrew the shah, forcing him to flee the country. Like other revolutions against U.S.-sponsored regimes, the government's end in Iran came suddenly, catching the West unprepared. *Time* magazine reported that "almost to the very end, the conventional wisdom of Western diplomats and journalists was that the Shah would survive; after all, he had come through earlier troubles seemingly strengthened."[6]

As in earlier cases, the United States lost an ally in the revolution. American businesses, especially the oil interests, suffered a heavy blow, and U.S. prestige took another hit in a foreign land. Furthermore, in November 1979 some students attacked the U.S. embassy in Tehran and seized fifty-three Americans as hostages. They were released unharmed but only after languishing in captivity for almost a year.

The Iranian revolution produced international aftershocks. Iran, a major oil exporter, sharply raised the price of oil in 1979, hurtling the planet into another bout of inflation and recession over the next three years. Unemployment soared around the globe, the impoverished Third World its chief victim.

Iran also got entangled into a full-blown war with one of its western neighbors, Iraq, in September 1980. The carnage lasted eight years before the battle-weary parties sued for peace. America and Russia took sides, with the United States supporting Iraq and the Soviets aiding Iran.

The second major event of 1979 was the Soviet assault on Afghanistan. On Christmas morning, Russian tanks and armor swept through Afghanistan's border, killed the ruling communist, President Amin, and installed a puppet, Babrak Karmal, in his place. All this was done with a ruthlessness reminiscent of the Bolshevik terror of 1917. The people of Afghanistan, known for their valorous defiance of Britain's supreme power in the nineteenth century, were outnumbered and outgunned, but they were also fighting for their homeland. The beleaguered Afghans carried on their fight with the Soviets for ten long years, until finally the invader was humiliated and forced to withdraw. Afghanistan thus turned out to be Russia's Vietnam. And just as Soviet assistance was crucial to America's surrender in Vietnam, U.S. aid to Afghan rebels turned out to be decisive in Russia's debacle.

The third major episode of 1979 involved a complete reversal of American monetary policy. Over the past three decades, the Federal Reserve had regulated the supply of money by targeting its discount rate, which governs other interest rates in the economy. The idea was that whenever market rates threatened to overshoot a target, the Fed would expand money supply and bring them down. During the 1970s, with inflation pushing interest rates upward, this policy led to a constant increase in the growth of money, which further ignited inflation.

The practice triggered strong criticism, especially from the Nobel laureate Milton Friedman, who denounced it as fuel for the vicious spiral of surging prices. Finally, in October 1979, under the stewardship of Paul Volcker, the Fed decided to reverse its thirty-year policy. From then on, the central bank would target monetary aggregates, or cash in the hands of banking institutions, rather than interest rates. As a result, money growth tumbled, and bond yields soared, but the inflation tiger was tamed in the 1980s. The world did suffer its worst economic slump since the 1930s but emerged stronger once price growth was subdued. Thus the sea change in Fed policy in the last year of the previous decade had wholesome as well as damaging effects on the world over the entire eighties.

1989: THE YEAR OF THE FALL OF THE BERLIN WALL

Finally, we come to 1989, the last year of the 1980s, when the Berlin Wall, the glaring symbol of the East-West divide, collapsed. More than anything else, the barrier that had partitioned Berlin into two halves ever since 1961 was emblematic of the cold war. In one stroke, a volcanic social upheaval ignited both the demolition of the wall in the month of November and the destruction of communism. It was perhaps the most momentous event of the twentieth century. The world was stunned, totally at a loss to explain why and how it had all happened with so little bloodshed, with such lightening swiftness, in the Soviet bloc yet, an area known for gore and violence ever since the Bolshevik uprising in 1917. Vaclav Havel, the celebrated novelist and future president of Czechoslovakia, was moved to remark that the spectacular fall of the Berlin Wall was evidence of divine intervention.

The collapse of the wall was the climax of a year that had consistently startled the world. One after another, Marxist regimes in Poland, East Germany, Hungary, Czechoslovakia, and Romania were convulsed or toppled by democratic forces in 1989, and with such speed that pundits and politicians in the West, especially on Capitol Hill and the White House, were taken by total surprise. As befits an event in the last year of a decade, the dismantling of the wall triggered a series of dramatic episodes in the 1990s. I will discuss them in detail in subsequent pages, but for now it will suffice to say that the wreck of the Berlin Wall sent the Soviet empire into an economic and political tailspin from which it has yet to recover. The effect of the event on Russia, its former satellites, and the rest of the world easily lasted through the next decade.

CONCLUSION

The foregoing pages have demonstrated my view that there is a pattern to be found in our recent history. For some reasons, a variety of social, economic, and political events around the globe have been woven into a historic tapestry ever since 1929, when the New York Stock Exchange suffered the worst debacle in its chronicle. The crash tore the world economy apart over the next decade. Interestingly, this was not an isolated incident, but the beginning of a pattern that lasted at least until 1989. Specifically, ever since the start of the Great Depression, we can see clear portents of coming catastrophes by looking at the last year of each decade. Between 1929 and 1989, there were seven such years, and not a single one went by without an epochal event somewhere on earth—one with global repercussions.

Each time, a bloody revolution, economic fiasco, or war erupted to traumatize the world for most of the next decade.

As we focus on 1999, the last year of the 1990s, the observed pattern weighs heavily on what we can expect this year, next year, and the coming decade. Before rushing to judgment about our future, however, we need enough information and analysis to reach reliable conclusions.

3

THE CYCLE OF INFLATION

I t is very hard to believe that history follows a pattern, that the seemingly discordant events of society, involving numerous people and institutions, each with its own interests and desires, could actually occur in regular cycles. Yet, as we've seen, there is at least one such pattern running through our century since 1929.

Now we will look at another neat arrangement of history, namely the long-run cycle of inflation. Specifically, we will see that ever since the 1770s, as far back as the data go, every third decade in the United States has been a peak decade of inflation, with the one exception of the period following the 1860s, due to the Civil War. Inflation cannot be sustained unless the state prints large amounts of money over many years. There may be other reasons for sizzling prices, but they are all temporary and cannot maintain the spiral of inflation. There have to be too many dollars chasing too few goods for an enduring rise in the cost of living. It is as simple as that.

The symbiosis between the two is so strong that if there is a cycle of inflation, then there must be an almost parallel cycle of money growth as well. This is precisely what will be demonstrated here. Thus historical patterns will be shown to exist in at least two more areas.

I first discovered these cycles in early 1983 and presented them in an article. They also underlined my 1985 book, *The Great Depression of 1990*. The cycles were shown to exist until the end of the 1970s, but now they can be easily updated almost until the end of the 1990s. It is interesting to note that new data actually reinforce the message of the two cycles and add to their reliability for forecasting.

THE CYCLE OF MONEY GROWTH

First of all, why do we examine money growth instead of money supply? The reason is that national output tends to rise every year because of growing population, capital accumulation, and improving technology. To buy this extra output, people need more cash, or its equivalent, such as credit cards, in hand; otherwise prices will fall and the economy will be disrupted, as no business can plan properly without the stability of future prices. Therefore, just to keep prices stable, money supply has to rise in proportion to the increase in production. In other words, as long as money growth approximates output growth, prices remain stable. Thus, if the GDP jumps by 4 percent, then money supply must also climb by 4 percent to avoid a prolonged price decline or negative inflation. For prices to rise and result in positive inflation, money growth has to outpace the growth of production and exceed 4 percent. That is why we examine the behavior of money growth over time and not just that of money supply. This is a technical point, but if you don't follow it, nothing much is lost. All you need to remember is that the money growth surge for a sustained period is a prerequisite for persistent inflation.

Let us now examine the empirical evidence. We can obtain consistent estimates of money supply going as far back as the birth of the American nation in 1776. The data used are for every tenth year. A simple transformation of these observations into rates of change per decade yields a vivid cycle, presented in figure 3.1. Here the rate of money growth is the percentage change per decade in the supply of money, which is measured as currency in the hands of the public plus demand and time deposits with commercial banks.[7]

The first peak of the cycle commences with the 1770s, which witnessed the birth of the American Revolution and an extraordinary use of the cash mint to finance it. Historians argue that money growth at the time dwarfed any preceding level in colonial America. Thereafter we see the long-term pattern emerge, reaching a crest

FIGURE 3.1

**The cycle of money growth in the
United States, 1750s to 1990s (in percent)**

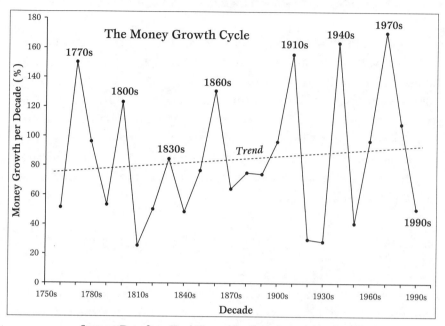

SOURCE: Data from Ravi Batra, *The Great Depression of 1990*
(New York: Simon & Schuster, 1987), 188; and *Economic Report
of the President* (Washington, D.C.: U.S. Council of Economic
Advisers, 1999), 407.
Note: Except for the aftermath of the Civil War of the 1860s, the
rate of money growth peaked every third decade in the
United States.

every third decade, with the singular exception of the two decades
following the Civil War of the 1860s.

Immediately after the Civil War, regarded as the most destructive
war in U.S. history, the pattern of money growth was disrupted. The
economy took about twenty years to recuperate, but once the nation's
recovery was complete by the 1880s, the cycle resumed its rhythmi-
cal course. It is testimony to the resilience of the cycle that even a cataclysm such as the Civil War, which shook the very foundations of
American society, could not swerve the money pattern for long.
Within the next three decades money growth crested in the 1910s,
which is the first inflationary peak of the twentieth century. Thirty
years later, the peak recurred in the 1940s and then again in the
1970s. Not surprisingly, in the eighties and the nineties, money

growth fell. Thus figure 3.1 shows that, *except for the post–Civil War interlude, the decennial rate of money growth crested every third decade over more than two centuries.* This is an amazing feature of the U.S. economy.

In the middle of the graph lies a dashed line, called a trend line, that reveals the behavior of average money growth. The trend is almost horizontal, revealing that American money growth, on average, has not increased much over a long period spanning more than two centuries. Some economists, including Milton Friedman, argue that money supply is the most crucial determinant of economic activity. If they are right, then according to the money growth graph, not much has changed about the U.S. economy over the long run, for the trend is only slightly positive.

THE LONG-RUN CYCLE OF INFLATION IN THE UNITED STATES

Inflation is a state of persistent increase in average prices. A one-shot upswing is not enough for the situation to be called inflationary. Moreover, it's not necessary that all products become expensive over time. As long as the average price level, measured by some kind of index, rises persistently, there is inflation.

Unlike the cycle of money growth, the cycle of inflation is not self-evident. We need to examine the data on the annual wholesale price index and transform them into decennial figures, a common practice among economic historians who seek to identify trends over centuries. To do this, we can either add up annual prices to obtain the aggregate price level in each decade or take an average of the aggregate by dividing it by eleven, the number of years in each decade, including the first and the last year. Either figure may represent the price level per decade. Once we transform the average price level into rates of price change or inflation, we can plot them in figure 3.2. Here, the long-run cycle of inflation emerges as another eloquent testimony to the resilience of the American economy.[8] It is elegantly displayed by the lines moving rhythmically up and down through twenty-five decades, beginning with the 1750s. Except for the post–Civil War period, figure 3.2 reveals that *over the last 250 years the decennial rate of inflation reached a peak every third decade and then usually declined over the next two.*

FIGURE 3.2
The long-run cycle of inflation in the
United States, 1750s to 1990s (in percent)

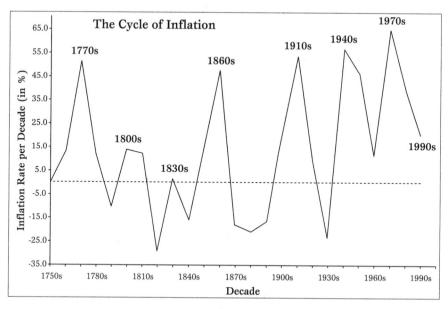

SOURCE: Data from Ravi Batra, *The Great Depression of 1990*
(New York: Simon & Schuster, 1987), 188; and *Economic Report
of the President* (Washington, D.C.: U.S. Council of Economic
Advisers, 1999), 401.
Note: Except for the aftermath of the Civil War of the 1860s, the
rate of inflation peaked every third decade in the United States.

The first inflationary peak appears in the 1770s, following which
the inflation rate declines over the next two decades and reaches
another peak in the 1800s. Again, it falls over the two subsequent
decades, rising to its zenith in the 1830s. This time inflation declines
for only one decade, but still the next peak appears thirty years later
in the 1860s. At this point the cycle is disturbed, but it begins anew
with the 1880s, because within three decades the peak reappears in
the 1910s, which is the first inflationary peak of the twentieth century. Thirty years later the cycle crests in the 1940s and then again
thirty years later in the 1970s. In the eighties and the nineties, the
rates of inflation tumbled.

The inflationary peak of the 1830s might appear curious, for it
occurs virtually on the zero line. But the decades immediately preceding and following the 1830s reveal negative rates of inflation.

Compared with these deflationary years, the zero rate of inflation represents at least relative inflation, though not inflation in the absolute sense. Thus it is not improper to regard the 1830s as the peak of the inflation (or deflation) cycle of the three decades between 1820 and 1850. Perhaps a safer statement regarding the cycle during the nineteenth century is that the inflation peak following each trough occurred every third decade, excepting, of course, the two decades after the Civil War. Here the troughs of the cycle occur in the 1790s, 1820s, 1840s, 1880s, 1930s, and 1960s, and except in the aftermath of the Civil War, each peak following the trough appears at an interval of thirty years.

INFLATION AND MONEY SUPPLY

What is the main cause of inflation? A great debate over this question occurred in the 1970s, but now a consensus has emerged among economists, who believe that inflation springs chiefly from prolonged monetary expansion. There may be other contributory factors, but they cannot sustain the spiral of rising prices in the absence of increasing growth in the supply of dollars. Thus a sustained rise in the growth of money is a prerequisite for the existence of inflation.

Figure 3.3 presents the paths of money growth and inflation together and shows that the two cycles run almost parallel to each other. Not only do their peaks match, but they were also both disturbed in the aftermath of the Civil War. The figure thus clearly reveals that the greenback printing press is the primary determinant of inflation. Every decade during which money growth crests is also a decade when the rate of inflation crests.

The cycles of money and inflation are extraordinary features of the U.S. economy. It is crystal clear by now that over long periods money is the sole determinant of surging prices. This suggests that only one of the two cycles is independent, because the inflationary rhythm is guided by the monetary rhythm. When you recognize that the supply of the greenback depends on dozens of unrelated and constantly moving factors, the observed pattern of money growth is simply astonishing.

Money is anything that society is willing to accept as a medium of exchange. The puny piece of paper on which a hundred-dollar bill

FIGURE 3.3
Money and inflation cycles, 1750s–1990s (in percent)

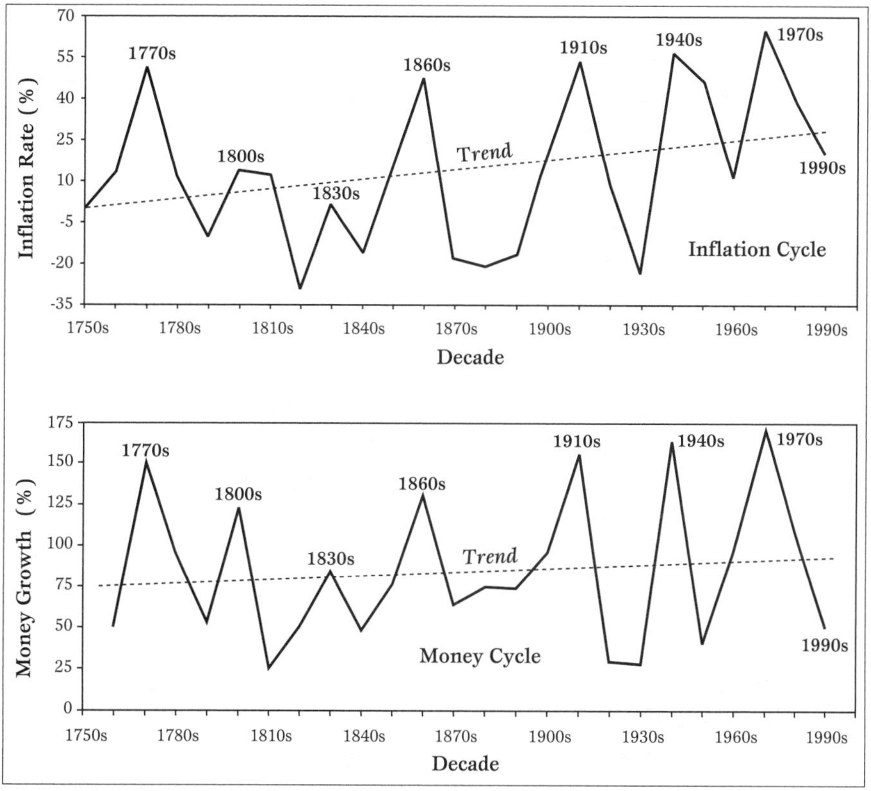

SOURCE: Data from Figures 3.1 and 3.2.
Note: The money and inflation cycles in the United States run
virtually parallel to each other. Not only do their peaks match,
but their troughs are also similar. Thus money growth is the
most important determinant of inflation.

is printed is inherently worthless, but you can buy a variety of things
with it, because it has been printed and stamped by the government
to facilitate commerce among people. In the distant past, only precious metals such as gold and silver were used as money, and no one
could even imagine accepting mere paper for goods and services. The
data used by this analysis go all the way back to the 1770s, and since
then myriad changes have occurred in the concept and shape of
money.

During the early nineteenth century, money took a variety of
forms, as gold and silver dollars coexisted with paper bills. The bills

themselves were issued by three sources—the federal government, U.S. banks, and state banks. The bulk of the currency, however, was issued by the state institutions. The situation changed dramatically after the Civil War, when a federal tax on state notes in 1865 effectively drove them out of circulation, and only notes issued by the treasury and national banks remained. Furthermore, the use of checks in business transactions grew so much that currency was no longer the primary form of money. Thus the Civil War and its aftermath constitute a major milestone in the annals of money and banking in the United States; no wonder both the cycles of money and inflation went out of kilter for about twenty years.

Another milestone in the use and form of money emerged in 1914 with the establishment of the Federal Reserve, the Fed, which serves as a central bank for the United States. The Fed was instituted mainly to control the total supply of dollars in the economy. Until then the availability of money was determined chiefly by the laws of supply and demand for credit. The establishment of the Fed, however, dramatically changed the landscape. Money growth now evolved under very different rules. Yet the cycle of money barely took notice.

Economists have long regarded the Fed as the most powerful institution regulating the U.S. and even the world economy. Yet the creation of the Fed made absolutely no difference to the rhythm of money growth, which continued to crest every third decade. Nor could anything else budge the money cycle: wars, revolutions, or economic debacles. The world has changed drastically since 1929, but the money cycle continues to chug along the course it first adopted in the late eighteenth century. By now credit cards, ATM machines, mutual funds, money market accounts, and a host of novel financial instruments have entered the arena of banking and finance, but the pattern of money growth has treated them with disdain, ebbing and surging as regularly as the tide.

The upper half of figure 3.3 reveals a trend line that is steeper than the trend line in the lower half. This suggests that over the long run, average inflation has slightly outpaced average money growth. In other words, today's economy displays an inflationary bias, a feature we should keep in mind in reading the future.

WARFARE AND THE CYCLES

The money cycle spans over three documentable centuries and presents an interesting challenge to those who argue that social events are random. The cycle displays seven peaks, of which as many as five occurred during periods of a major local or global war. The 1770s saw the American Revolution, the 1800s the Napoleonic wars in Europe, the 1860s the Civil War, the 1910s the First World War, and the 1940s the Second World War. Each time the warring states, confronted with grave danger, chose to finance the escalating cost of the conflict by printing copious amounts of money, which in turn sparked a round of booming prices.

How did Napoleon's myriad battles, in which America was not militarily involved, affect the U.S. rate of money growth and inflation? Napoleon came to power in 1799 and almost immediately plunged into the task of glorifying France at the cost of its neighboring nations. With war raging in Europe, the United States exported large quantities of foodstuff and raw materials for which the Europeans paid with precious metals, which in turn swelled money growth and prices in the United States. So it was that the first decade of the nineteenth century became a peak period of the money and inflation cycles.

Even though the wars themselves were over by 1815, their aftershocks were potent enough to affect two full decades. Not only the 1800s but also the next decade encountered inflation, although the price surge during the 1810s was somewhat subdued. Once inflation takes hold for a few years, it leaves a lasting impression on the human psyche. People adjust their behavior so as not to be caught again by price surprises. They shun money, especially paper money that depreciates over time, and start hoarding goods. Thus inflation fuels further inflation, as increased hoarding of products propels their demand and hence prices. Of course, the process ends as the state shuts down its money mint at the end of the war, but not before it has plagued society for a decade or more.

What about the other peaks of the cycles, the 1830s and the 1970s, both of which largely escaped bloody conflicts among nations? Although these periods avoided major conflagrations, even there warfare did have some role to play in the surge of money and prices.

During the 1820s, the economy experienced serious deflation, which is the opposite of inflation. Money growth was extremely shallow at that time and the cost of living fell sharply. In the following decade, there were minor though perennial tussles between the U.S. government and Native Americans, but their expense was large enough to escalate government spending, requiring the printing of money in the form of treasury notes. From 1835 to 1842 a seven-year conflict known as the Second Seminole War cost the federal administration $50 million. Since the entire federal budget between 1830 and 1840 varied annually from a mere $15 million to $24 million, hostilities with the Seminoles consumed a big chunk of government spending. As a result, even though the conflict didn't cost too many lives, it did generate larger money growth and halted the deflation in prices. The inflation rate during the 1830s was no longer negative.

Warfare was also involved during the 1970s, though much more indirectly than in any other peak decade. The so-called Yom Kippur War began in October 1973, as Syria and Egypt launched a surprise attack against Israel. America backed the Jews, and Russia the Arabs. In response, an international oil cartel called the Organization of Petroleum Exporting Countries (OPEC), which was dominated by the Arab nations, imposed an oil embargo against the West and effectively the rest of the world. Petrol prices skyrocketed.

To its surprise, OPEC learned that oil prices could be raised substantially by trimming production. So even after the hostilities ended in less than a month, the cost of petrol actually climbed. The war by itself should have had no lasting impact on U.S. money growth and inflation; product prices would have surged for a couple of years due to costlier energy but then come back to their normal level of stability. But the administration chose to fight the recessionary and inflationary consequences of the oil surge with monetary expansion. Money growth jumped, and a temporary problem of inflation swelled into a decade-long spiral.

The discussion presented above should give us pause. Except for the singular exception of the aftermath of the Civil War, the American economy reveals that every third decade has been the peak decade of money growth and inflation, starting as far back as the 1750s. Furthermore, some kind of war, directly or indirectly, was involved in generating these cycles. If this does not prove historical determinism, nothing else will. Economic, political, and social events clearly seem to be woven into an inexorable and identifiable tapestry of history. Of course, how we respond to the war is the stuff of which the cycles are made, but it appears that some kind of innate conditioning leads us to the same type of behavior whenever we face a given circumstance or crisis. Frequently governments print money when trouble springs from the battle front, or from an economic slump. And if the slump is triggered by inflationary pressures, monetary expansion begets escalating inflation without curing the recession.

However, none of this means that there is a three-decade cycle of warfare as well. Nor does it imply that in modern times major wars have usually occurred at the interval of three decades, for there were bloody conflicts in other decades as well: America fought a war with Britain from 1812 to 1815, with Mexico in 1846 and 1847, and with Spain in 1898. All it signifies is that the U.S. response to warfare fits with its three-decade rhythm of money and inflation. There were also sanguinary conflicts in the fifties and sixties that fell outside the realm of the three-decade pattern. Both the Korean War and the Vietnam War were costly in terms of defense spending and lost lives. However, in both cases the money spigots were kept closed.

Warfare is perhaps a perennial condition of humanity, but its financing has varied somewhat over time to generate the regular economic cycles. In fact, the 1973 Arab-Israeli battles were short lived and didn't militarily drag America into them. Yet in the aftermath the United States responded by printing oodles of money, and in the process generated the highest peaks of the money and inflation cycles. Thus it is not warfare that has been following a regular pattern but rather the human response to it.

THE LAST YEAR OF A DECADE AND THE CYCLES

The cycles are also linked to the historical pattern outlined in the preceding chapter, wherein the last year of each decade since the 1920s had a major impact on the global economy. The stock market crash of 1929 and the subsequent depression generated a trough of both the cycles in the 1930s. The start of the world war in 1939 and its aftershocks in the 1940s gave rise to cyclical peaks.

The expansionary effects of fiscal policy discovered in the largest peacetime deficit of 1959 sparked a long economic boom, so when output grew sharply and money supply did not, inflation for the 1960s was subdued until, of course, 1969, when prices surged to anticipate the trends in the 1970s. In 1979 Federal Reserve chairman Paul Volcker, followed by Alan Greenspan, decided that enough was enough and resolved to restrain the flow of money. Consequently, money growth and inflation tumbled over the next two decades and neatly blended with the cyclical journey that had begun more than two centuries before.

Thus it is evident that global events seem to fall into regular cyclical patterns. For our purposes, the money cycle, and its offshoot, the inflation cycle, makes the task of economic forecasting much easier, as we shall see subsequently.

4

MY FORECASTING RECORD

In 1978, to the laughter of many and the applause of a few friends, I wrote a book on world history and titled it *The Downfall of Capitalism and Communism*, predicting that both systems would collapse by or around the year 2000. Thus began for me a new career, fraught with the risks as well as acclamation, of a forecaster. In spite of its manifold hazards, I have continued to remain in that profession, and the current work is no exception. I have persisted with the business of predictions and written many more books since 1978. Some of my prophecies have been general and some specific. A menu of the forecasts I have made in recent years appears in table 4.1.

THE 1978 FORECASTS

Of the thirty-three forecasts listed in table 4.1, if I am permitted to say so, only two have been partially or totally wrong. Contrary to my prophecy, the Dow Jones index as well as the over-the-counter Nasdaq index were at all-time highs in April 1999, and the 1930s-style depression has not yet materialized. The table also includes predictions for which some time remains. Other than the two just mentioned, all the remaining prophecies have materialized in virtually the way I had foreseen. I will shortly return to this matter and argue that even my forecasting errors seem to dovetail with the pattern of those that have come true and now appear to be on their way.

TABLE 4.1
My Forecasts, 1978–1997

Forecasts Made in 1978[a]

1. Soviet but not Chinese communism will collapse around the millennium.
2. A revolution will occur in Iran in 1979, and the priesthood will take over.
3. Starting in 1980, there will be a seven-year-long war between Iran and Iraq.
4. The rule of money, or monopoly capitalism, will come to an end in the United States around the year 2000.
5. Army commanders would become famous before the fall of monopoly capitalism.
6. Pornography, promiscuity, crime, and divorce will climb until the dominion of money ends in politics.
7. Income and wealth disparities will skyrocket.
8. Women would play increasingly active roles in business and politics.
9. Family values and spirituality will take a back seat.
10. The rule of money will give way to a global golden age.

Forecasts Made between 1980 and 1983[b]

11. The American economy will prosper for seven years between 1983 through 1989.
12. Inflation will gradually subside in the 1980s.
13. Interest rates will fall in the 1980s.
14. Share prices will break records every year between 1983 and 1989.
15. Farm and oil prices will plummet in the 1980s.
16. Bond values will soar in the 1980s.
17. Industrial mergers will surge around the globe.

a. These forecasts were made in Ravi Batra, *The Downfall of Capitalism and Communism* (London: Macmillan, 1978; reprint, Dallas: Liberty Press, 1990), chaps. 8–10; and Ravi Batra, *Muslim Civilization and the Crisis in Iran* (Dallas: Venus Books, 1980), chaps. 7 and 8.
b. I made these forecasts in Batra, *Muslim Civilization and the Crisis in Iran,* ibid, and in an article written in early 1982 but published as "The Long-Run Cycle of Inflation in the United States," in the *Renaissance Universal Journal,* Vol 2, April 1984, 14–17. The forecasts were repeated in Batra, *The Great Depression of 1990,* 22.

18. European countries such as Britain, Germany, and France will suffer a serious slump in 1986, facing postwar peaks of joblessness.

19. From 1989 to 1990 share prices will crash all over the world, leading to a seven-year-long depression.

20. Traditional values will make a comeback soon after the end of the rule of wealth in society.

Forecasts Made in 1988 for the 1990s[c]

21. The U.S. dollar will crash by the end of 1994.

22. Inflation and interest rates will tumble again in the 1990s.

23. Real estate values will plummet in many areas of the United States.

Forecasts Made in 1991[d]

24. Every year of the 1990s will be a year of drama, marked by unprecedented change in government, economy, or religion somewhere in the world.

25. President George Bush will be defeated by a Democrat.

26. A third political party will start in the United States.

27. Japan will suffer great political instability.

Forecast Made in 1992[e]

28. The North American Free Trade Agreement (NAFTA) will depress the Mexican economy and U.S. real incomes.

Forecasts Made in 1996 and 1997[f]

29. Stock markets will start crashing by the end of 1997.

30. The global speculative bubble will burst by August 1998.

31. The major battle between American bulls and bears will come in the summer of 1998.

c. Such forecasts appeared in Ravi Batra, *Surviving the Great Depression of 1990* (New York: Simon & Schuster, 1988), chap. 2.

d. I made these predictions in a lecture in Rimini, Italy, in October 1990, when the Italian government awarded me a Medal of the Italian Senate for correctly predicting the downfall of communism, in my macroeconomics class at SMU in spring 1991, and again in several lectures delivered in 1993 and published in a Japanese book, *Takashi Asai* (Future Economic Institution) (Tokyo: Tokuma Shoten, 1994), chap. 3.

e. Cf. Ravi Batra, *The Myth of Free Trade* (New York: Macmillan, 1993), 190–92.

f. These forecasts were made in Ravi Batra, *The Great American Deception* (New York: John Wiley and Sons, 1996), 174, and Ravi Batra, *Stock Market Crashes of 1998 and 1999: The Asian Crisis and Your Future* (Dallas: Liberty Press, 1997), 155–58.

32. Federal Reserve chairman Alan Greenspan will lower interest rates when share markets begin their fall in the United States.
33. Even as share markets crash in Asia and Latin America, the U.S. domino will sustain itself and be the last to fall.

My forecasts have mostly relied on the premise that history follows a discernible pattern, a view I share with the likes of Arnold Toynbee, Oswald Spengler, Karl Marx, and St. Augustine, among others. These are celebrated historians, and even though their ideas have been denounced at times, their breadth of vision far outshines that of their detractors. The accuracy of most of my prophecies indicates that there must be something right about the ideas underlying them; there must be some validity to the philosophy of historical determinism, which posits that history follows a natural, possibly providential, design.

Let's examine the first ten forecasts listed in table 4.1, most of which appeared in *The Downfall of Capitalism and Communism.* The Soviet empire has disintegrated right before your eyes; some critics say Chinese communism still stands, but my forecast excluded the Chinese variety, which is likely to persist for a while. The priesthood dominates Iran and has been doing so since 1979. Starting in September 1980, the country fought an eight-year war with Iraq. Thanks to the Gulf War, army generals such as Colin Powell and Norman Schwartzkopf have become celebrities. Similarly, women are more active than ever before in business and politics while income and wealth disparities have skyrocketed. Few worry about family values and personal integrity, even as crime, pornography, and divorce become rampant. Of course, the golden age and the fall of monopoly capitalism have not materialized, but their time has yet to come.

THE 1980–1983 FORECASTS

Let's now proceed to forecasts 11 through 20 in table 4.1, which appeared in *The Great Depression of 1990.* Following a severe recession in the early eighties, the seven years between 1983 and 1989 were prosperous, while inflation, interest rates, and oil and farm prices tumbled from their levels in the previous decade. Share prices broke records every year between 1983 and 1987 but then plunged in a stunning crash, which was anticipated in the second edition of *Great Depression.* Both bond prices and mergers jumped in the eighties. In 1986 France, Britain, and Germany suffered rising unemployment. All these forecasts were one way or another linked to the three-decade cycles of money and inflation examined in the preceding chapter.

THE 1988, 1991, AND 1992 FORECASTS

We now turn to predictions 21 through 28 in table 4.1. In 1994, thanks to the devaluation of the Mexican peso, the dollar collapsed, although not until the month of December; thus this forecast barely came true. In April 1995 the dollar went on to hit an all-time low of 80 yen. Inflation and interest rates have been tumbling since 1990, and by 1998 they were the lowest since the 1950s. In many large states, such as New York, California, and Florida, real estate values crashed in the early 1990s. With regard to my forecast about NAFTA, the devaluation of the peso in December 1994 catapulted Mexico into a deep depression. Real wages and the GDP both plummeted in a hurry. Even in 1999, real earnings of Mexican workers were below their pre-NAFTA levels. At the same time, U.S. real incomes began to fall after rising slightly in 1993. As soon as NAFTA was adopted in January 1994, real wages in both Mexico and the United States responded in the way I had foreseen a year earlier.

Every year of the 1990s has been full of drama and intrigue. The drama commenced with the stock market crash in Tokyo on the first trading day in 1990, followed by Saddam Hussein's invasion of Kuwait in August. Barely two months later, East and West Germany were united as a by-product of the collapse of the Berlin Wall. In January 1991 the Gulf War pitted the meager army of Iraq against not just U.S. military might but the whole world. An overwhelming victory in the conflict took President George Bush to the height of his popularity, his public approval rating surpassing 80 percent. Barely six months after the war, an abortive military coup in the Soviet Union accelerated the fall of communism. Soon after this, a third-party movement, led by Ross Perot, emerged in the United States in 1992. He won an unprecedented 19 percent of the vote in the presidential election and contributed to Bill Clinton's unexpected victory at the expense of the once invincible George Bush.

Japan's Liberal Democratic Party, ruling the country since 1950, collapsed in 1993 and paved the way for subsequent economic and political turmoil. In 1994 Nelson Mandela put an end to apartheid in South Africa and became that country's president. The same year witnessed the signing of peace treaties between implacable and ancient foes, the Jews and Palestinians, with slow but steady progress in coming years. This was followed by the Republican control of the House of Representatives for the first time in forty years. In April 1995 the dollar, as previously stated, sank to its all-time low; the year also saw the start of a depression in Mexico and the longest U.S. government shutdowns, which lasted from November 1995 all the way to January 1996. All this, and what immediately follows, demonstrate that each year of the 1990s turned out to be dramatic.

THE 1996–1997 FORECASTS

Let's now focus on my predictions made since 1996. A currency meltdown started in Thailand in July 1997 and quickly spread to all the Asian Tigers, encompassing eight countries. Stock markets crashed, and overnight some countries such as Indonesia, Thailand, Malaysia, and Korea slipped into a devastating recession. Then came Japan's turn. Struggling ever since its share price crash in January 1990, Japan sank even deeper into the slump in 1997 and 1998.

Share price crashes rippled around the world at the start of 1998, while the U.S. economy and stock markets continued to flourish. However, when August came, the Dow Jones index fell about 19 percent in one month, whereas the Nasdaq index tumbled as much as 25 percent. Many of the small cap stocks lost more than 50 percent of their value from their peak reached in July. Thus the global speculative bubble burst open in the month of August 1998, as predicted. In September and October, the financial world was in a panic. Just as Asia was reeling, Russia defaulted on its international debt, and Brazil was expected to follow suit. It is at that point that my thirty-second forecast came true, and Federal Reserve chairman Alan Greenspan engineered a series of cuts in the rate of interest. Once that happened, my final prediction came to pass. Nearly half of the world was in recession by April 1999. Europe was beginning to slow down, but the U.S. juggernaut continued its forward march. The American economic pace in fact accelerated in the last quarter of 1998, as the GDP climbed at a 6 percent annual rate. Thus the American economy continues to be an oasis of prosperity in the midst of an increasingly depressed world.

Epoch-making events normally occur once in a century, but ever since the fall of the Berlin Wall on November 9, 1989, the world has witnessed a series of them. The crash of the wall itself was a once-in-a-lifetime occurrence, but many more such events are likely in the near future.

Thus you see virtually all the predictions I made over the two decades between 1978 to 1997 have already come true. Only forecast 19 did not fully materialize, because share prices crashed in Japan in 1990 but not in the United States, and the world faced only a recession, not a depression. An interesting question now presents itself: When someone makes a great many prophecies, and almost all come true, then what can be said of the one case where the accuracy was only partial? In other words, what happened to the great depression of 1990, the title of my work first published in 1985?

THE U.S. ECONOMY, 1990–1998

According to official figures, a recession started in the United States in June 1990 and ended nine months later in March of the following year. The nation's output fell by a tiny fraction, less than 1 percent. Thus government figures display only a minor damage to the economy from the slump of 1990. But then you wonder why President George Bush, with an all-time-high public approval rating of 84 percent in March 1991, lost in an electoral college landslide to Bill Clinton barely twenty months later. Our economists view recession as a decline in the nation's output over two consecutive quarters. By this measure the recession was over in March 1991, the same month that produced the highest approval rating for the president, because the output began to rise. Now this is interesting. The president won accolades from his handling of the Gulf War, and the economy began to recover, yet he lost to a virtually unknown governor of a small state, Arkansas.

The truth is that the slump of 1990, though not a full-fledged depression of the type in the 1930s, was much more serious than revealed by official figures on output. The public said so at the ballot box and threw a once-untouchable president out of office. If we apply the conventional concept of recession to the 1930s, as the GDP began to rise, the depression was over by the end of 1933, a year when the unemployment rate hit 25 percent of the labor force. How ridiculous does that sound? Even in 1939, the jobless rate was over 15 percent. The point is that the state of the economy can not be gauged by output figures alone. You have to examine the trends in many areas including joblessness, real wages, and consumer optimism.

I am not alone in my view of the 1990 downturn. Harvard professor John Kenneth Galbraith called it a recession cum depression; economist David Levy characterized it as a "contained depression." Lawrence Hunter, deputy chief economist for the U.S. Chamber of Commerce, dubbed it a "never-ending recession." Even Massachusetts senator Ted Kennedy, no critic of Bill Clinton's, described it as a "quiet depression" as late as 1996.[9]

According to output figures, the U.S. economy started humming in early 1991; then why did so many luminaries take issue with that characterization? In a poignant commentary on the state of the economy, *Time* magazine openly wondered in January 1992, "Well, why are Americans so gloomy, fearful and even panicked about the current economic slump?"[10] The answer came from the state of real family income in America coupled with all the downsizing that had occurred in the early 1990s.

Since 1970, an increasing number of women have joined the labor force, so real family income has been rising in spite of stagnant real wages for individuals. According to the *Economic Report of the President,* median family income was $43,290 in 1989, just a year before the slump. In 1990 it fell to $42,400, and in 1996 it stood at $42,300, not only below the 1989 level but also below the 1990 figure.[11] Even five years after the recovery is supposed to have begun, median family income had not caught up with the preslump figure. This is why Pat Buchanan defeated the front-runner Bob Dole in the early 1996 Republican primary. On that occasion, journalist Jason DeParle, a staff writer for the *New York Times Magazine,* wrote: "Call it what you will, but class anger is back. Who could have imagined that a win in New Hampshire would come to a man who called the stock market un-American? Or that Bob Dole would pose, even fleetingly, as a critic of corporate America."[12]

National output figures told one story, but family income told another. Mark Twain used to say that there are lies, damn lies, and statistics. It is clear now that the official spin on the state of the economy has masked its true character, creating a false impression of growing prosperity.

This, however, is only part of the distorted picture. Let me give you an inside story of what actually brought about the seemingly unprecedented U.S. prosperity in the 1990s.

After Japan suffered a stock market crash in January 1990, it responded to the crisis by slashing interest rates. The idea was that low borrowing costs would encourage businesses to expand their investments, prompt households to make purchases, and cushion the banks from tons of bad debt so that the share price debacle would inflict minimal damage. However, for a variety of reasons, which are discussed later, this medicine failed, and the country's economy continued to sink at a slow but unmistakable pace.

Most Japanese banks survived as their deposit costs tumbled, but in a nation shell-shocked by the debacle there was little business and consumer demand for their loans. So they turned to other countries to expand their lending business or find lucrative investments. Despite a faltering home economy, they had plenty of funds to lend or invest, because the Japanese are among the biggest savers in the world. Some of their money went to the Asian Tigers, but a substantial part came to the United States, which had a huge appetite for foreign funds to finance its gargantuan budget deficit. Funds also poured into America from many other nations that had a bulging hoard of dollars acquired from their trade surplus. China alone had a $34 billion surplus in its U.S. trade in 1995.

From 1990 to 1995, the federal red ink in America amounted to $1.5 trillion, of which about a fourth, some $400 billion, was financed by foreign funds. An equal amount from abroad was invested in other American assets such as stocks, factories, and real estate. Thus about $800 billion of foreign money poured into the United States during the first half of the 1990s, and all the country could show for it was a declining median in family income, along with a loss of real wages. Stock and bond prices had skyrocketed because of foreign investment, but a vast number of Americans had suffered lower incomes.

With Japan continuing to sink into the abyss and the world awash in dollars, the inflow of foreign funds to the United States accelerated after 1996. The U.S. trade deficit had already become a blessing in disguise, and now it turned economic recovery into a full-blown boom. Normally, a country with a growing trade shortfall has to raise interest rates to attract foreign funds that in turn finance that shortfall. As a result, the economy and financial markets go into a slump, imports shrivel, and foreign commerce moves into balance. This has been the experience of all countries all through recorded history.

But in the 1990s, the laws of nature turned on their head. The U.S. economy and financial markets increasingly benefited from the trade deficit. As the deficit zoomed, so did American prosperity. A rising shortfall meant an ever-increasing hoard of dollars in international hands; people abroad didn't know what to do with all that foreign currency. Foreign governments or central banks ploughed the dollars right back into American assets, U.S. interest rates fell again, and a virtuous circle, sparked initially by the 1990 crash in Japan, turned into a gusher. In 1997 Asian currencies went into a tailspin, spurring a big rise in America's already enduring and large trade deficit. But that only helped the United States, because a larger inflow of external capital meant even lower interest rates.

The Asian crisis affected the U.S. economy in two ways, one positive and the other negative. The negative effect came from surging imports of manufactured goods that generated further downsizing in major industries. The positive impact sprang from falling interest rates that continued to fuel a housing boom, especially as people moved into ever larger homes. When a family buys a residence, it also likes to purchase many other things—appliances, furniture, paintings, rugs, and so on. Thus a housing boom is the best thing that can happen to an economy. In this way the salutary effect of the Asian crisis far outweighed the negative impact, so the U.S. economy and financial markets kept humming even as other nations stumbled.

On April 1, 1998, the United States orchestrated another dose of financial deregulation in Japan, ostensibly to cure the Japanese crisis. But its effects were the same as those of the Asian turmoil. Deregulation permitted the Japanese people and insurance companies to invest money abroad, a privilege heretofore available only to their banking institutions.

Uncle Sam, no longer rich but in desperate need of incoming largesse, has become the largest debtor in the world, but since the debt is not in foreign currency, its ill effects will take longer to erupt. Foreign debt has already crippled seemingly strong economies— Thailand, Malaysia, Indonesia, South Korea, the Philippines, Brazil, and others, whereas obvious laggards such as Mexico and Russia are gasping for breath. The United States is still standing tall despite its mountain of debt, but since its liabilities are not in terms of a foreign currency, it will be the last domino to fall. The country doesn't need to raise interest rates to attract foreign exchange, which is what is killing the other debtors.

This is the inside story of America's sizzling prosperity in the late 1990s, even as the rest of the world crumbles. As the federal deficit ballooned in 1990 and thereafter, the slump of that year could have turned into a full-fledged depression, but a flood of Japanese money brought interest rates down and saved the day. In spite of that inflow, there was a good deal of suffering for six long years until 1996. After that, as the foreign inflow accelerated, a tepid recovery turned into a full-blooded boom. Is this a real boom or a mere postponement of the day of reckoning? With billions of dollars in loans even a pauper can become a tycoon and gloat about his riches. But one day the loans come due with interest, something that has already bedeviled many parts of the world. The U.S. hour of judgment is almost here, and then the great depression, postponed in 1990, could make a ferocious comeback.

5

FREE-MARKET FUNDAMENTALS:
SUPPLY AND DEMAND

What you have read up to this point is mostly history and its interpretation. My prognosis has been simple and descriptive. But now we must cross the minefield of technical analysis. In order to see where we are headed we have to comprehend how an economy works, what it needs to remain prosperous and stable. We now have to enter the complex arena of tables and graphs in order to pinpoint the faults of prevailing ideas. What you are about to go through requires a little more focus and concentration, but the reward will be a richer understanding of our economic system and the means of its reformation. I promise I will not deviate far from the commonsense notions of simple supply and demand.

When Adam Smith, revered as the father of modern economics, wrote his masterpiece, *The Wealth of Nations,* in 1776, he pioneered a new and elegant defense for what is normally called the free-enterprise system. Although the Industrial Revolution had started two centuries before he was born, capitalism was still in its infancy. Under the influence of religion pervasive in his time, the public was generally suspicious of the profit motive and of individualism, which they thought could lead to anarchy. Interests of the state, not of the people, were paramount in the minds of leading thinkers.

Smith championed a new course and defended the general pursuit of self-interest as well as profits. He argued that all human actions are rooted in self-preservation and that self-interest and personal ambition are not vices but virtues, leading to hard work and prosperity.

Smith contended that left to themselves businesses and workers are motivated by self-interest to put their capital and labor to uses where they are the most productive. A producer of goods seeks maximum return from his investment, whereas an employee wants the highest salary for his skills and diligence. Facing keen competition from other companies, a businessperson has to build high-quality products at the lowest possible prices, whereas to get ahead of fellow workers, everyone has to work to his best potential. This is how self-preservation works.

The mechanism that brings the best out of employers and employees is what Smith called "the invisible hand" of a free market, where businesses compete for consumers' money in pursuit of profits, and consumers seek reliable products at the cheapest price. In their quest for profits, companies produce only those goods for which there is demand and employ technology and resources in a way that maximizes productive efficiency. In a free-market economy characterized by intense competition among firms, everyone is happy: investors earn maximum returns, and consumers are satisfied by high-quality products available at the lowest possible prices ensured by the maximum efficiency. This is the miracle performed by the invisible hand in spite of, or rather because of, human greed and acquisitive behavior.

Efficient operations guarantee that society's resources are put to their best use, generating the highest living standard from available technology. Smith thus assailed the myriad regulations that in his day perpetuated monopolies or restrained business competition, for they impeded the working of a free market. He championed small-scale enterprises as a continual source of new competitors. This point is very important, because modern monopolists have invoked Smith to rationalize their income levels. Adam Smith did not denounce avarice, which is inborn to most of us, but he did attack the state institutions that restrain competition and in the process enable some to be enormously wealthy and force others into destitution. He defended the profit motive but not profiteering.

It is well known that a pioneer is respected everywhere except at home. The same fate awaited Smith. Britain, where Smith was born, failed to pay heed to its brilliant economist and continued to protect the state trading monopolies. However, a newborn republic, the United States of America, adopted the practices he had preached. The spirit of individualism sizzled among America's freedom fighters, who were generally averse to federal intervention in personal matters such as the pursuit of profit in a business enterprise.

The new republic followed Adam Smith in all respects except in his advocacy of free trade. The British scholar generally favored the abolition of import tariffs, except in matters of self-defense and retaliation against the tariffs of other countries. But U.S. presidents, from George Washington to Abraham Lincoln, essentially sealed the American borders from foreign goods by adopting high import duties. American firms at home did not have to face unfettered foreign competition in their quest for profit and industrialization, but they encountered more than enough competition at home to enjoy the benefits of Smith's free enterprise.

The young republic, at the turn of the nineteenth century, was predominantly agrarian, meeting almost all its needs for manufactured goods from imports, including textiles, metals, and ships. Less than 5 percent of its labor force was engaged in industry, the rest employed in farming or services. Tariffs at the time averaged about 15 percent, but they jumped after 1815, stayed high in the coming decades, and reached their zenith of 65 percent in the 1860s, soon after the Civil War.

Insulated from foreign competition, the nascent U.S. industry expanded at a brisk pace. America was blessed with vast, fertile land, plentiful raw materials, a Calvinistic work ethic, a fast-growing population, and, above all, a huge number of small-scale enterprises. In short, all the prerequisites for the success of the invisible hand were present.

Since the country was just starting to industrialize, the early enterprises were small and exuberant, unable to corner any market. They provided keen competition to each other. It is the power of domestic rivalry that becomes a dynamic force in a free-market economy. Americans imported capital and technology—but not many goods—from Europe, combined them with domestic factories and labor, and sold their products primarily to the consumer at home. The rest is history. By the end of the nineteenth century, the United

States, starting practically from scratch, had forged ahead of the established economies of England, France, and Germany and emerged as the world's economic leader. The invisible hand of Adam Smith had provided a most visible success story to the globe. Free enterprise, henceforth, became the mantra of the experts, economists and politicians alike.

SUPPLY AND DEMAND

The working of the invisible hand is today described as unfettered supply and demand, with producers and workers providing the supply and consumers the demand. In the early history of capitalism, the economy was basically very simple. The government tended to be small, consuming only a tiny fraction of society's resources. Paltry state budgets couldn't begin to support the vast bureaucracy needed nowadays to manage a host of official economic functions. However, the basic ingredients of a modern economy are much the same as they were in the nineteenth century.

Supply and demand are the twin engines of economics, and they will remain so forever. A sound economy, regardless of size and complexity, requires a balance between the two forces. The invisible hand of a free market means that supply and demand are free to operate, and as long as the two function without constraints, the economy stays healthy and prosperous. When social institutions or the state interferes in the economy in such a way that one or both forces are monopolized, then market balance is destroyed. The result is either high unemployment, inflation, or both.

Interestingly enough, state intervention or society's disinterest in a free-market economy can produce sizzling prosperity for a few years, but in the long run the laws of nature take over. Take, for instance, the Roaring Twenties, the decade immediately preceding the agony of the Great Depression. Business investment, productivity, new technology, GDP, profits, and stock prices all soared to generate a period of unprecedented optimism and prosperity. Everyone came to believe that all you needed to be rich was to own shares in some company, any company. But hidden behind the hoopla was a growing gap between supply and demand. While consumers had not altered their behavior, producers had. Merger after merger created industrial giants and vast profits. While the force of demand was unconstrained, that of supply had been cornered to produce over-night millionaires, and the government did nothing to restore com-petition. Supply and demand were no longer free to operate. For a while the formula that tolerated monopolies worked to perfection, but in the long run the invisible hand of the market took over to gen-erate the world's worst depression.

In the pages ahead, we shall see that whenever the markets are free, prosperity is broad-based and lasting, and whenever they are not there may be a temporary illusion of affluence that is followed by widespread poverty. I am a great believer in free markets, but my con-cept of economic freedom is at variance with that of some econo-mists. I believe in the power of internal competition and that the government should be ever so vigilant in enforcing antitrust laws to maintain this challenge. Foreign competition, in my view, is not a necessary ingredient.

According to many of my peers, however, free markets mean that the state should let businessmen, especially tycoons, tinker with the economy. If they want low taxation, then offer it to them, even if this may mean high taxes for the poor and the middle class; if they indulge in megamergers, don't stop them, even if domestic competi-tion suffers and regional monopolies mushroom; if they raise their own salaries, while downsizing others, stand idly by. Some call this supply-side economics. To me it is a recipe for economic disaster, for it destroys the free working of the force of supply. When monopolies replace competitive firms, the force of demand is still free to function, but that of supply is constrained; and while there may be fabulous prosperity for the few, and a broad-based boom creating copious jobs, there will be a calamity in the long run.

Freedom signifies an arena in which everyone can enter, not one in which only the powerful flourish. That is why antitrust laws need to be strictly enforced to sustain the working of the invisible hand. When producers in every industry, just like consumers, are too numerous to be visible, that is when the invisible hand functions at its best. The free market, in other words, requires plenty of invisible or small-scale enterprises. When a few companies become large enough to corner the markets, then it is the duty of the state to break up the monopolies or at minimum not permit mergers among large, profitable firms. This, at least, is the concept of free markets espoused by Adam Smith.

THE LABOR MARKET

The laws of supply and demand apply to all segments of the economy, including those seeking and offering jobs. However, economists have traditionally neglected the labor market, focusing primarily on the exchange among products and services. In complex modern economies, a large number of goods, services, and assets are traded daily, weekly, monthly, or annually. Markets exist for everything that enters the purview of exchange. There are markets for food, automobiles, electronics, furniture, houses, appliances, education, health care, labor, land, capital, raw materials, credit, and even money. In addition, assets such as stocks, bonds, futures, options, and so on are also traded daily. Thus numerous markets exist nowadays, and state vigilance to ensure their freedom has never been greater.

Scholars have conventionally focused on product markets, neglecting the exchange that takes place for assets and resources. Popular macroeconomic theories, today and in the past, concentrate on national demand and supply for goods and services, paying perfunctory attention to the behavior of share prices, worker productivity, and wages. However, we shall soon see that the labor market is the nucleus of a macroeconomy. If there is an imbalance in this arena, then all other markets function abnormally. When the national labor market is distorted, the markets for goods, services, and assets are distorted as well.

Adam Smith, among others, concentrated on the behavior of producers and consumers, but everybody is a laborer first and a consumer later; similarly, all producers need labor to generate a product. That is why it turns out that the labor market is at the heart of a smoothly functioning economy, and every other activity is directly or indirectly linked to it.

Some people believe that the term *labor market* should be abolished, because it relegates human beings to the status of commodities. It is true that labor is unique: no worker can be bought and sold, at least not in our times. Furthermore, unlike commodities, raw materials, stocks, and bonds, people have feelings. They need a proper work environment, safety procedures, and flexible work hours. As a product of exchange, labor is clearly different, but in a modern economy, employers rent labor in much the same way you lease an appliance from a rental store. When someone applies for a job, he or she may have found the opening listed in a newspaper, which also includes advertisements for many other products. The employee signs a contract with the employer just as someone enters into an agreement with an auto dealer to lease a car. Thus labor skills are bought and sold in much the same way as other services.

When you rent a house, you have obtained the housing service for a certain price but not purchased the house itself. The labor market, where workers offer their productivity to an employer at a certain price, functions in much the same way. Some people, however, run their own business and essentially work for themselves. They are called self-proprietors or self-employed workers and are considered part of the labor force.

Like most goods and services, labor markets may be local or national. If employers and workers search for jobs locally, as they do for most secretaries, janitors, and auto mechanics, the market is local; if the buyers and sellers of labor services look for positions around the country, as do doctors, lawyers, accountants, professors, and engineers, then the market is national.

Some workers, locally as well as nationally, are represented by unions. Even though union membership has plummeted since 1980, when Ronald Reagan was elected president, there are still over fifteen million workers in the United States who do not directly sell their skills to producers. Most unionized industries are in the manufacturing sector, including automobile, electronics, tractors, and airplanes. General Motors, Ford, and Boeing, for instance, have to bargain about wages and working conditions with labor leaders. Some services such as airlines, trucking, and education are also represented by unions. In the case of organized labor, employers normally have to deal with a union regarding the hiring, firing, and seniority decisions. Some federal and state employees are also represented by unions.

NATURAL DEMAND

Whether or not workers are organized, they and their salaries are the main or natural source of society's product demand. The idea of demand is easy to follow in any industry but difficult to comprehend at the national level. About fifteen million cars and trucks are sold annually in the United States; someone needs these four-wheelers and creates a demand for them. Thus consumer demand in any one industry is expressed in terms of physical units: x number of autos, for example, or y number of teachers needed by schools and colleges, and so on. However, the concept of demand for all goods and services together cannot be expressed in physical units, because you can't add apples to bananas.

National demand has to be described in terms of a common denominator such as aggregate or total spending on newly produced goods and services in the economy. Spending on raw materials must be excluded from this concept, because no one wants them for their own sake; they are needed to produce consumption goods or machines, which in turn are needed to embody new technology and to produce other products. Thus business spending on raw materials is excluded from the estimate of national demand. What is included? Practically every other type of expenditure on newly produced goods.

Who spends money in the economy? Mostly laborers and employers, precisely the people involved in supplying the products. Thus national demand and supply are interconnected concepts. The main source of consumer demand is wages; people normally avoid using their interest and rental income for consumption, unless they are retired and no longer earn a regular salary, and much of the aggregate consumption comes from active workers, not retirees. In 1997 aggregate consumption in the U.S. equaled $5.4 trillion, whereas compensation of employees and self-proprietors added up to $5.2 trillion. Clearly, almost the entire level of consumer spending came from wages or work-related incomes. In 1980, on the other hand, consumption was at $1.7 trillion, whereas labor income equaled $1.8 trillion. That year the people saved a lot more than they did in 1997. When wages rise, workers spend more; when they fall, spending declines.

In order to account for the effect of prices on national demand, we should examine inflation-adjusted spending. Economists like to study what is called real aggregate spending, which is adjusted for changes in prices. Real consumer expenditure responds positively only if the real wage climbs; here the real wage is the inflation-adjusted level of one's salary. If your income and prices both double, there is no change in your real wage; your real spending will also then be constant. Thus the term *real* is added to any figure after it is adjusted for inflation.

Such adjustment is usually done with the help of an average figure described by a price index. The CPI, for instance, is an average price of all products commonly entering into public consumption. Another well-known price index is known as GDP deflator, which deals with all goods and services and is used to adjust the dollar value of GDP to obtain what we call real GDP, which is an estimate for national output. The dollar salary is normally divided by the CPI and then multiplied by one hundred to obtain a person's real wage. Consumer spending out of real wages may be termed natural consumer demand.

This demand is natural for two reasons. First, the purpose of all production is to meet the consumption needs of the people, of whom about half are in the labor force. Workers support families, which spend money to meet their daily needs for food, clothing, education, health care, housing, and entertainment. These are the needs that must be met for self-preservation. Although Americans enjoy among the highest living standard in the world, almost 13 percent of U.S. residents subsist below the poverty line; about 40 percent have no medical insurance. Virtually half of Americans have less than $1,000 in the bank at any moment.[13] Any spending used to meet these necessities may be described as natural. Of course, the meaning of necessities changes over time. Because of educational requirements and large outlays on commuting for work, real income for meeting necessities has sharply gone up in recent years.

Second, natural consumer demand requires that people meet most of their needs without incurring debt. If a large part of personal spending comes from borrowed money, it cannot be termed natural, because the money has to be paid back from future earnings, which may or may not prove sufficient. Thus natural consumer demand may be defined as one where people meet their basic needs primarily out of their incomes without going into debt.

What about borrowing money to buy a house, car, or an appliance? These goods, especially homes, last a long time, and loans obtained to finance their purchase are compatible with the concept of natural demand as long as they are reasonable and manageable. When a person acquires a house, he or she replaces rental expense with a monthly mortgage. As long as your monthly house payment stays clear of your savings, your debt may be said to be reasonable and compatible with natural demand. The same applies to the purchase of a car and appliances. The test of whether consumer demand is natural lies in what happens to personal savings and/or consumer debt over time. If debt and income go up in the same proportion, all consumer demand may be said to be natural; if not, some increase in debt may be said to be artificial, unsupportable by the person's or society's means.

Consumers are not the only buyers in society. Businesses also spend money in the economy; they buy or build machines and office buildings to generate their products. This type of spending is called business investment, of which a substantial part is dedicated to replacement. Every year part of the plant and equipment constructed in the past breaks up or becomes obsolete, and companies have to replenish this just to keep their production from falling below the level of last year. This type of spending is called replacement investment and is financed primarily from funds that businesses set aside for the depreciation of capital. The *Economic Report of the President,* an annual publication of the U.S. Council of Economic Advisers, calls it capital consumption, which is linked to existing demand. If consumer demand were to fall for any reason, businesses would be reluctant to replace their depleted stock of capital.

Businesses also spend money to meet new consumer demand, to upgrade their equipment, or to utilize new technology. Much of the spending on computers in recent years has come from corporations in their desire to improve worker productivity. Companies finance this type of investment primarily in two ways—from their profits or loans obtained from banks or the public. Debt-financed investment has to be paid out of future earnings, which may or may not materialize. Here too investment may be called natural if it is financed out of depreciation allowances and current profits. This way, we may define natural demand as consumer and business outlays without the excessive use of debt.

ARTIFICIAL DEMAND

Whenever people and nations live beyond their means, the spending so generated may be termed artificial, in the sense that it cannot last forever. Natural demand is durable, even permanent, but artificial demand must face a day of reckoning. There is no free lunch anywhere in the world. As long as the nation's peacetime debt rises no faster than its GDP, which is a measure of society's earnings, no problem may arise from artificial demand. During wars and other emergencies, of course, this type of rule does not apply.

The worst type of artificial demand is one where a person or a nation persistently borrows money for current consumption. Since the loans have to be repaid, debt-financed consumption enhances today's living standard at the expense of the future. It is perhaps one of the most cowardly acts, because it saddles our children with the burden of debt. Debt-financed investments may be condoned, because they are likely to enhance our future earnings, but debt-financed consumption should be sanctioned only when survival is at stake. In 1998 U.S. consumer debt broke new records; in some months, the public spent more money than it earned, something reminiscent of the 1930s, when indeed millions of Americans worried about survival. But 1998 was a boom year, and if a large part of consumer demand was artificial in good times, it portended problems in the future.

In modern economies, governments affect national spending through taxation and direct purchase of goods and services. State budgets in the nineteenth century were usually small and had little impact on the course of their economies. But since the Second World War, most governments have grown in size and now exert a substantial influence on public well-being. State spending injects money into the economy and adds to aggregate demand, whereas tax revenues have just the opposite effect.

If the government has a balanced budget, with spending matching the tax revenue, national demand is more or less unaltered; with a deficit budget, however, demand rises; it falls with a surplus budget. Since the early 1970s, when the world economy suffered the so-called oil shock that quadrupled the international price of oil, most governments have been running on red ink. The budget shortfalls mushroomed in the 1980s, especially in the United States, with the federal government borrowing hundreds of billions of dollars every year to finance its excess spending. It is only under President Bill Clinton that the deficit has been decreasing; it even went into surplus in 1998.

The debt-financed budget deficit is another instance of artificial demand, because it has to be paid back by future generations through extra taxation or higher interest payments. In 1970 the federal government paid about $14 billion in interest on its debt; by 1997 the figure had jumped to $290 billion, an almost twentyfold rise. Even if inflation is taken into account, this was a monumental jump in federal obligations and has to be paid out of current revenues. The present generation bears the burden of past profligacy by the federal government. Some governments, doing as the Romans did, finance their deficits in the old-fashioned way—by printing money. This is what occurred in ancient Rome. In this case, no debt is left for posterity, but excessive use of the money mint can cause serious inflation. There is no easy way to justify budget deficits, and they must be included in the artificial category for raising national spending or demand.

Another type of artificial demand is a country's trade surplus, which may be positive, negative, or zero. A negative surplus is also called trade deficit, which is a drag on national production. The trade surplus too is an unnatural way of generating demand for home products, because the country not only becomes dependent on foreign prosperity, it may also generate global friction by forcing a production loss abroad. One nation's surplus is another's deficit. Through surplus trade a country may be able to maintain its industry only at the expense of production in some other country. Japan in the 1990s is a prime example of a nation with a stagnant economy coexisting with a vast trade surplus. If the surplus is so good, why is Japan still struggling to escape its long recession? Domestic, not foreign, demand is the best and reliable source of prosperity.

Aggregate spending equals natural plus artificial demand. For the economy as a whole, whenever consumer, corporate, or government debt as a percentage of GDP rises over time, artificial demand is created, suggesting that there is something wrong with the fundamentals of demand and supply. The situation should be rectified as soon as possible, or else serious problems will arise. The nation may postpone facing these woes in the short run, but in the long run it will suffer high unemployment, inflation, or both. Most economies today, including that of the United States, have substantial artificial demand, which augurs poorly for the future.

NATIONAL SUPPLY

Like national demand, national supply becomes comprehensible only if it is expressed in terms of the national currency; otherwise you have to engage in the fruitless exercise of adding the production of apples and bananas. The GDP, which is the retail value of newly produced goods and services during a year, is the same thing as national supply. If our objective is to see how the economy is performing over time, this figure should also be adjusted for inflation to obtain real GDP.

In order to generate production, companies have to invest money from their own profits or from loans from banks or the public; they may also sell their shares to investors to raise funds for capital formation. After acquiring enough funds, the companies build plant and equipment and hire labor to produce a desirable product. Most businesses offer high-quality and reliable goods to attract customers, so profit maximization requires that employers find skilled and motivated workers, and use the latest technology. This way goods are produced with minimum production costs and maximum worker productivity.

Labor productivity is thus the key to profitability in a competitive world, where efficiency and company survival go together. In today's society, however, product quality can be masked behind attractive packaging. Glitzy commercials can conceal, at least for a while, the true worth of a commodity. Large companies, with millions available for advertisements, can fool the public for some time and get away with production of shoddy goods and services.

You may have noticed that even in recent recessions prices seldom fall. The true test of a free-market economy is that when national demand contracts, prices decline. This is what used to occur in the past. Since the 1970s, however, prices keep rising regardless of booms or slumps. Cars, shoes, tuition, health care, medicines, and so on become costlier in an annual ritual. The recession of the early 1980s was the most serious since the 1930s; national demand plummeted for goods and services, but still the cost of living continued to rise at an unhealthy pace. Unemployment soared and people's ability to buy goods tumbled, yet the annual rate of inflation persisted at a solid 6 percent. How were companies able to do this? How could they raise prices in the face of plummeting demand? Through the power of commercials that generate what is called quality competition rather than price competition.

Through advertising, big corporations create an impression of quality superiority in the minds of their patrons, and are able to lift prices even with falling costs and demand. For all practical purposes, there may be no difference in driving a car using gas sold at either Exxon or 7-Eleven. Yet, people are ready to pay extra pennies for the privilege of using Exxon, even though the quality difference may be more imaginary than real. Such is the power of advertising.

Most large modern corporations are regional or segmented monopolies. A pure monopoly is one that is the only provider in a market; electric and water utilities are common examples of such companies in states and cities. Outside of utilities, however, pure monopolies seldom, if ever, exist today. But some corporate giants are near monopolies or regional monopolies. Microsoft may have a near monopoly in computer software; its Windows network is said to control as much as 90 percent of the market for operating systems. In aircraft Boeing is also a near monopoly. General Motors, by contrast, is a regional or partial monopoly, controlling about a third of the auto market in the United States.

Whenever companies are large enough to raise prices even in recessions, they may be called regional or segmented monopolists. Economists call them oligopolies. A regional monopoly, unlike a single supplier controlling 100 percent of the market, exercises limited power over its prices. A single seller may, of course, raise its prices at will depending on demand and cost conditions, but even a regional monopolist has some ability for price gouging, because through advertising it can hook millions of people to its products. So when the company raises prices a little at a time, it loses some, but not very many, buyers. It has monopoly power in its own segment of loyal customers, in its own niche, so to speak. And if there are ten or fewer businesses supplying a market in a vastly rich country like the United States, each price augmenting company can count on others to raise their prices. This way goods can become expensive even as national demand tumbles.

Regional monopolies do compete fiercely with each other. Most industries in America are dominated by a few giant firms; they face stiff rivalry from foreign but not domestic firms. In automobiles, for instance, the Big Three of General Motors, Ford, and Chrysler control about 70 percent of the market. In cigarettes, breakfast foods, aluminum, steel, soap, and communications, only a few companies are predominant. Phillip Morris and RJR Nabisco do compete fiercely in the tobacco industry, but competition is limited mostly to quality, not price.

Because of brand loyalty among their patrons, the companies can easily raise prices without fear of customer revolt, especially when they are reasonably certain that their competitors will follow suit. People believe there is a qualitative difference among the products of different firms, and are willing to pay a small premium over the brands offered by other companies. This way each corporation can act as a monopoly within its own arena and has the ability to earn much higher profits than would be possible in a world of smaller enterprises with limited resources for costly commercials. And it makes no difference if companies are owned by foreign or domestic enterprises, as long as they are located on your own soil, a subject that will be explored in detail in chapter 12.

Thus Adam Smith's invisible hand no longer operates on the supply side of the economy. Markets are free neither in America nor in most other countries. In Western Europe the market structure is much the same as in the United States; inside Japan domestic firms compete fiercely but mostly in manufacturing. In Japanese service industries, such as freight and insurance, the lack of price competition is as remarkable as in the United States. But the worst type of regional or pure monopolies afflict the Third World. The concept of competition is alien to some countries in Asia, Latin America, and Africa. The industrial landscape in Brazil, Mexico, India, Argentina, and Pakistan, for example, is dotted with corporate behemoths that offer poor-quality products at extortionate prices. As we shall soon see, this is the main reason why Asia is now going through an economic turmoil. In fact, we will discover that the main reason for high unemployment and inflation in any economy is the lack of keen rivalry among firms in various industries.

WAGES AND PRODUCTIVITY

Supply and demand for goods are linked to the workforce through wages and productivity. What happens in the national labor market is the key to a country's economic health. Supply and demand for workers determine wages and employment. Skilled and motivated workers are the backbone of high efficiency, but what is perhaps crucial is that company wages reflect labor productivity. When new technology raises hourly output, then fairness demands that workers are properly compensated for their hard work and skills. This is not only a question of ethics but of labor peace and social prosperity as well.

Wages are the main source of demand, productivity the main source of supply, and if the two are not in sync with each other, then national supply and demand cannot be in balance for long, and eventually the economy runs into major trouble. For a while the balance between the two forces can be maintained by raising artificial demand through excessive business investment, or through the expansion of consumer debt, money supply, corporate debt, government budget deficits, and even exports, but these are mere palliatives that may mask the problem for some time. Artificial spending is the stuff of which economic disasters are made. Frequently it culminates in recessions, but occasionally it has even spawned depressions and inflation—even hyperinflation. Whenever and wherever a country has suffered a major depression, you will find a persistent and substantial wage-productivity gap. The bigger the size of artificial demand, the greater the eventual trouble.

A SIMPLE ILLUSTRATION

When the labor market is distorted in the sense that real wages lag behind productivity, the entire economy behaves irrationally. Let us take a simple example in a very simple economy. Suppose there are one hundred workers in a society, and each produces $5 worth of output. Worker productivity is then $5, and if everybody is employed, total output or supply will be $500. U.S. experience of the 1950s and the 1960s reveals that a high-growth economy with practically no unemployment and inflation requires that about 80 percent of output go to labor and the remaining 20 percent to the owners of income-producing property or capital, which is also an important resource contributing to productivity. (Capital owners usually earn incomes through their labor as well, so the 20 percent share is not their only source of earnings). Under this rule, wages will be 80 percent of output, or $400, and profits the rest, or $100.[14]

Keeping the argument as simple as possible, let us suppose that initially all wages are consumed and all profits are invested into new technology and the replacement of worn-out capital so that consumption spending is $400, investment spending is $100, and the aggregate spending is $500. In this case, the economy functions smoothly, for both national supply and demand for goods equal $500.

Now assume that owing to new technology, worker productivity doubles to $10, so the value of output generated by one hundred workers rises to $1,000. If wages and consumption also double to $800 and the profits and investment to $200, again national supply and demand for products will remain in balance, this time each equal to $1,000. However, suppose wages rise only to $600, while profits go up to $400. Consumption now equals $600, and it is clear that investment spending must now be $400 lest national demand be short of supply, resulting in overproduction. Would businesses be willing to put all their profits into new investment, when consumer spending grows slowly? The answer is most likely not.

If you are investing $200 when your sales are $800, you are not likely to increase your investment for business expansion when your sales go down to $600. If companies realize that the current demand for their goods is inadequate, they will trim their investment even below $200. The purpose of capital spending, after all, is mainly to meet consumer demand; you would expand your business only in proportion to your sales. If sales fail to materialize, investment will decline. With consumer demand less than $800, the companies will invest even less than $200, in which case total spending will fall way short of supply, businesses will be stuck with unsold goods, and lay-offs will have to follow. Thus the simple example makes it clear that when wages lag behind productivity, distorting the labor market, the product markets will also be out of kilter.

It is of course possible that, for a while, the companies may not be aware of the shortfall in consumer demand; their high profits may convince them to expand their capital expenditures all the way up to $400 and to buy more machines. In this case, demand and supply will each equal $1,000, and the economy will reveal no signs of the potential imbalance possible from the slowdown in consumer spending. The growth process, however, will continue. With investment sky-rocketing to $400, the use of new technology and worker productivity will climb even faster.

Suppose in the next round output per employee jumps to $20, so total supply, with full employment of labor, soars to $2,000; if wages and consumer demand rise only to $1,200, then investment must climb to $800 to maintain the balance between supply and demand. It is clear that with wages lagging behind productivity, the growth process will become explosive, requiring ever-increasing doses of business investment to maintain high employment and the living standard.

This process is purely artificial in the sense that businesses will be selling a large portion of their goods to each other rather than to consumers to sustain their prosperity. It's like a Ponzi scheme in which you have to create sellers to buy your products and sell them to other sellers. Such schemes always collapse. When firms raise their capital spending and buy more machines from other companies, in reality they sell goods to each other, because consumers certainly have no use for plant and equipment. Sooner or later, a point will come when the companies are unable to sell all their output, and a recession or a depression will result. If the growth process continues for a long time, then the potential overproduction becomes so large that a depression becomes inevitable.

It is noteworthy that the power of this logic in no way depends on the simplicity of our assumptions. In the real world, some workers do save, and not all profits may be invested. Furthermore, there is a large government sector today in most economies, which additionally have to reckon with the ills of inflation. Labor income also may not initially amount to 80 percent of output; these assumptions are not crucial to the argument. What is critical is that real wages grow slower than the rate of productivity resulting from new technology and business investment.

What could be done to rectify the problem? Since the fundamental source of the imbalance in both the labor and product markets is that wages trail productivity, the solution is clear. Either a law should be passed that all output be divided proportionately between labor and capital, or some institutions should be created such that wages grow in sync with hourly output. This, of course, has not been done anywhere in the world, even though the wage-productivity gap, hereafter called the wage gap, has been soaring all over the globe for the last three decades. Then how has the balance been maintained between demand and supply for products?

The two forces of the market must always be in balance; otherwise, the global economic systems will explode in a storm of instability, which has not happened in the United States at least since 1990 and in Asia from 1990 to 1997. Some may even dismiss the global recession of 1990 and suggest that the world escaped a major slump between 1983 and 1997. The wage gap inevitably results in demand gap, which equals the difference between national spending and the economy's maximum potential output. Stated another way, how has the world, especially the United States, succeeded in eliminating or reducing the demand gap in the wake of a large wage gap persisting for decades?

Almost all nations have followed the same recipe to maintain the market balance. Although a variety of artificial means is available to raise demand to the level of supply, most countries have resorted to high consumer and government debt. Investment spending, as shown above, can also be augmented to plug the demand shortfall, but this measure may generate more problems than it solves. For business investment initially increases national spending, but later stimulates productivity. As we've seen, to plug the demand gap, the country will have to allocate ever increasing sums for capital formation, and the problem will only grow over time. There is one nation that has tried this method—Japan.

In most regions, now including Japan, government deficits and debts have skyrocketed. Is it a coincidence that this phenomenon coexisted with the soaring wage gap? Clearly not. In fact, the logic of the argument is that this was inevitable: governments around the globe were forced to do this to maintain superficially healthy economies. Unable and unwilling to eliminate the wage gap, this is all they could do in the name of sound economic policy.

THE U.S. ECONOMY, 1959–1998

Let us explore the postwar behavior of the American economy. While examining any time period, consistency in the relevant data is important to avoid misperceptions. As much as possible, the statistics should be obtained from the very same study. I have collected economic figures from a highly reliable source, the *Economic Report of the President,* issued in 1999. This is an annual publication of the U.S. Council of Economic Advisers and offers a variety of statistics, including real wages and productivity, which, among other things, are presented in table 5.1.

The data, displayed in five-year intervals, go as far back as 1959, which is the starting point of our analysis. Using the *Economic Report of the President* and others, we could combine the wage-productivity series and go as far back as 1947, but the data consistency would be lost because the other publications use slightly different definitions.

If we divide the index of output per hour in the business sector by the index of real employee compensation, both available from the *Economic Report of the President,* we obtain a measure of the wage gap in the United States. If real incomes rise in sync with labor productivity, which is the same thing as hourly output, then the figures in column 2 should be more or less constant. In 1959 the wage-gap index stood at 80, and rose steadily thereafter, at first slowly and then in a torrent, to reach an all-time postwar high of 105 in 1998. Clearly wages trailed productivity over time; in three decades the wage-gap index soared by almost a third.

According to our hypothesis, when wages trail productivity, natural demand stagnates, so artificial demand must rise to maintain the balance between supply and demand. Two measures of artificial demand are consumer debt and the government budget deficit. Columns 3 and 4 present consumer credit and the government deficit

TABLE 5.1

Wage Gap and the Index of Artificial Demand in the
United States for Selected Years, 1959–1998 (in percent)

Year	Productivity[a] Real Wage	Consumer Credit GDP	All Government Deficit GDP	Index of Artificial Demand
1959	80	11.0	−2.4	8.6
1964	83	13.0	−2.4	10.6
1969	83	13.0	−3.0	10.0
1974	85	13.6	−0.9	12.7
1979	89	13.5	−1.3	12.2
1984	96	13.2	1.8	15.0
1989	98	14.3	0.3	14.6
1994	102	13.8	1.3	15.1
1998	105	15.5	−0.5	15.0

SOURCE: Data from *Economic Report of the President* (Washington, D.C.: U.S. Council of Economic Advisers, 1999), 384–424.

[a] Column 2 furnishes the wage-gap index, which is obtained by dividing two other indexes, one dealing with output per hour, or labor productivity, and the other with real employee compensation, or national real wage.

as a percentage of the GDP. The two are added to obtain the index of artificial demand shown in column 5. The table reveals that as the wage gap climbed, so did consumer debt, reaching an all-time high of 15.5 percent in 1998. As a result, the artificial demand index was also close to its peak that year.

The figures for the government deficit are very interesting, because as late as 1979, the government budget, contrary to popular belief, displayed a surplus, not deficit. For national demand, what matters is the budget shortfall at all levels of government—state, local, and federal. It is true that the federal government has had a deficit budget between 1969 and 1997, but between 1959 and 1974 the state and local governments had so much revenue that there was an overall surplus. The overall government deficit was actually negative and in surplus, which peaked in 1969.

The official culture of red ink really began in the early 1980s, peaked in 1984, but persisted for a long time thereafter. Finally, in

1998 there was a surplus again, the first in eighteen years. With a record-high wage gap, the index of artificial demand, and hence the potential demand gap, was also close to an all-time high in 1998, suggesting that any erosion of business or consumer confidence could lead to massive trouble in the economy.

THE STOCK MARKET

As mentioned earlier, when the labor market is distorted in the sense that employees are not properly compensated for their productivity-raising skills, other sections of the economy behave irrationally. Among the first to be infected by the growing virus of the wage gap is the market for stocks and related assets. Over the long run, U.S. share markets have produced an annual return of about 12 percent on invested funds, but in some decades their yield far exceeded the historical norm. This happened in the 1920s and, on a much larger scale, in the 1980s and the 1990s. Each time the wage gap and artificial demand soared. This must be more than a coincidence, as is clear from a study of table 5.2, which, for the 1920s, displays the same information as the previous table. The wage-gap index just before the start of the decade was at 111, but climbed steadily thereafter, reaching a high of 156 in 1929; the index of consumer debt, not surprisingly, jumped rapidly, reaching a high of 6.9 percent that year.

At the time, state budgets were in balance and the federal government enjoyed a surplus, as displayed in column 4; when this is subtracted from figures in column 3, we get a measure of artificial demand in the 1920s. Clearly, the index was then much lower, but, then as now, it soared to unprecedented heights. In many instances, what matters is not just the absolute level of any figure but also its rate of change. In trying to analyze what triggered a crisis, the answer usually lies in something that drastically changed. The index of artificial demand, though still quite low in 1921, more than doubled by 1929, and the stock market followed, a symbiosis clearly displayed in figure 5.1. The Dow Jones Index (or the Dow), jumped from 72 in 1920 to 381 by August 1929, a vertical climb of over 400 percent in just nine years, clearly outpacing the historical norm of 12 percent a year by a wide margin. The public rejoiced, unaware that the share market euphoria was rooted in the quicksand of artificial demand.

THE CRASH OF THE MILLENNIUM | 73

TABLE 5.2

Wage Gap in Manufacturing and the Index of Artificial Demand in the 1920s, 1919–1929 (in percent)

Year	Productivity Real Wage	Consumer Debt GDP	Government Surplus GDP	Index of Artificial Demand
1919	111	3.1	1.5	1.6
1921	128	4.3	1.4	2.9
1923	130	4.4	1.3	2.1
1925	148	5.1	1.0	4.1
1927	154	5.6	1.0	4.6
1929	156	6.9	0.8	6.1

SOURCE: Data from *Historical Statistics of the United States: Colonial Times to 1970* (Washington, D.C.: U.S. Department of Commerce, 1975), series D 685, D 727, D 802, F 32, X 409, Y 493.

Note: The wage-gap indexes in tables 5.1 and 5.2 are not comparable because of differences in the definition of wages.

The same thing happened between 1982 and 1999, as revealed in figure 5.2. In June 1982 the Dow hit a low of 804, but then began a long and steady climb, never to look back at the bad old year that witnessed a serious recession. Share prices can climb for a variety of reasons, some of which I examine in subsequent chapters, but the soaring wage gap is among the most potent stimuli. It is easy to see why. The rising wage gap is one prerequisite for a phenomenal rise in profits that, in turn, sparks a share market boom. The other precondition is the jump in hourly output, so the fruit of soaring productivity goes primarily to the owners and controllers of capital.

The growing wage gap alone is not sufficient to trigger stock market returns above the historical norm. In the 1970s, for instance, the real wage plummeted while productivity remained more or less constant, causing a rise in the wage gap but hardly a movement in the Dow, which averaged 906 in 1968 and then 844 in 1979. Real incomes fell because of rising oil prices, inflation, and globalization of the U.S. economy, but the same factors that depressed wages also depressed profits; consequently, the rising wage gap failed to spark a share price boom.

FIGURE 5.1
The wage gap and the Dow Jones index, 1919–1929

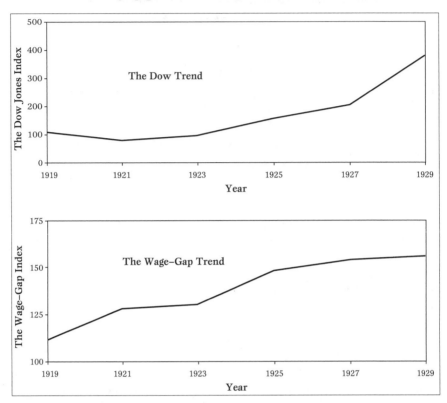

SOURCE: Data from P. S. Pierce, *The Dow Jones Averages: 1885–1990* (Homewood, Ill: Business One Irwin, 1991). *Note:* During the 1920s, the Dow jumped as the wage gap climbed.

What about the times when the wage gap fell or at least did not rise? This happened in the 1960s and in the first two decades of the twentieth century. Table 5.1 reveals that the wage gap was more or less constant from 1959 to 1969, rising a miniscule 6 percent in ten years. Both productivity and wages soared during this decade, which enjoyed spectacular GDP growth of 4.4 percent per year, while share prices rose only 45 percent during the entire period. It is true that the growth rate during the 1960s was not the fastest ever in American history, but per capita GDP growth certainly was (per-capita GDP is output per person). Honors for the sharpest growth rate goes to the 1900s, and there also the wage gap fell slowly but

FIGURE 5.2
The wage gap and the Dow Jones index, 1979–1999

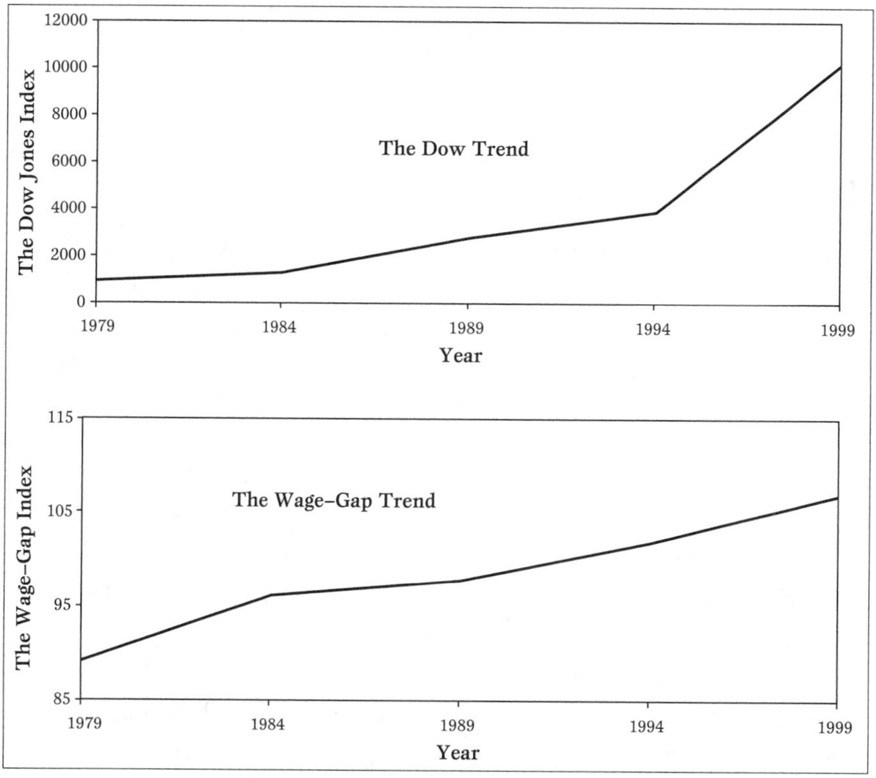

SOURCE: Data from table 5.1 and *Economic Report of the
President* (Washington, D.C.: U.S. Council of
Economic Advisers, 1999), 436.
Note: As the wage gap rose steadily after 1979, the Dow skyrock-
eted. The 1999 Dow figure is its March peak at 10,007, and the
1999 wage gap is estimated by the author at 107.

steadily. There again stock markets failed to zoom, but the general
living standard soared.

During the 1910s, however, the wage-gap index was more or less
constant, and neither GDP growth nor share prices sizzled. The culprit again was stagnant productivity, perhaps caused by the First
World War, which entangled the American economy from 1915 to
1918. Thus, in the American annals, there are only two peacetime
decades—the 1900s and the 1960s with no major war—during
which living standards jumped at the fastest rate, and in both cases
the real wage kept pace with hourly output. The evidence clearly

demonstrates that when wages grow in sync with productivity, prosperity is not only widespread but also expands rapidly. That is when demand and supply grow in tandem, and the balance between the two pivotal forces is preserved without any increase in artificial spending.

REASONS FOR THE RISING WAGE GAP

We have seen that when productivity and the wage gap rise, share prices zoom and may create an illusion of prosperity with the help of artificial demand, and when the wage gap stagnates or falls, share prices crawl but general affluence soars and endures. Interesting questions arise at this point: What governs the behavior of the wage gap? When does it fall or rise? Like most puzzles in economics, this one also depends on the laws of supply and demand. In the modern world, labor is like any other commodity, and its price—the wage rate—is set by the extent to which employers need workers and households or wage earners need work. Common sense and fairness dictate that when someone becomes more productive, he or she should be rewarded for higher skills. Unfortunately, in the case of labor, common sense does not always prevail, even when markets are completely free.

Demand and supply for labor do set the market wage, but that may or may not conform to worker productivity. As a simple illustration, consider the factories set up in Mexico by multinational firms like General Electric, IBM, and General Motors. Wages in Mexico are about $1 per hour, whereas in the United States they are about $20 per hour for the same type of work. If a Mexican worker produced one-twentieth of his U.S. counterpart's output then Mexican wages would be closer to labor productivity. But Mexican productivity, aided by technology, cannot be that low. Even if literacy in Mexico sharply trails that in the United States, the productivity differentials cannot be as large as the wage differentials.

Even with high technology, many functions are routine. How much education do you need to operate a vacuum cleaner, for instance, or, for that matter to drive a truck, a tractor, or a railway engine? Some functions in new capital equipment do require a high level of skills and education, but a vast number are merely repetitive work, which does not take long to learn. The productivity of Mexican workers is not much lower than that of their U.S. counterparts, yet they earn a mere fraction of their northern neighbors. Obviously their reward pales before their contribution. Why? The answer comes from the laws of supply and demand.

In hiring labor, an employer, even a small one, has an advantage over job seekers, especially in overpopulated countries with a large pool of unemployed workers. A company seeks to hire those who meet its needs of skills and education; it needs productive workers but pays wages set by the market. If the pool of job seekers is large relative to labor demand, then wages will be low; the smaller the pool, the higher the wages. The supply of labor is generally beyond the control of market forces, at least in the short run, because people have to work to survive, but the demand for labor depends on many factors, including wages, competition, globalization, and new technology.

Given a choice between two workers of equal skills, an employer will always select the one asking for a lower wage. Labor demand rises as wages fall and declines as wages rise. Competition among workers themselves tends to depress their salaries. That is why labor unions are usually able to generate high incomes for their members as well as nonmembers. Falling union membership may partly account for the wage deterioration in the United States since 1980.

By contrast, competition among businesses tends to generate extra hiring. Suppose there are two grocery stores in your area. Because of keen rivalry between them, they both offer quality products and good service at low prices, and to attract customers, they hire polite and informed mangers, keep the floors spotlessly clean, offer you help in locating the goods you need, and so on.

Now suppose some big shot comes from out of town, buys both the stores and merges the two into one company. The grocery competition in your area is gone. Soon you will notice a rise in grocery prices, poorer service, and a fall in product quality. These are the natural consequences of mergers and declining competition. In addition, the new store will reduce the demand for workers. It will keep only one manager and fewer floor sweepers, cashiers, and helpers. When firms become less competitive, their employment falls, and so do market wages. The proliferation of mergers since the 1970s, or the industrial dominance of monopoly capitalism, is one reason why wages have failed to keep up with rising productivity in the United States, Canada, and Europe. Vanishing business competition is also why the wage gap soared in the 1920s.

Another reason is the increasing globalization of the world economy. This trend tends to depress wages all over the globe, including the Third World, which has been a major recipient of new investments by multinational corporations. Until about 1970, the United States, Europe, and Canada imposed high tariffs on the imports of manufactured goods such as cars, consumer electronics, machinery, textiles, and so on. As a result, the multinationals limited their production of goods and technology to these three areas, where much of the world's demand was.

Then came the U.S.-sponsored policy of free trade, which led to the reduction of most tariffs. This gave the multinationals an open invitation to start factories in the Third World, where labor productivity was lower but wages much lower. This way production occurred far away from the areas of demand, for the impoverished Third World people could not afford the high-tech products produced by global corporations. The businesses set up these companies only to take advantage of subsistence wages, because now they could bring their products back into the rich countries without worrying about those high tariffs. Thus Nike produced its footwear in Indonesia, GM set up factories in Mexico and Brazil, and IBM established itself in Taiwan only to trim their labor costs. In the process, U.S. labor demand in manufacturing fell relative to supply, and wages could no longer keep pace with productivity.

While it is easy to see why the activities of multinational corporations tend to depress the U.S. wage rate, it is more difficult to assess their impact on wages in the Third World. But even there the results are the same. With vast overpopulation, few developing countries need capital guzzling technologies. Instead they need to employ labor-intensive methods of production. However, to compete with global corporations, local firms in the Third World are also forced to employ machines that displace workers. The end result is a reduced demand for local labor from the available pool of the world's capital.

Furthermore, the developing economies are under no pressure to adopt policies that bring wages closer to productivity, because they know that multinational goods produced on their soil will be exported back to the rich countries. They don't need to generate demand at home. Otherwise they might try to legislate a minimum wage above the level of subsistence and then create more demand at home to absorb domestic production.

Let us now consider the effect of technology, which by itself has an ambiguous impact on labor hiring. New inventions almost always lead to the displacement of labor. Call any company today, and instead of being connected to a person, a recorded message asks you to press a variety of buttons on your phone to get the information you want. It is very annoying to the listener but reduces labor cost for the business. New technology has largely displaced the telephone operator who in the past used to answer all queries. Automation tends to reduce the demand for labor and raise labor productivity. This is one reason that unions are always wary of high technology that aims to deplete their ranks. But scientific discoveries also generate new products that expand the need for both capital and labor.

The range of goods available in a typical American home today defies the imagination. Refrigerators, air conditioners, room and water heaters, carpets, marble floors, radio, television, telephones, cameras, VCRs, computers, electric and microwave ovens, and so forth are standard items in many U.S. households. These are all the by-products of new inventions. Thus technology, while always raising productivity, has an ambiguous impact on labor demand. But it is indispensable to the rise in our living standard. Americans today can afford all these gadgets, because the latest equipment enables them to produce a far greater output per hour than in the past. While automation displaces workers, new products require workers; on the whole, high technology need not trim labor demand.

However, without tariffs the new-product technology may not generate additional labor demand and counter the effects of automation. In the past, when tariffs were high, new gadgets were mostly discovered and produced in America; automation was then no more than a nuisance, because those displaced and downsized could easily find lucrative jobs in new industries. Workers from obsolete or declining sectors could quickly move into high-tech sectors at the same or higher wages, because new technology displaced labor but also created more attractive products. When the railroads could no longer provide new jobs, workers switched to automobiles; when the textiles industry shriveled, employees moved to appliances. When the radio market was saturated, those laid off migrated to the production of televisions.

That was the heyday of U.S. industry. Tariffs ensured that the new inventions were translated into factories on American soil. Today, however, while new products are still discovered in America, their production occurs abroad. Robotics, fax machines, photocopiers, and VCRs are all inventions of American science, but the bulk of their production occurs in low-wage countries, because their importation is mostly free from taxation. Hence Americans downsized by mergers and automation are unable to find high-paying jobs in new-tech industries. New technology still raises productivity but trims the demand for U.S. labor, generating in the process a growing wage gap. Therefore, as we've seen, the rising wage gap in the United States is the result of an array of forces such as union decline, increasing globalization, and monopoly capitalism.

WALL STREET LOGIC

During the 1990s, with share markets routinely setting records in the United States, wary investors occasionally wondered about the economic fundamentals, especially as the Tokyo market continually crashed while the Dow soared to unprecedented heights. To reassure the public, Wall Street economists, analysts, and financiers offered the same explanations fashionable in the 1920s. True, the stock euphoria of that bad old decade ended in ruins, but this time around, they were certain, things were different. Didn't they sing the same hymn in Japan in the 1980s?

Financial analysts and brokers, frequently interviewed on CNN, CNBC, and other business-related TV programs, along with the columnists of popular newspapers and politicians basking for years in the glow of the soaring Dow, all agreed that this time the fundamentals were sound. In other words, the share manias of the past were admittedly irrational, because they were not backed by a strong economy. But this time around things were entirely different. What were those fundamentals on which so many agreed?

One mantra that I heard again and again was that we now had low inflation, low interest rates, and low unemployment, a combination that had not occurred since the mid-1960s. It is true that the thirty-year U.S. Treasury bond yielded a meager 5 percent at the end of 1998; the inflation rate was just 1.5 percent and the unemployment rate was below 5 percent. The information was correct, but it was misinformation nevertheless. Not a single analyst reminded the public of 1929, when inflation was zero, the bond yield 4 percent, and unemployment 3 percent. In terms of the so-called Wall Street fundamentals, that fateful year, 1929, looked great. Yet the stock market crashed, and the Great Depression began. During the 1990s, no one mentioned the ballooning wage gap and consumer debt since 1980, the twin economic evils of the 1920s.

A stratospheric stock market, in the wake of a growing demand gap, is cause for worry, just as it was in the 1920s. The government officials who gloated about it at the time proved to be incapable of stopping the crash of 1929. Unfortunately history is repeating itself, except in a vastly magnified way. The administration trio of Bill Clinton, Robert Rubin, and Alan Greenspan, chief architects of the debt and share market bulge of the 1990s, paid no heed to the growing wage and demand gap. One day they would regret their unprincipled policies, which partly account for the deepening crisis engulfing half the world. Their artifacts are unlikely to carry illusory American prosperity past 1999, the final year of the decade.

6

ECONOMIC MIRACLES
AND FAILURES

Of all the miracles reported in history, in scriptures, novels, and other tomes, the one concerning growth and prosperity is perhaps the most difficult but meaningful to perform. Yet three nations—Germany, Japan, and South Korea—have done just that following the Second World War. All three, practically destroyed in the global conflict, rose like a phoenix out of the ashes.

What do they have in common besides devastation? In each case, it transpires, real wages grew strongly with productivity for a long time. For a variety of reasons such as keen domestic or foreign competition, enlightened social conscience, or strong unions, the trio's labor income kept up with its earnings of capital. The three together form a group of overachievers. Their economies expanded briskly, eliminating poverty and generating affluence for the vast majority of their people. Theirs is a Cinderella story of unmatched success that carries great lessons for other nations.

JAPAN

Of all the postwar economic miracles, Japan's is the most dramatic. With its phenomenal rate of growth and development, the country quickly became a role model for its neighbors, especially the so-called Asian Tigers, including the four Little Tigers—Hong Kong, Taiwan, Korea, and Singapore. The Tigers adored how their neighbor, a mere

| 83

cluster of tiny islets devastated by atom bombs, first regained its feet, swiftly penetrated the markets of the world's richest country, the United States, and then became an economic superpower, all in a matter of thirty years. They watched how a protectionist Japan, endowed with few natural resources except an educated and dedicated workforce, rebuilt an industrial machine and then turned it into an export locomotive, first concentrating on low-tech goods and then excelling in high-tech industries.

Postwar Japan is an amazing story of recovery, reconstruction, and economic excellence. The country literally galloped out of embers and developed into a giant in just a quarter of a century. Whenever America grows at the rate of 4 to 5 percent per year, its economists consider it a great achievement. But from 1950 to 1973, the growth rate in Japan exceeded 10 percent. That torrid pace of growth over such a long period has not been duplicated by any other country in recorded history. In the process Japan went through a face-lift, eclipsing the stigma and shame of defeat in the war. Instead, the nation offered a development model to other aspiring countries.

Since 1990, however, Japan has suffered political instability arising from recession or stagnation. Its real estate and stock markets are in turmoil, and its banks and insurance companies still reeling under pressure. All this has taken some of the gloss off the Japanese miracle, but the country remains the second-largest economy on the planet. Moreover, the United States is now heavily dependent on Japan's savings, which have financed a major chunk of the U.S. federal debt. America, regarded as the world's premier economy, has borrowed more than $1 trillion from Japan since 1982.

Japanese growth during the 1950s was slightly below 10 percent per year, while in the 1960s it was slightly above that figure. But in both decades the vast majority of the population prospered. Labor productivity soared, and so did the average real wage. During the early 1950s, unemployment dogged the nation and kept wage gains paltry relative to productivity gains. By 1960, however, joblessness plummeted, and wages began to keep pace with torrid growth in output per hour.

Table 6.1 presents indexes for real wages, productivity, the wage gap, and per-capita GDP from 1960 to 1997. The GDP per person, after adjustment for inflation, rose from a mere ¥0.77 million in 1960

(U.S. $2,139) to as much as ¥2.07 million in 1975 (U.S. $5,750). This is a jump of 168 percent in just fifteen years. The real wage index before taxes went up from twenty-three in 1960 to seventy-three in 1975, a rise of 217 percent over the same period. Similarly, manufacturing productivity made a leap from fourteen to fifty-one, or a climb of 264 percent. These are stratospheric numbers.

The development experience of most countries reveals that once unemployment vanishes, growth slows down. Production normally expands through increased employment of capital and labor, and once the workforce has been absorbed in the factories, output growth

TABLE 6.1

The Indexes of Wage Gap and Per-capita GDP in Japan, 1960–1997

Year	Real Wage Index	Productivity Index	Wage-Gap Index (%)	Per-capita GDP (1990 = 100)
1960	23	14	61	0.77
1965	32	21	66	1.12
1970	50	38	76	1.77
1975	73	51	70	2.07
1980	75	64	86	2.46
1985	81	77	95	2.85
1990	95	95	100	3.40
1995	107	109	102	3.80
1997	110	119	109	3.80

SOURCE: Data from *International Comparisons of Manufacturing Productivity and Unit Labor Cost Trends, 1997,* (Washington, D.C.: U.S. Department of Labor, Bureau of Labor Statistics, 1998), 10 and 23; *International Financial Statistics* (Washington, D.C.: International Monetary Fund, various issues).

Note: A word of caution is desirable regarding the use of indexes in economics. They are used for analysis over time, but not for comparisons among various things at a time. Thus comparing the real wage index with the productivity index in 1960 or in any other year is not permissible because of different formulas used by the Bureau of Labor Statistics in their construction. In reality, real wages can never exceed labor productivity, but the real wage index, which is not the same as actual real wage, can exceed the productivity index, which is not the same as actual productivity. The sole purpose of index numbers is to facilitate comparisons over time. Thus column 2 reveals that the real wage in 1965 exceeds that in 1960, and so on. Various indexes can, however be divided to see how they perform over the long run, and that is what has been done here. Thus column 4 is obtained by dividing column 3 by column 2 and then multiplying by one hundred to get the percentage.

is unable to match past performance. Japan, however, was exceptional, as its economy continued to sizzle even after 1960, when joblessness all but vanished. The reason lies primarily in the relative stability of its wage-gap index, which was sixty-one in 1960 and seventy in 1975. This index is obtained by dividing column 3 by column 2 and then multiplying by one hundred to express it as a percentage.

The wage gap actually rose somewhat, but the rise was extremely small, given that hourly output in manufacturing more than tripled between 1960 and 1975. Over these fifteen years the gap rose at the rate of a miniscule 1 percent a year. With wages soaring in sync with productivity, national demand kept pace with output. As a result the country needed little artificial demand to cope with soaring production. Consumer debt was practically unheard of, the government budget deficit was more or less zero, and foreign trade was in balance. Corporate debt varied from industry to industry, but overall the country met its investment needs from a high level of savings. As a result, even Japan's exceptional rate of investment did not generate the problems associated with artificial demand.

The rise in real wages was almost uniform during this period. With unions remaining strong in a high-employment economy, labor incomes grew steadily and sharply between 1960 and 1975, as did hourly output. National productivity gains reflected growing efficiency in many areas, including agriculture, manufacturing, construction, and services. This was balanced growth in which all key industries prospered, and the wage-gap index changed very little.

How did Japan accomplish its economic miracle? Through the import of capital and technology, harnessed under an umbrella of protectionism. Slowly but surely the country became the world leader in the areas of electronics, shipbuilding, and petrochemicals. The biggest prize, however, went to the auto industry, which today is dominant around the globe. The industry started slowly in the early 1950s. Some fledgling but dynamic companies like Toyota and Prince developed on their own, whereas Nissan, Isuzu, and Hino obtained technology from Europe and the United States. They took some time to build plants and master the art of complex manufacturing. Beginning with small cars, they excelled at the task by the end of the decade. Honda and Subaru joined them in the early 1960s, and after 1965 Japan became a major exporter of cars. Today high-quality Japanese cars of all sizes, luxury, and variety crisscross the globe.

Rapid industrialization requires capital accumulation and savings. During the 1950s and 1960s, Japan needed capital, and its people rose to the occasion. They educated themselves, worked hard, and saved large portions of their incomes. When wages rise rapidly, it is, of course, easier to save more, but self-discipline is still necessary. Too much thrift could have caused the problem of overproduction, inducing national demand to trail national supply, creating excess production in the process. This, in turn, would have led to production cutbacks and unemployment.

In Japan, however, corporations went on an investment binge and absorbed people's savings, which rose from 5 percent of national income in 1950 to as high as 25 percent in 1975. As long as investment spending soaks up idle funds, demand is large enough to absorb national output, and there is no problem of excess production. In fact, the high rate of saving fostered capital formation, new technology, and growth.

Rapid growth and prosperity demand diligence and character; they also demand government policies based on common sense. The economic model followed by Japan between 1950 to 1975 was purely nationalistic, designed to wipe out the stigma and shame of annihilation in the Second World War. But it was enlightened nationalism. The country adopted a highly protectionist stance that permitted little foreign challenge to vulnerable domestic industries. Barriers were set up to minimize imports, even as the state encouraged exports to obtain the raw materials and technology needed for speedy industrialization. Without foreign competition, how did Japanese firms become efficient enough to successfully battle their U.S. counterparts inside the United States? The answer lies in Japan's intense domestic competition.

Japanese experts may have derived this strategy by studying the economic history of the United States, discovering the true secret of prosperity. America itself had become a global industrial giant in the nineteenth century by encouraging the formation of small firms under the protective shield of tariffs as high as 100 percent. These companies faced little threat from established giants from England, France, and Germany, but they competed vigorously against other domestic firms inside the United States. They imported capital and technology, and in a few decades became strong enough to challenge the hegemony of Europe.

Japan was a worthy pupil in this regard. Intentionally or not, the country developed along the time-honored U.S. model, and with hard work and pluck, its youthful industries began to outcompete the American behemoths on their own turf. Prior to the war, Japanese industry consisted of many regional monopolies organized under the umbrella named zaibatsu. They kept wages low and profits high, blocked the entry of other entrepreneurs, and virtually used their workers as serfs. After its military defeat, Japan was occupied by the American army. Operating under the belief that the zaibatsu had supported Japanese militarism, the Americans forced its monopolies to dissolve. This was the great gift of occupation authorities to Japanese industry, which could not have abolished monopolies on its own. As we've seen in the United States, it is very difficult to fight the wealthy interests that control politics, even if their actions are destructive for the nation.

Along with the policy of encouraging domestic but not foreign competition, the government of Japan set out to balance trade. In 1950 the country did not have much to export; nor did it have the raw materials needed in the production process. The yen was a nonentity at that time, and the nation faced a crippling paucity of foreign exchange. The need to import raw materials, plant, and equipment meant that Japan occasionally suffered from a trade deficit, which was financed by foreign capital. This type of trade deficit produces high growth, because the import surplus is used for investment, which will increase production in the future. From that increased production will come an export surplus, which will balance trade over time—say, over one or two decades. This is the course that the United States followed in the nineteenth century, and Japan duplicated it after 1950 with even greater success.

Whenever the trade deficit threatened to be out of control, the Bank of Japan, the nation's central bank, raised interest rates to reduce investment spending and hence imports. This strategy effectively maintained parity between exports and imports. From 1950 to 1973, Japan's trade was balanced, with any deficits prior to 1965 wiped out by surpluses thereafter.

The policy of balanced trade was matched by one of balanced budgets, a major accomplishment at the time. Governments in other developing countries were profligate in their spending. But in Japan there was no need for budgetary red ink, as wages kept pace with soaring productivity, and domestic demand did not need any artificial prop.

In addition to foreign trade, the authorities tightly controlled the banking system. This was essential to avoid any waste of capital, which was in short supply. The stock market was underdeveloped, so companies could not raise funds by selling shares to the public. Their voracious appetite for investible funds had to be met by the government through its central bank. Since most financial institutions needed official help, the Bank of Japan came to exercise great control over them. This way, the state kept a tight leash on the activities of commercial banks, especially some of the large houses known as City Banks.

Government lending to large banks has become an important way of supplying funds to industry. The Bank of Japan regulates the supply and demand for money by adjusting its discount rate, a rate that the City Banks pay to the central bank for loans. These loans are the most important way cash currency has been supplied to the private sector. The Bank of Japan regulated the activities of commercial banks through a policy called window guidance. The banks were told when and where to increase their loans. The discount rate and window guidance were frequently used to face the crises created by trade deficits.

Because of fast economic growth, prices rose rapidly. The average inflation rate per year was 5 percent from 1950 to 1973. Normally, inflation spurs interest rates, but in Japan, for two reasons, they declined gradually from the mid-1950s until 1970.

First, the Bank of Japan kept the discount rate low and made plentiful loans to City Banks to create rapid growth of money. Second, and more important, the economy generated few speculative activities that waste capital. The high level of savings provided sufficient funds to commercial banks and, in spite of torrid money growth that frequently exceeded 15 percent per year, limited the inflation rate to an average 5 percent. The real rate of interest, that is, the real cost of money, is the market interest rate minus the rate of inflation.

After 1955 interest rates steadily declined and varied between 6 percent and 8 percent. With inflation at 5 percent, real rates of interest rarely exceeded 3 percent, an exceptionally low level that stimulated business investment.

Alas, some of the rational policies followed by Japan since the war were abandoned after 1975. Under the influence of extremist economists, domestic as well as foreign, logic gave way to dogma, and the nation began to suffer. Intolerance for mergers yielded to benign neglect. Companies grew so large that union influence on wages waned. Once wages began trailing productivity, other economic ills slowly developed and culminated in the bubble economy of the 1980s. Finally, in 1990, the bubble ruptured, and Japan sank into a prolonged recession that dogged its economy throughout the decade, with no end in sight.

Reforms after the war were dictated either by General MacArthur or by plain sense. As the nation prospered, many bright young men and women went to prominent U.S. universities to study economics. There they were trained in the virtues of deficit budgets, stock and commodity speculation, financial deregulation, and company mergers, and they dutifully passed these lessons on to their policy makers.

Japan also abandoned its concern for balanced trade and became interested in exports for their own sake. Not only were they now needed to import raw materials, plant, and equipment, they were considered necessary for economic growth as well. The balanced trade policy was replaced by a trade surplus policy. Slowly but surely, Japan became dependent on foreign markets, and the era of rapid growth came to an end. Even while the country was busy conquering world markets, its internal base grew feeble. Now Japan is groping its way through the worst crisis since the Great Depression.

In retrospect, Japan's biggest mistake was jettisoning its procompetition policy. Mergers began to occur in the 1960s and increased sharply during the 1970s. As a result, the industrial concentration ratio, which is the market share in an industry controlled by the top three firms, slowly approached U.S. levels. Small competitive firms gradually turned into regional monopolies.

While firms continued to challenge each other vigorously, the shift to power in fewer hands weakened the ability of unions to secure wage gains in sync with the efficiency gains. Japanese firms were still very competitive with respect to those in other countries, but labor bargaining suffered in the process. As a consequence, wages failed to keep up with productivity. As we see in table 6.1, the wage-gap index increased glacially from 1960 to 1975 at the rate of 1 percent a year. Over the next fifteen years, however, the annual rise in the wage gap almost tripled, as the index rose 43 percent from 1975 to 1990. We already know that a soaring wage gap spawns a variety of new and unexpected problems, which then have to be fixed through artificial means involving the creation of debt by consumers, corporations, or the government.

Today Japan is facing dwindling employment and real incomes, but the roots of this crisis go back to the 1970s. To be sure, some of the new developments, such as the oil shock of 1973, were beyond the nation's control, but many others were policy mistakes.

Although the Finance Act of 1947 permitted the issuance of construction bonds to finance the infrastructure, at first these bonds were not issued. Until 1965 Japan's budgetary policy was one of strict balance. From 1965 to 1974, construction bonds were indeed used to finance deficit spending, but they were small and their purpose was to stimulate business investment. Strictly speaking, construction bonds did not represent a government policy of deficit budgets.[15]

A true deficit budget policy, where state spending rises sharply to combat unemployment, began in 1975. That year, deficit-financing bonds, or "deficit bonds" as they are often called, were issued for the first time in postwar Japan. At first these bonds were regarded as temporary, and it was assumed that the budgets would be balanced again as soon as possible, at least by 1980. However, the deficit actually increased that year, more or less persisted until 1998, and is expected to continue far into the future. The year 1975 was thus a watershed year and inaugurated a clear departure from the government's earlier stance of balanced budgets.

As Japan's wage gap soared, natural demand fell relative to national supply. The rising government deficit was one way to plug this shortfall; another was to adopt the mercantilist policy of surplus trade. The country began to depend on foreign demand. Japan had suffered occasional, but small, trade deficits until the mid-1960s. These were investment-driven deficits that created new high-paying jobs and expanded productive capacity. This in turn created export surpluses to pay for earlier import surpluses.

The trade surplus first arose in 1967 and then began to grow. It led to a great outcry in the United States, which had not seen a deficit since 1896. Japan's surplus became an international issue by 1970, because it resulted in a great outflow of dollars. The old exchange rate of 360 yen to the dollar was now a relic of the past. In the interest of balanced trade, the yen should have been revalued upward, but the Japanese government resisted this move. The entire nation had acquired a deep-seated memory of how foreign exchange shortages in the 1950s had constrained the rate of growth and resulted in higher interest rates and periodic recessions.

Even though industrialization had completely transformed the country into a manufacturing giant, Japan continued to live in fear of external shocks, a fear reinforced by the jolt of oil prices in 1973, even though the nation withstood the jolt better than any other country. For a variety of reasons, an irrational attitude that exports had to be maintained and increased at all costs had taken root in the Japanese psyche. Even today this myth impedes rational policy.

The economic crisis between 1973 and 1975 convinced the policy chieftains that future growth would have to come from exports. Instead of expanding the domestic demand base as they had done in the first period of growth, they now turned to overseas demand. The Bank of Japan periodically intervened in the foreign exchange market to restrain the rise of the yen when it threatened Japanese exports, but even this policy only slowed the currency appreciation. So obsessed were companies and the government with exports that they persuaded the unions to limit their wage demands; this was the only way to boost exports in the face of an appreciating yen.

If the yen rises, the only way to augment foreign sales is to lower your own prices, for which it is necessary to keep wage gains far below productivity gains. In other words, the desire of the government and companies to raise the export surplus in the wake of yen appreciation caused an ever increasing gap between real wages and labor productivity.

Thus regional monopolies, feeble unions, and the country's obsession with surplus trade limited real wage growth. The resulting jump in the wage gap created the need for growing budget deficits in order to maintain the balance between domestic supply and demand. In 1976 Japan's trade surplus was $3.7 billion. By 1985 it had grown to $49 billion. So it was that Japan became increasingly dependent on foreign markets and on the stability of its exchange rate.

A growing wage gap inevitably generates a speculative bubble in share markets, which in turn may spawn bubbles in other assets such as real estate and precious metals. This is what happened in Japan. Between 1960 and 1975, when wages kept good pace with soaring productivity, the index of share prices tripled. Stock markets surged but no faster than manufacturing productivity, which also tripled. This was no speculation or market mania, as booming share prices simply reflected a booming economy. This was real, not paper, prosperity.

Following 1975, however, the wage-gap index soared at a rate of 3 percent per year, and the inevitable happened. Stock prices sizzled, with the market index rising by 700 percent over the next fifteen years. Between 1975 and 1990, productivity nearly doubled, but share prices surged eightfold. The gargantuan imbalance in the share markets sparked frenzied speculation in land and housing. Of course, everyone in Japan celebrated. Politicians gloated, financial brokers danced in ecstasy, historians sang hymns of Japanese glory, and prudence disappeared. But then came 1990, the year of reckoning. First share prices crashed, followed in turn by real estate, consumer confidence, and business investment. With them came soaring bankruptcies, shattered families, and the highest rate of unemployment ever recorded in Japan. Such are the long-term woes of a growing wage gap, and the resulting concentration of wealth.

To summarize, from 1950 to 1975, Japan adopted a series of policies that sparked rapid growth and durable prosperity: balanced budgets, balanced trade, tight regulation of banks, high domestic competition but little foreign competition, land reform, and lifetime employment. During this period, real wages surged, both before and after taxes, income and wealth disparities tumbled, and Japan emerged as a global economic giant.

However, after 1975 these policies were abandoned one by one. Budgets were no longer balanced, balanced trade gave way to surplus trade, banks were deregulated, high competition yielded to regional monopolies with strong control over unions, and income inequality climbed. As a result, in spite of respectable economic growth and productivity rise, huge imbalances appeared in the markets for land, stocks, property, foreign trade, and housing, and so on. The combined result of all these imbalances was the bubble economy, which burst at the start of 1990.

Officially, a recession began in April 1991 and was over by 1993. In reality, the economy showed few signs of revival even at the end of 1998. In fact, the country had suffered the worst crisis in terms of unemployment, corporate bankruptcies, bank failures, official confusion, budget deficits, and debt since the last great depression in the 1930s. At the beginning of 1999, the government promised to end the recession by raising state spending by as much as $200 billion; this would be the eighth such promise relying on fiscal red ink since 1990, and like its predecessors, this one too would fail. It is vividly clear that the cure lies in the same rational policies that had transformed Japan into an industrial powerhouse in just twenty-five years—policies that were later jettisoned under the influence of U.S.-trained scholars and an addiction to exports.

Tragically, after 1975 the living standard stagnated in spite of rising productivity. The Japanese people continued to make sacrifices in terms of high savings and long working hours. Today Japan stands in danger of chaos and a cataclysmic depression, but the cure is very simple, as we shall discover in the final chapter dealing with economic reforms.

GERMANY

If Japan is the powerhouse of Asia, Germany is the juggernaut of Europe. Both countries were devastated in the war, and both astounded the experts with their superlative economic performance. The formula for German success has been more or less the same as that of Japan. The Second World War turned the nation into a vast inferno, destroying its infrastructure and industry. Moreover, the country was split into two estranged parts, with the eastern part containing the bulk of the area's arable land and natural resources. However, these handicaps could not constrain German ebullience and ingenuity for long. Drawing on a hallowed tradition of precision, quality, and craftsmanship dating back to the turn of the century, the nation recovered quickly from the wounds suffered in the conflagration of the 1940s.

Germany's reputation stems not from its spectacular growth but from its subjugation of inflation. According to table 6.2, which examines the trends in its real wages, productivity, per-capita GDP, and share prices, German growth performance was indeed above the world average, but it was not much stronger than that of its immediate neighbors to the south. Its per-capita GDP jumped a healthy 54 percent over fifteen years between 1960 and 1975, but it was nowhere close to the performance of Japan. What earned high marks for Germany was its rock-solid currency, the deutsche mark. Unlike Japan, where inflation surged with high growth, Germany was a bastion of price stability. In 1970 one German mark was worth twenty-eight cents; in 1998 it was worth sixty cents. So strong was the mark that it became an international currency in the 1970s, challenging the hegemony of the almighty dollar. Germany's economy is the largest in Europe and the third largest in the world. The irrepressible nation rebuilt itself in the old-fashioned way: through high savings, business investment, and quality control. In many industries, Germany defines the standard of craftsmanship. The nation has special strengths in chemicals, machine tools, steel, and cars. Lufthansa, Volkswagen, BMW, and Mercedes-Benz are reputed German trademarks around the globe.

Unlike its Asian ally, Germany adopted a policy of laissez-faire, pure and simple. While Japan feared foreign competition in the early stages of development, Germany had no such qualms. The European powerhouse challenged global rivals soon after the war, and its companies quickly began to outcompete their counterparts in England, France, and Italy. It imposed low duties on foreign products, especially those exported by its neighbors, most of which were socialist economies rendered inefficient by the lack of internal competition and by wasteful state planning. Their goods were no match for the intensely productive labor force and factories of West Germany.

By 1960 Germany consistently enjoyed an export surplus, which in turn enabled the mark to become the dominant currency inside Europe. German products set the standards for quality and durability all over the world. What is even more interesting is that unlike Japan after 1975, Germany's export locomotive did not trample the

TABLE 6.2

The Indexes of Wage Gap, Per-capita GDP, and Share Prices in Germany, 1960–1997 (1990 = 100)

Year	Real Wage Index	Productivity Index	Wage Gap Index (%)	Per-capita GDP	Share Price
1960	23	29	126	17,440	34
1965	33	39	118	20,650	28
1970	47	52	111	24,660	29
1975	61	66	108	26,870	29
1980	75	77	103	31,620	31
1985	81	89	110	33,800	68
1990	96	99	103	30,590	100
1995	109	112	103	35,710	103
1997	113	124	110	36,700	150

SOURCE: Data from *International Comparisons of Manufacturing Productivity and Unit Labor Cost Trends, 1997* (Washington, D.C.: U.S. Department of Labor, Bureau of Labor Statistics, 1998), 10 and 23; *International Financial Statistics* (Washington, D.C.: International Monetary Fund, various issues).

Note: From 1990, the figures are for unified Germany.

rights of its workers. Its real wages rose even faster than its soaring productivity. With regard to the spread of prosperity, Germany fared better than Japan. As revealed by table 6.2, the wage-gap index fell steadily for German workers over the twenty years from 1960 to 1980. This could have caused a series of trade deficits. With salaries outpacing productivity, demand should have outpaced supply, so that the excess demand had to be met with an import surplus. But this did not happen.

The wage-gap tumble meant that there was little, if any, artificial demand in the economy. There was no consumer debt of any consequence nor any budget deficits at the state and federal levels. Corporations also were mostly free from debt. Total demand comprises natural and artificial demand, and if the artificial stimulus to the economy is zero or negative, the nation can have a trade surplus even if real wages grow faster than its productivity.

Many American economists, including Alan Greenspan, argue that rising wages hurt business investment as well as employment.

They oppose the minimum-wage legislation, which they say ends up harming teenaged and unskilled workers by forcing their layoffs.[16] This is a self-serving argument, because it tends to support the wealthy interests that finance such research through the award of grants and distinguished professorships. The German development experience clearly belies this dogma, which is a standard menu in almost every economics text used in American universities. From 1960 to 1970, even as the wage-gap index plummeted from 126 to 111, the rate of unemployment was below 1 percent in Germany, but three times as high in its neighbors as well as in Canada and the United States. Nor did the wage-gap tumble trim the German rate of investment, which held steady at about 25 percent of the GDP.

Even during the 1970s, when oil prices skyrocketed, Germany out performed most other oil-importing countries except Japan. Today there are seven advanced economies known as the G-7 (or group of 7). They include Germany, Japan, Canada, the United States, France, Britain, and Italy. During the 1970s, the wage gap in Germany continued to sink, and its joblessness tripled; yet its rate of unemployment was just half that in other G-7 countries, where the wage-gap index went in the opposite direction and soared. The moral of our story thus far is that rising wages create no problem so long as productivity rises as well; in fact, trouble arises when wages fail to keep pace with growing efficiency.

The German experience also supports our view that a growing, or at least constant, wage gap is a prerequisite to a stock market boom. Since the gap fell in Germany from 1960 to 1980, we should expect share prices to be no better than stagnant. This is precisely what happened. The German stock market index actually declined from thirty-four in 1960 to thirty-one in 1980, in spite of soaring pro-ductivity.

As long as foreign competition sprang mostly from its socialist neighbors, the German economy did very well. After 1980, however, Japan and the Asian Tigers fixed their sights on Europe, and an intense trade battle with Asia began to exact its toll. Germany, along with its neighbors, faced new pressures and problems. Until that piv-otal year, the country had been a big beneficiary of the growing inter-national trend toward open markets and the U.S.-inspired policy of globalization. The bulk of its trade was with high-wage countries, which were unable to counter the German juggernaut. But when Asia challenged Europe on its own turf, the German industrial machine faltered.

Globalization no longer offered a win-win situation. The competition from Asia not only hobbled German exports in Europe and elsewhere, it also led to capital flight from Germany into the newly industrialized countries that included the Little Tigers and the so-called Asian cubs, or Baby Tigers, such as Indonesia, Malaysia, Thailand, and the Philippines. German multinationals opened factories abroad in search of low wages to counter the Asian challenge. Investment at home suffered. After 1980 the rate of investment slowly but unmistakably declined, and the unemployment rate inched up gingerly but steadily. By 1985 joblessness had hit a worrisome 8 percent of the workforce.

When foreign competition heats up and investment sinks at home, labor demand grows slower than labor supply. Under these circumstances, wage growth must slow down, or unemployment will jump. If employment is to catch up with expanding population, income growth must then trail productivity. Low joblessness and surging wages cannot coexist in the face of heated foreign challenge and a declining rate of investment.

Under strong unions, German wages continued to soar at almost the old pace, so the wage-gap index was virtually unchanged even after 1980, fluctuating between 103 and 110. Something had to give. If workers continued to insist on an ever-growing pay scale, then they had to live with the specter of rising unemployment. Another interesting development occurred with respect to stock prices. After 1980 productivity continued to sizzle and the wage gap no longer fell, thus paving the way for the share market boom. German shares also benefited from the speculative bubbles then arising in Canada, the United States, and Japan. This so-called law of substitution posits that under normal circumstances, when stock markets surge in a major economy, they follow suit in other countries. Between 1980 and 1998, German shares jumped almost 400 percent.

An interesting paradox is that share markets surged even as labor redundancies soared. From 1960 to 1980, stock prices had sagged, with unemployment practically nonexistent. Paper assets shriveled, but the real economy prospered. After 1980, however, joblessness spread its tentacles far and wide, but stock markets boomed. It is clear that share market affluence may have nothing to do with durable prosperity for the public; it may only reflect the opulence of the few, not the benefit of the masses.

The German miracle, already blunted by globalization, faced a new jolt in October 1991 when East and West Germany were reunited. Ideologues don't heed their failures, and Helmut Kohl, now the chancellor of a larger, unified nation, was no exception as he rushed to open the formerly closed markets of the East to fierce competition from abroad. Free trade was supposed to give the East the affluence of the West. What the chancellor failed to realize was that the benefits of increased foreign rivalry may be elusive and come only in the long run, but its destructive impact shows up immediately. Not surprisingly, whatever little industry the East brought into unified Germany was immediately destroyed by the foreign challenge, resulting in massive layoffs. By 1994 East Germany's unemployment rate roared to 40 percent.

Most economists blame the crash of the East on its backward technology and relatively unskilled labor, but not on free trade. This sounds like a lame excuse, especially when the benefits of free trade to lift the East were touted so eloquently, and when the federal government spent as much as $500 billion to upgrade the capital base of the acquired territory.

German unification was followed by the dissolution of the Soviet Union and the democratization of its former satellites such as Poland, Hungary, and Czechoslovakia, all of which invited foreign capital and offered a vast pool of low-paid labor. The result was another round of German capital flight, shrinking investment at home, and increasing joblessness. When high-wage industrial jobs migrate abroad, either factories must shed workers at home, or real wages must trail productivity. German unions refused to ease their wage demands, so today the country is saddled with a jobless rate exceeding 10 percent and more than four million people looking for work. Both figures are postwar highs.

Germany faces a tough dilemma today. It must discard ideology and adopt meaningful economic reforms to enjoy a pre-1980-style economy, when wage growth was high, unemployment was nonexistent, but share markets were sluggish. Those were the good old days of real prosperity linked to the tangibles of real earnings and production, not paper assets of shares and their derivatives.

KOREA

The third postwar economic miracle is that of South Korea, its development strategy sharing aspects with Germany and Japan. Lacking in natural resources, and decimated by the Second World War, Korea was a latecomer to the club of developing economies. At the dawn of the 1950s, it was drawn into a costly war with its neighbor, North Korea, which had ended up with the bulk of the region's natural resources. Thus Korean energy was initially diverted toward the production of weaponry and self-defense. As a result, Korea's economic performance, in spite of substantial aid from the United States, was initially no better than mediocre.

In the 1960s Korea set its sights on a program of rapid industrialization and development. As if to make up for lost time, it rushed into a frenzy of saving and investment. In 1961 the vibrant nation had harnessed only 12 percent of the GDP into investment, but by 1970 the figure jumped to 23 percent and by 1990 to an unheard of 37 percent. Like Germany, Korea came to rely heavily on foreign commerce, with trade constituting as much as 78 percent of its GDP in 1980, and like Japan, it adopted a policy of covert and overt protectionism.

American economists have recently blamed Korea for crony capitalism, which occurs when the authorities confer favors on rich industrialists, awarding them lucrative government contracts and low-interest loans. Banks also reward their own directors and officers with low-cost money regardless of whether the projects are viable or make any economic sense. Similarly, people with contacts in high offices get preferential treatment in obtaining import licenses and sinecures. In short, crony capitalism is unfair, unethical, and hugely inefficient, since relatively undeserving people end up in managerial positions. There is a grain of truth in this characterization of the Korean economy, which is dominated by four major conglomerates that are similar to regional monopolies in the United States. The four groups are Hundai, Daewoo, Samsung, and Lucky Goldstar.

However, as we saw with Japan, even though much of the Korean industry is monopolistic and shielded from foreign competition, the companies owned by the four cliques offer intense rivalry to each other. As Harvard economist Michael Porter confirms, an "essential underpinning of Korean comparative advantage is the fierce and even cutthroat rivalry that characterizes every successful Korean industry. . . . A pioneer makes the initial entry, but other competitors soon follow."[17]

Thus we encounter two different and diametrically opposite notions about the Korean system: one that views it as essentially unethical and corrupt and another that extols it for its strong internal competition. As usual the truth lies somewhere in the middle. Korea is an amalgam of corruption and competition, and for a long time the system worked extremely well. For a variety of reasons the country achieved a balance between supply and natural demand, and the economy grew at a phenomenal pace. As with Japan until 1975 and Germany, Korea's wage gap was either static or shrank over the long run, as can be clearly seen from table 6.3, which displays the steady increase in Korean real wages and productivity in manufacturing from 1967 to 1997. Over these thirty years, employee output climbed more than tenfold, whereas real earnings soared elevenfold. In other words, real wages shot up even faster than the monumental jump in productivity. As a result, the wage-gap index was 120 in 1967 and 113 three decades later; it fell slightly during that period, although its progress was uneven. In 1990 it sank to its lowest level, the year the Koreans harnessed as much as 37 percent of their output for investment. With wages skyrocketing in sync with productivity, natural demand kept up with domestic supply, and businesses became confident enough to sharply raise their capital spending. Clearly, then, the main spur for investment comes from home demand, which in turn relies crucially on real incomes. That is why it is important that wages keep up with productivity. When this happens, even crony capitalism cannot cripple the economy.

Korea clearly followed the proportionality rule of development or the law of balanced growth and reaped huge rewards in terms of general affluence. Its per-capita GDP shot up sevenfold between 1967 and 1997, and since demand kept up with supply there was little need for artificial stimulus to the economy. The budget deficit as a

TABLE 6.3

The Indexes of Wage Gap, Per-capita GDP, Budget Deficit, and Share Prices in South Korea, 1967–1997

Year	Real Wage Index	Productivity Index	Wage-Gap Index (%)	Per-capita GDP (1990 = 100)	Share Prices (1990 = 100)	Deficit GDP
1967	13.3	16.0	120	867	NA	0%
1970	19.8	23.3	118	1,051	5.6[a]	0
1975	26.4	35.6	135	1,459	11.7	0.4
1980	45.7	55.9	121	2,026	14.6	1.1
1985	59.5	77.2	130	2,729	18.6	0.9
1990	100.0	100.0	100	4,185	100.0	0.7
1995	141.0	154.0	109	5,734	123.0	–0.4
1997	151.0	171.0	113	6,307	60.0	NA

SOURCE: Data from *International Financial Statistics Yearbook: 1998* (Washington, D.C.: International Monetary Fund, 1999), 540.

[a] The share price index starts from 1972.

percentage of GDP was either zero or minimal. In fact, there were several years, such as 1995, when the budget was actually in surplus.

Korea has the largest economy of the Asian Tigers. Although it has been protectionist toward imports, its growth strategy has been oriented toward exports. Some people confuse an export-focused economic policy with free trade, but the two may, in fact, be very different. Free trade means low or zero taxes (also known as tariffs) on imports. In other words, free trade is an import-oriented policy, which may or may not be combined with export-led development. Actually, most of the Tigers have export-driven economies rather than free trade, a strategy that has produced exceptional growth rates, as high as 10 percent per year, although it is noteworthy that Korea's emphasis on exports has declined sharply since 1980 without hurting its pace of development.

In the early stage of industrialization, Korea, like Japan and the other Tigers, focused on light manufacturing that required little capital but considerable skilled labor. In other words, early industrialization concentrated on labor-intensive manufacturing. Once surplus labor was absorbed by light industries, and qualified workers were hard to find, the country went after high-tech enterprises that required more capital per person. This way productivity rose even faster than before and also made large wage gains possible for workers. The fruits of industrialization then spread among the general population. That is why Korean income disparities pale before those in many advanced and developing economies.

The state has played an active role in Korea's economic development. In the early 1970s the government turned to heavy and chemical industry to build six industries through increased tariffs and subsidized credit. Wages were controlled and banks told to lend money to priority sectors. The idea was that the six enterprises, including steel, chemicals, shipbuilding, and electronics, would become world-class competitors and promote exports. The program was a success in some respects and a failure in others.

The nation's export drive was indeed successful, but the tight control on the financial system led to some weak banks that had to be bailed out. Even today the banking system operates under some controls. Eventually, the government abandoned the heavy and chemical industry program, liberalized trade, and loosened its grip on banking. The wage-gap index surged in the 1970s, but in recent years the wage controls have also been abandoned, and worker earnings have risen dramatically.

Since the mid-1990s, increasing trade liberalization has resulted in growing trade deficits, which create big problems because Korea has a large foreign debt. As long as trade is in surplus, the debt can be easily managed. Otherwise it can create major currency and economic woes. Heavy industrialization, especially petrochemicals, have also contaminated rivers and lakes.

A notable feature of the economy after the mid-1980s was financial deregulation. Until the early 1980s, Korea maintained large tariff or nontariff barriers against the imports of capital-intensive, high-tech industries, and restricted foreign access to banking, insurance, and stock markets. However, as the decade progressed tariffs were gradually lowered and foreign investments permitted in financial sectors. Capital became far more mobile internationally than ever before. As a result of trade liberalization, Korean imports soared, with a negative impact on the balance of trade.

Trade deficits normally hurt growth, but Korea saw a marked increase in foreign investment in its factories as well as stock markets. The negative consequences of the trade shortfall were thus neutralized and growth remained strong, but share prices went into a frenzy. From 1972 to 1985, though share prices tripled, they grew no faster than productivity, suggesting that the stock market boom was supported by a solid economy with expanding production. But between 1985 and 1990, just as foreign money flowed in, the stock price index jumped more than fivefold in just five years, and it grew another 23 percent by 1995, while productivity rose only 100 percent. Thus share markets galloped ahead of the underlying economy, and a speculative frenzy developed. After 1995, a sell-off began that in 1997 turned into a full-blown crash, which dealt a crippling blow to the economy, sending it into a spiral of falling output and rising prices. Thus financial deregulation eventually did what even crony capitalism could not; namely, it produced a recession that continued well into 1999, with no end in sight.

The heavy inflow of foreign money debilitated the economic institutions in a system permeated with crony capitalism. As international dollars flowed into Korean banks and share markets, those with political connections received even more generous loans. The conglomerates themselves rushed into a borrowing spree and managed to acquire copious foreign currency debt, leaving them vulnerable to the financial storm that engulfed the Asian Tigers after mid-1997. Starting with Thailand, a series of competitive devaluations struck the group, especially those like Korea that were saddled with a lethal mix of a large trade deficit and foreign debt. The Korean won collapsed, and the country suffered a serious recession, with higher inflation as well as unemployment.

MEXICO

So far we have focused on economic overachievers, countries that were able to accomplish speedy industrialization and widespread affluence. We have discovered that the secret of their outstanding performance was a continuous balance between supply and natural demand via the law of balanced growth between real wages and productivity. We will now turn to a group of economic underachievers, whose growth strategy should be avoided. This group consists of Mexico, India, and Brazil, nations that are well endowed with natural resources, yet keep hopping from crisis to crisis, never realizing their full potential because of official corruption, faulty economic policies, or both.

The growth record of this trio has been mediocre, its income and wealth disparities drastic, and its foreign debt out of control. What else does the trio have in common? A toxic mix of regional monopolies long shielded by a thick wall of protectionism that has resulted in a soaring wage gap and a perennial imbalance between supply and natural demand. Name any economic ill, and this group has suffered it at one time or another: mass unemployment, simmering poverty, hunger, hyperinflation—all coexisting with princely luxury for a few industrialists and political barons.

The United States has long been regarded as a haven for the company CEO, whose average annual compensation runs into the millions. Brazil has a tiny economy compared with many nations, yet its CEOs pocket a pay scale second only to that of their American peers. Some of the rich in Mexico and India, countries where the unskilled earn less than a dollar per hour, are even billionaires.

Let us start with Mexico, a country that despite its proximity to the United States has an economy remarkably different from that of its northern neighbor. Mexico is well endowed with oil, agriculture, and other minerals. Much of its workforce is relatively low skilled, and for a long time the country protected its industries from foreign competition, while its giant neighbor to the north switched to free trade. Finally, in 1994, after protracted negotiations, Mexico joined Canada and the United States in a free-trade agreement called NAFTA and opened its borders to competition from North America.

NAFTA was inaugurated with great fanfare and grandiose expectations. Unfortunately, like many other treaties between the United States and Mexico, this one also worked to the serious detriment of the Mexicans. Within a year of NAFTA's adoption, Mexico suffered a crippling depression along with inflation. Unemployment shot up, while real earnings plummeted by a third. The economy revived somewhat in 1997 and 1998, but wages still did not. In a system riddled with monopolies, wages are always the last to recover.

NAFTA's aftermath was not the only crisis that Mexico has faced

over the three decades between 1968 and 1997 (table 6.4). The CPI
starts at a paltry 0.1 and ends up with an eye-popping figure of 364,
or a jump of 363,900 percent in thirty years, clearly not an enviable
record. The 1960s is the last decade that enjoyed a modicum of price
stability. The CPI climbed 7-fold in the 1970s and then a hyperinfla-
tionary 142-fold in the 1980s. Stability did return during the 1990s,
when the volcano of inflation cooled but continued to simmer.

Along with hyperinflation came a gargantuan foreign debt.
Throughout the postwar period, whenever Mexico established a U.S.
connection, its poor ended up paying a hefty price, while its rich wallowed in affluence. During the 1970s, when OPEC hiked the price of
oil by more than 1,000 percent, Mexico, being a large exporter of oil,
was a major beneficiary, but it frittered away its newfound wealth
through official graft and corruption. Millionaires emerged during
the decade, but the people grew poorer, as is evident from column 2
in table 6.4. The manufacturing real wage actually shriveled in the
1970s.

Meanwhile, OPEC, of which Mexico was not a member, accu-
mulated a vast horde of petro-dollars that were deposited with large
multinational banks—Citicorp, Chase Manhattan, Bank America.
Eager to find borrowers for burgeoning funds, the banks persuaded

TABLE 6.4

The Indexes of Wage Gap, Inflation, and the Budget
Deficit in Mexico, 1968–1997 (1990 = 100)

Year	Real Wage Index	Productivity Index	Wage-Gap Index (%)	Consumer Price Index	Government Deficit GDP (%)
1968	2.0	5.7	285	0.1	1.5
1970	2.0	6.0	300	0.1	1.0
1975	1.0	7.0	700	0.3	3.8
1980	1.1	8.2	745	0.7	3.0
1985	0.9	8.2	911	7.1	7.6
1990	1.0	8.1	810	100.0	2.8
1995	0.9	8.3	922	225.0	0.6
1997	0.8	8.2	1,025	364.0	1.3

Source: Data from *International Financial Statistics Yearbook: 1998* (Washington,
D.C.: International Monetary Fund, 1999), 624.

the Mexican authorities to formulate a grandiose development plan that they could readily finance. The government then borrowed billions for ill-conceived projects, most of which failed. The bulk of the loans ended up in the pockets of politicians and bureaucrats, but the country was stuck with a large foreign debt that continues to proliferate. Today, after paying billions of dollars to its creditors every year, the Mexican government and various companies still owe as much as $200 billion to financial institutions abroad. This is a crippling burden for a country whose annual production barely exceeds its foreign debt.

The primary source of Mexico's seemingly unending troubles are its regional monopolies that have forced a vast rise in its wage-gap index over the years. The index was 285 in 1968 but zoomed to a shocking 1,025 in 1997. Mexico's economy is riddled with graft, fraud, and wealth disparities. The situation is so bad that real wages have been tumbling in spite of rising productivity. With a vast imbalance in the labor market, the rest of the economy has been simply out of kilter. When foreign debt was low, the government budget deficit was high, as in 1975 to 1980. In the 1990s the deficit as a percentage of GDP fell sharply, but then external debt jumped even more. In 1985 both the debt and the deficit were out of control.

As in Japan in the 1950s, Mexico must break up the internal monopolies to harness its ample natural resources for general prosperity. This will lower the wage-gap index and restore balance in all areas of the economy. Until then the nation will lurch from one crisis to another.

INDIA

India's affliction, not so virulent in some respects but more deadly in some others, is remarkably similar to Mexico's. The Asian giant has not suffered from hyperinflation, nor has it enjoyed the comfort of steady prices. The country's main ills are overpopulation, unemployment, and poverty, yet their cause is much the same—regional monopolies, both state and private.

India won independence from British rule in 1947 and immediately vowed to build its economy. It had to overcome many handicaps such as illiteracy, low savings, little experience with capital formation and industrialization, lack of skilled labor, a vast refugee problem, and so on. But its hurdles were no tougher than those faced by Korea and Japan, both of which were crippled by the war and, unlike India, had few natural resources.

India adopted a mixed-economy model in which state enterprises competed with private companies. The country received generous foreign aid from Britain, the United States, and the Soviet Union, yet its economy could never get out of first gear. What went wrong? India adopted Soviet-style centralized planning and modified it slightly by tolerating private industries in certain areas. Thus railroads, airlines, electricity, and communications were reserved for the state, whereas in textiles, steel, banking, and machine tools, state and private enterprises existed side by side.

State monopolies are woefully wasteful and inefficient, but when they also face strong unions they suffer massive losses and become a huge drain on the public treasury. Labor unions in state-owned enterprises forced restrictive work schedules, inflexible operating hours, and no-layoff policies. Facing scant competition from other firms, they produced shoddy goods and constantly created red ink.

By contrast, private firms wallowed in money and profits, especially in areas where they competed with state-owned companies. State businesses were no match for private monopolies, which paid low wages but charged the same high prices set by their inefficient rivals. Flush with profits, company stalwarts took de facto control of political parties that needed money at the time of elections. Thus India's democracy became "corruptocracy." Today almost every bureaucrat, from top to bottom, is on the take, and the only way to get anything done is to grease someone's palm.

India's love affair with monopolies is as consistent as it is incomprehensible. The country generally distrusted international corporations and shunned contact with them. But when direct foreign investment could not be avoided, economic planners reserved the vast domestic market for one or two foreign firms. Instead of opening a particular segment to all foreign companies, which would fiercely compete with each other over quality and price, they granted monopolies to foreign concerns in a number of industries. The multinational corporations loved this arrangement, which enabled them to earn vast sums from paltry investments.

A quick glance at table 6.5 reveals the absurdity of India's strategy of development. Even after four decades of planning, the country lacks reliable data on real earnings that may be used to form a wage-gap index. So we have to rely on a proxy, consumption as a percentage of the GDP. If the wage gap grows over time, then, absent credit cards and consumer debt, consumption spending should fall relative to total production, creating in the process a rising consumption gap.

The second column of the table confirms this view. In 1967 India's consumption spending was as much as 82 percent of the GDP, but it plummeted to 59 percent by 1996. The magnitude of this fall is simply breathtaking, dwarfing even the vast rise in the wage gap in Mexico, where the comparable consumption figure dropped from 74 percent to 66 percent over the same time period. The consumption collapse cannot be explained away by the minisucle rise in India's savings rate. Clearly, wages must have drastically lagged behind productivity.

Not surprisingly, India had to live with a constant budget deficit, as shown in column 5, and a soaring stock market, as confirmed by column 4. With all those imbalances, per-capita GDP moved at a snail's pace. From 1967 to 1985, it rose from 3.8 to 5.2, or by 37 per-

TABLE 6.5

The Indexes of Consumption Gap, Per-capita GDP, Budget Deficit, and Share Prices in India, 1967–1997 (1990 = 100)

Year	Consumption-Gap Index (%)	Per-capita GDP	Share Price Index	Government Deficit GDP (%)
1967	82	3.8	16.7	4.2
1970	75	4.1	21.1	3.2
1975	73	4.3	20.7	4.1
1980	73	4.3	32.4	5.5
1985	68	5.2	41.4	8.5
1990	62	6.4	100.0	5.8
1995	59	7.3	322.0	7.3
1996	59	7.5	247.0	6.0

SOURCE: Data from *International Financial Statistics Yearbook: 1998* (Washington, D.C.: International Monetary Fund, 1999), 484.

cent over eighteen years, hardly a stellar performance by a country that received hundreds of billions of dollars in foreign aid. Japan and Korea did four times better. After 1985 India liberalized its economic policy, permitted greater domestic and foreign competition, and its per-capita production responded accordingly, rising from 5.2 to 7.5, or by 44 percent over eleven years.

India still has a long way to go. Today it is gasping for breath under the stranglehold of official graft; private conglomerates; state monopolies; a large underground, tax-evading economy; and a general state of confusion. Jawaharlal Nehru, the country's first prime minister, had great intentions but very little common sense. To help the poor he chose a "socialist pattern of society" development path. This, unfortunately, turned out to be a slippery slogan that played into the hands of tycoons, who hated the thought of a competitive or free-enterprise economy. In the name of socialism and public well-being, they exploited the country's natural resources to stuff their own pockets, offering, in return, massive environmental pollution. There seems to be no light at the end of India's ever-deepening tunnel.

BRAZIL

Whenever an economic crisis struck the world during the 1980s and 1990s, Brazil featured prominently in it. The country has jumped from one calamity to another just like Mexico and India, even though it is endowed with a vast amount of fertile land and is rich with minerals.

Brazil has the ninth-largest economy in the world, with a GDP of over $600 billion in 1999. In terms of population and production, it is the biggest economy in South America, though not the richest in terms of per-capita income. That distinction belongs to Argentina; Brazil is a distant second. But even here aggregate figures can be misleading. Barely 10 percent of Brazilians gobble up nearly half of their nation's output; almost 60 percent subsist on farming, mainly producing and exporting coffee, corn, wheat, tobacco, sugar, and fruits. The poorest 10 percent of the public lives on just 1 percent of the GDP. Thus a large majority of the population is destitute.

Brazil is among the newly industrialized countries. Its auto industry contributes as much as 12 percent to the economy, but the country also produces a variety of minerals—iron ore, coal, silver, oil, and gold. The first thing that catches your eye in table 6.6, which captures the essence of Brazil's performance from 1967 to 1997, is the trend in the CPI, which starts at one in 1967 and rockets to one hundred million in 1990, a testimony to the extent to which inflation has ravaged the Brazilian economy in the past.

Few words can capture the ethos of what transpired on the inflation front in Brazil. This is the mother of all hyperinflation. But there is more. By 1994 the CPI had surged to twenty-five billion. These numbers are beyond comprehension, placing Brazil in a class by itself. Needless to say that it was sparked by relentless government spending and the printing of money.

After a quarter century of furious price increases, it occurred to the country's president, Fernando Henrique Cardoso, that hyperinflation was not a sane way to do business. In 1994 the local currency, the real, was pegged to the U.S. dollar in order to restore domestic and international confidence in the currency. The idea was to restrain price increases by keeping a tight leash on mints that in the past had printed bushels of money. Thanks to the new policy, the inflation tiger was quickly tamed, and between 1995 and 1997, prices

TABLE 6.6

The Indexes of Consumption Gap, Inflation, Per-capita GDP, and the Budget Deficit in Brazil, 1967–1997 (1990 = 1 million)

Year	Consumption Gap Index	Consumer Price Index	Per-Capita GDP	GOV. Deficit GDP (in %)
1967	72	1	38	1.5
1970	64	2	44	0.6
1975	66	4	62	0.5
1980	71	37	76	2.5
1985	67	362	74	11.1
1990	60	100 million	80	9.3
1995	65	41 billion	85	6.8
1997	62	51 billion	89	8.0

SOURCE: Data from *International Financial Statistics Yearbook: 1998* (Washington, D.C.: International Monetary Fund, 1999), 264.

rose only a mild 25 percent over two years. (The ten billion increase in the CPI is about a quarter of 1995's base figure of forty-one billion.) The rate of inflation in 1998 was a once unthinkable 4 percent.

What is more interesting is that in spite of traumatic inflation, Brazil's real per-capita GDP grew at a healthy compound annual rate of 2.9 percent over the three decades between 1967 and 1997. This record compares favorably with the performance of a stalwart like Germany, which, by contrast, has been a bastion of price stability. Between 1967 and 1980 Brazilian growth was even stronger but failed to significantly improve the lot of farmers and the urban poor; income and wealth disparities surged so fast that poverty and hunger continued to stalk the land.

Regional monopolies in Brazil are so powerful that they have literally minted money, while paying abysmal wages to their employees. As with Mexico and India, the chasm between wages and productivity, reflected in the rising consumption gap, has soared. In 1967 72 percent of the GDP went into people's consumption; by 1997 the figure had dropped to 62 percent. Brazilian experience suggests that unless monopolies are split into smaller competing companies, no amount of growth may suffice to eradicate hunger and poverty. The wage and consumption gaps in Brazil jumped just as fast as those in Mexico with predictable imbalances in other sectors of the economy. One such imbalance was the persistent budget deficit that surged from a paltry 1.5 percent of GDP in 1967 to 11 percent in 1985 and remained stubbornly high at 8 percent in each of 1997 and 1998. Another was a mountain of foreign debt, reaching $228 billion by the start of 1999.

Brazil and Mexico have the dubious distinction of being the largest foreign currency debtors in the world. Both have to generate a large export surplus just to pay interest and principle on their external liabilities each year. In 1998 alone Brazil had to fork out some $50 billion to service its foreign obligations. This continues to put a tremendous strain on the country's economy. A study by economist Walter Mead, using data provided by the U.S. International Trade Commission, suggests that while Brazil's manufacturing productivity is about 59 percent of the U.S. level, Brazilian employee compensation is barely 10 percent of the U.S. rate.[18] Such is the handiwork of the nation's mighty monopolies, which have created perhaps the widest chasm between wages and productivity on earth. No wonder Brazil is plagued by the world's largest foreign currency debt, and a vast domestic debt at the same time.

A third imbalance in the system showed up in Brazil's stratospheric stock market. Share price returns in terms of the local currency are simply unfathomable because of Brazil's hyperinflation, but even when expressed in terms of the dollar, they were better than impressive. Between 1987 and 1996 the stock market jumped 700 percent in just ten years and another 60 percent the next year.

Brazil was the darling of international investors, who gave it a resounding vote of confidence in 1997, when currency crises erupted in Asia and began to decimate the Tigers and Japan. Foreign capital fled the Asian markets but, after an initial hiatus, returned to the South American giant. Brazil and all of Latin America, especially its largest trading partner, Argentina, then heaved a sigh of relief.

The Asian turmoil had unleashed a firestorm that could not be quenched by the United States or the International Monetary Fund (IMF), even though they engineered a series of costly bailouts for Thailand, Indonesia, and Korea. The storm next engulfed Japan, which was already reeling from a recession. Within a year, in October 1998, Russia defaulted on its external debt, and, because of its heavier debt burden, the international spotlight fell on Brazil.

Once again Brazil survived the onslaught, with the help of a conditional bailout of $41 billion by the IMF, but international confidence in debt-ridden economies was shaken. Capital, both domestic and foreign, began to flee the country. Brazil's foreign exchange reserve fell by $40 billion in the last three months of 1998 alone. As 1999 opened the country found it difficult to raise taxes and trim its ever-present budget deficit, which was a precondition of the IMF loan. Consequently, capital outflow accelerated. Vast amounts of reals were converted into dollars and fled to the United States.

In order to defend its currency, Brazil had already raised its interest rates to as high as 40 percent, making the local currency more attractive to all investors, domestic as well as foreign, but the lure of a lucrative return faded before the threat of currency depreciation, which becomes inevitable if foreign reserves plummet. In the first week of 1999 Brazil raised the interest rate further, to 50 percent, but could not slow the capital flight. It was now clear that the real could be no longer pegged to the dollar. On January 13, the local currency was devalued by 8 percent and then allowed to float freely a few days later. Within two weeks, the real lost 40 percent of its value relative to the dollar. In the end, despite advice and help from the IMF, Brazil met the same fate as the Asian Tigers and Russia—currency collapse, stock market crash, and a steep recession.

For the U.S. investor, Brazil's devaluation was more ominous than the Asian turmoil. Large American banks—Citicorp, Chase Manhattan, Bank America, and others—had lent over $15 billion to the country. Some two thousand American businesses had invested more than $27 billion in the economy. Ford Motors, General Electric, Whirlpool, Motorola, and Lucent, all with a big presence in São Paulo, faced heavy losses in their local operations.

Furthermore, if Brazil went down, so would the rest of Latin America, which absorbed 20 percent of U.S. exports. Thus Brazil's troubles were far more portentous for the United States than the tumult in Asia.

7

ECONOMIC CONSEQUENCES
OF THE MILLENNIUM BUG

There is something sinister about the end of a millennium that instills awe and fear in us humans. Toward the end of the last one, the world braced itself for imminent doom, a sentiment reinforced by frequent wars, famines, and plagues. Fear was so great that the affluent in France donated all their wealth to monasteries to save their souls from perdition. Citing Nick Hanna, author of *The Millennium*, John Moroney remarks that in 999 debts and prisoners were pardoned, and errant spouses even admitted to their adultery.[19]

The planet was paralyzed by the dread of meteors, asteroids, lunar and solar eclipses, sunspots, witches, and inconceivable natural calamities. People around the globe, inspired by priests, offered their money and oblations to the gods; animals were sacrificed in droves to the deities.

A thousand years later, some clergymen continue to prey on the gullible, but few people fret about the end of the world. Yet there may be more to worry about this time around. For one thing, in addition to the religious doomsayers, we now have some secular ones as well. They have a small but growing following that could mushroom into a serious menace for the economy. For another, the peril this time springs not from the stars or the heavens but, ominously, from the earth itself. The culprit is more mundane, the handiwork of man, not some wrathful gods. It is popularly called the millennium bug, which is much more tangible and real than the imaginary ghosts of the medieval past.

Variously known as the year 2000, or Y2K, problem, a computer glitch, or a virus of the zeros, the millennium bug is supposed to bite us in or around the year 2000. It is a symptom of our excessive dependence on science and technological change, or as Chris Taylor of *Time* magazine declares, it is "a fitting conclusion to a 40-year story of human frailties: greed, shortsightedness and a tendency to rush into new technologies before thinking them through."[20]

THE PROBLEM

Plainly speaking, the Y2K menace arises from the fact that affordable computers built as late as the early 1990s were programmed to use a shortcut in reading dates. We all do the same ourselves. For instance, we write 99 for 1999, or 98 for 1998, and so on. Older computers use a similar shortcut, so when 2000 arrives, they will only see 00 in their memory. We would know that the two zeros represent the dawn of a new millennium, but the computers, if they decipher the zeros at all, could mistake them for 1900. At this point, the machines could simply freeze or spew erroneous data, which in turn could infect other computers. Thus the millennium bug is a massive virus that could paralyze not only the nation but also the whole world.

Since we know the nature of the dilemma, why can't we fix it? Why can't we just reprogram old computers or replace them with the far more powerful new ones? We can, but the cure is costly and extremely time consuming.

The Y2K predicament had its origins in the 1950s, when computers were still a novelty; the machines were slow, they had barely enough memory, and mainframe systems occupied large rooms. To economize on money and memory, a programmer devised the strategy of using the last two digits to represent any given year. No one bothered to change the practice, even though computer quality, design, and memory made quantum leaps over the coming decades. The year 2000 was out of sight and therefore out of mind. But no more. Now we're in a mad scramble to fix the glitch or face the music of massive disruptions. There is hardly an American business, school, university, hospital, municipality, state, or branch of the federal government that is not dependent on the computer. If this technology breaks down, life as we know it will come to a sudden halt.

Millions of computers have been put to work since the 1950s; many have special software designed to handle very specific functions. Replacing them all would require a few trillion dollars. Then why can't we just reprogram them? We could, except that billions of billions of lines of instructions and codes are involved. Just reading them would require thousands of new programmers, who are not readily available. The Y2K jumble is incredibly tedious and time consuming.

Since American life is inconceivable without computers, their malfunction could seriously disrupt all sectors of the economy. Jim Lord, a computer and software expert and a retired naval officer, outlines a series of troubles that could arise the moment the clock ticks 01-01-00. In his own words, these are:

1. Incorrect payment of government benefits such as Social Security, welfare, food stamps, and pensions.
2. Rampant medical malpractice as patients are refused, misdiagnosed, or treated for the wrong condition.
3. The collapse of banks and insurance companies as well as stock brokerages and exchanges.
4. Massive business failures as tens of thousands of companies declare bankruptcy rather than take on the costs of repairing their computer systems.
5. Massive and persistent outages of electrical power, water, sewage treatment, and telephone service.
6. Widespread disruptions in emergency services such as police, fire fighter, and ambulance.
7. The most severe traffic jams ever seen.
8. The greatest explosion of lawsuits in history.[21]

Others are even more ominous. Their prophecies include airplane crashes, nuclear plant explosions, misfiring missiles, accidental launch of atomic weapons, and disruption of food distribution chains. I am not a computer expert, and like most of you I am inclined to dismiss the apocalyptic part of their premonitions. Barnaby Feder and Andrew Pollack, two reporters at the *New York Times* put the matter into perspective: "The direst predictions of what will happen—financial chaos, societal strife, food shortages and persistent, widespread blackouts—are highly improbable. But it is not hard to find reputable alarmists—computer experts who say they will not fly or schedule surgery at the onset of the year 2000."[22]

As Richard Lacayo of *Time* magazine puts it: "The problem is that there is no clear agreement, even among sober experts, of how bad the Y2K computer problem will be."[23] Most people perhaps should take some precautions such as keeping meticulous records of bank and stock statements, mortgage payments, cancelled checks, 401(k) plans, withdraw some extra cash, buy a few candles and flashlights, and even store some food. But I personally wouldn't move to a cave or purchase a water tank. I may also not fly on the first few days of the new year but will certainly see a doctor, if necessary. A study by the U.S. Senate recommends that we should prepare for the glitch as we would for a one-week-long fierce storm. *Newsweek* correspondent Jane Quinn settles the matter nicely for us: "Think of Y2K as a hurricane being tracked off-shore. It might strike the coast with gale force, or it might gradually blow itself out. Both possibilities are supported by plausible stories. Do you board up the windows or not?"[24]

Yet the apocalyptic predictions have performed a stellar service by waking us all up to the gravity of the situation and by prompting complacent businesses to take timely action. If the situation turns out to be as bad as the alarmists think, then life would certainly become very uncomfortable, especially in the United States with its great dependence on technology, but the world would survive, albeit at some economic cost. Let's take a look at what those costs and their likely effects might be.

PREPARATIONS UNDER WAY

As late as 1995, governments and businesses took the millennium bug lightly. But in 1996 Y2K-related spending surged, especially in the banking industry, which is therefore better prepared than other sectors of the economy. This is a great relief, because financial institutions are the lifeblood of our system. Most scholars agree that large money centers are in good shape, and are, to use the technical jargon, Y2K compliant, but small banks may not be. U.S. regulators are prepared to merge any noncompliant banks into large ones at the end of 1999, so that the public, in their view, does not need to withdraw extra money. However, some Y2K faithful recommend keeping a month's worth of cash in bank vaults. This sounds like good advice. The federal reserve will print an extra $50 billion of notes and make them available to the banks just in case they face a stampede of panicky customers.

Public utilities also seem to be fully prepared, but unpredictable snafus could easily hurt their industry, which is dependent on embedded systems, where computers or microchips are embedded in another piece of equipment. It is very laborious to discover how many electric transformers have these chips hidden in them. In fact, such chips seem to operate in most modern gadgets today—cameras, TVs, VCRs, automobiles, appliances, even toilets. Therein lies the intractability of this problem. Experts say that only a tiny percentage of modern appliances are sensitive to dates, but with billions of hidden chips being used by companies, even a 1 percent failure rate could cause havoc in the economy, especially among utilities.

There is tremendous energy waste in America. Cable and network TV, for instance, runs all night even though few people may be watching. Most businesses are lit twenty-four-hours a day, even though the lights could be turned off from dusk to dawn without seriously hurting production. Restaurants and shopping malls throughout the South keep their air-conditioning thermostats so low in summer that you need a sweater to avoid the chill. Even if the electric utilities have not fully fixed their software by the year 2000, there is so much latitude in America to conserve power that even frequent outages might not do the harm suggested by the doomsayers. The Y2K bug may even induce some healthy habits in us, as we waste less energy and in the process clean up the environment.

Among various branches of government, many say they are or will be close to compliance by the end of 1999. The Pentagon and the Social Security Administration seem to be in good shape, and, you may be happy to know, so is the nation's tax collector, the IRS. The Nuclear Regulatory Commission and the Securities and Exchange Commission have required utilities and financial firms to submit Y2K proposals. They have taken the threat of an atomic or financial meltdown seriously and are continuously monitoring the situation. The New York Stock Exchange tested its Y2K compliant computers in 1998, and everything went well. Some branches of state, federal, and local governments perhaps will be unprepared for the millennium glitch, but they, and for that matter anyone else, could switch to manual handling of the problem, the way they did in preelectronic times. It won't be easy and there could be lengthy delays, but life would go on.

ECONOMIC CONSEQUENCES

All the preparations for Y2K, especially those yet to come, will be very expensive, and could have grave economic consequences. Already, there have been some disruptions in the credit card industry, which issued cards with expiry dates ending in 2000, and in some cases the computers simply went dead, or refused to authorize purchases for cardholders in good standing. These were no more than a nuisance, and the problems were quickly fixed. In all, 40 percent of the largest companies in Europe and the United States have suffered minor difficulties, because some software had to use dates in the millennium year and thereafter. Still, the predicament has proved costlier and more complex than many experts had anticipated. Merrill Lynch, for instance, had to raise estimates for the compliance cost by 33 percent at the end of 1998. By most forecasts, the Y2K glitch will cost $1 trillion to $2 trillion around the globe. Thus businesses will be saddled with a huge expense, which they will likely pass on to their customers. This could also crimp their investment and capital formation.

Within the business community, large corporations flush with profits and resources are in the best position to deal with the millennium bug. There is evidence that big business will be able to handle the problem. Thus multinational corporations like General Motors, Exxon, Bank America, International Harvester, Upjohn, among hundreds of others, are likely to modify or replace their computers and continue to do business as usual. Experts think that at least half of the computers in use today will be fixed in good time, which suggests that the other half could shut down or cause errors.

While big firms have been feverishly working on the glitch, small companies lack the resources and even the willingness to tackle something they can't see at the moment. Most of them are behind schedule in their compliance plans, and many have done nothing at all. But millions of them provide parts and components to large firms, and this makes large companies as vulnerable as their small suppliers. Eventually, some small firms may have to merge with their patrons to survive, but will probably not opt for mergers until they have no choice, and by that time it could be too late to avert business disruptions.

If the Y2K bug seriously impedes our transportation system, national productivity will suffer. Massive traffic jams resulting from the breakdown of traffic lights could cause delays in the distribution of goods and services across the fifty states. If it takes longer to haul goods across the highways or the railroads, then national productivity will suffer. The same will happen if commuters spend extra hours on the roads.

Today many people work at home, gathering information about the world from the Internet. The millennium bug could hit them especially hard. Their productivity could plummet from computer malfunctions or power outages. If they decide to commute, traffic jams could really become catastrophic.

Faced with uncertain electrical supply, the companies will have to invest in gas- or oil-fired generators. That will keep the work going, but sharply raise their production costs. Even if the utilities are well prepared, they may have to ration power supply and give priority to home owners, or limit some businesses to power use in daytime and others to nighttime. All this will raise costs and crimp productivity.

The economic effects of the Y2K imbroglio will be similar to those of an energy shortage that raises production costs for companies and heating or cooling costs for the households. The last time energy prices soared was in the 1970s, when oil prices jumped throughout the decade because of production cutbacks by OPEC. In 1973 alone, the price of petroleum climbed 400 percent. The economic effects of that event have been well documented, and the Y2K glitch could have similar consequences.

Let us not forget lawsuits in our litigious society. Some software companies, like Intuit, Macola, and Symantec, already have been sued to see if they are obligated to offer free upgrades to programs that won't work past 1999. So far the suits have gone against the plaintiffs. Many others are still pending, and some others have been settled out of court, with minor damage to the software industry. But the lawyers have already chalked up some solid gains, and the party has just begun. The main reason that some plaintiffs lost is that they could not produce instances of actual damages, but if suits can be filed in anticipation of harm, just imagine how extensive the litigation will be when the millennium year is actually upon us. The legal industry is salivating at the thought of hundreds of lucrative class action suits. Some experts believe that while the Y2K glitch would be mostly over by the end of the year 2000 or thereabouts, the lawsuits will plague companies for years. These additional business costs will have economic consequences similar to those of production costs arising from other sources.

THE STAGFLATION OF THE 1970S

When oil prices jumped in the 1970s, the world went through a horrendous crisis involving rising unemployment as well as prices. A barrel of oil cost $2.50 in 1973 and over $12.00 in 1974. The world economy went into a tailspin almost overnight. Energy costs climbed, commuting became expensive, and productivity suffered. The rate of inflation was only 3 percent in 1972, but soared to 6 percent in 1973 and then to 11 percent the following year. Similarly, in 1973 the unemployment rate was only 5 percent, but had swollen to 8.5 percent in 1975. Oil prices kept rising all through the decade and jumped again at the end of 1979. By 1982 the jobless rate in America was the highest since World War II, with inflation peaking in 1980 at 13.5 percent.

Let me hasten to add that such rates of unemployment and inflation were not typical of the whole decade; with each oil price hike, they lasted one or two years, but they were large enough to cause economic devastation. In fact, the consequences of the energy shortage were so painful and so different from any in recent memory that they gave rise to new economic terms and concepts. One of them was the idea of stagflation ("stag" from stagnation and "flation" from inflation together make up stagflation), which signifies high inflation and unemployment.

Another was the concept of a misery index, which simply adds up the rates of price increases and unemployment to gauge the agony in the economy. In 1982 10.7 million people were jobless, almost penniless in a system afflicted with soaring prices. Such was the tumult of stagflation caused by rocketing energy costs. There were, of course, other reasons for the roaring inflation, such as the Treasury's printing oodles of money, but the energy crisis was the initial trigger.

Stagflation was just a euphemism for what transpired in society. The years 1975 and 1982 were actually years of inflationary depression that fortunately faded quickly. If the twins of high inflation and unemployment had lasted a little longer, the misery of the 1970s could have matched that of the 1930s. Imagine being jobless and watching your savings depreciate month after month due to soaring prices. At least during the 1930s, consumer prices fell sharply, and the real earnings of those employed actually went up. During the 1970s, by contrast, real wages plummeted for the vast majority of people.

Energy plays a crucial role in virtually every activity, so its price significantly impacts a nation's economic performance. Factories need energy to operate. Homes require it for cooling, heating, and lighting. An oil price hike plagues the U.S. economy in a variety of ways. First, production costs climb for the producers, who then have to trim their output of goods and services. Second, since America imports more than half its requirements for oil, a rise in energy prices adds to the trade deficit, which is a major drain on the country's GDP.

Why should supply fall when production costs rise? A simple example will illustrate the point. Suppose you own a sofa factory and have $100 for investment. If the production cost is $20 per sofa, you can build five sofas with your capital; if the cost increases, say, to $25, then you can make only four sofas. Thus supply declines as the cost of production jumps.

In economics, almost all questions can be answered through the medium of supply and demand. When supply falls relative to demand, prices have to rise, while output must decline. This is exactly what happened in some years in the 1970s and then in the early 1980s. During the 1970s oil prices rose frequently. As a consequence, the country went through the wrenching experience of low output growth, leaping inflation, and worrisome unemployment.

We have already seen that the millennium bug will raise production costs and trim productivity. Both effects tend to hurt the supply side of the market and work like a rise in the price of oil. What transpired in 1975 is likely to be duplicated in 2000; both inflation and unemployment will then be adversely affected. How wide the effect will be is anybody's guess. Since even computer experts are uncertain about the true magnitude of the problem, it is hard to speculate about the extent of the misery to come. One thing, however, is certain. The inflation picture will definitely deteriorate over what we have seen in the late 1990s, where the CPI has been rising at less than a 2 percent annual rate. The Y2K glitch could also produce a nasty surprise in terms of unemployment, because unlike the oil price hike that only raises business costs, this will raise costs and hurt the nation's productivity at the same time.

On the optimistic side, the glitch is not going to persist long past the year 2001. Unlike energy prices in the 1970s, the computer virus is likely to be a one-shot affair, so its aftereffects may not linger long after the millennium year. Lawsuits will, of course, continue, but their effect on production expenses is unlikely to be strong in an $8 trillion economy. Companies will either have to fix the problem or go out of business, and most of them will borrow or use their savings to do the job. In a worst-case scenario, they could switch to the old-fashioned ways of work; this would be expensive and seriously reduce output per hour, but it won't bring life to a standstill.

On the darker side, Barnaby Feder and Andrew Pollack cite Edward Yardeni, the chief economist for Deutsche Bank Securities in New York, suggesting there is a 70 percent chance that the Y2K bug "will cause a worldwide recession equivalent to the one that followed the 1973 oil shock." If this happens, we are in for a stunning setback, because, as mentioned above, both inflation and unemployment shot up following that event.[25]

GLOBAL REPERCUSSIONS

While the petroleum price hike during the 1970s afflicted all oil-importing countries, it offered a bonanza to OPEC. Oil exporters flourished at the expense of energy importers. In 2000, however, there will be no winners. The bug will bite the whole world, and its effects will depend on how dependent a country is on its computing machines. Other nations are even less prepared than the United States. In Europe, Britain and Germany seem to be three months behind the United States in terms of readiness, whereas most other countries are six to twelve months behind.

Japan, despite its long recession, is the closest to America in the race for compliance, which is likely to impact a nation's competitive position in world markets. However, Japanese banks, already weakened by their financial losses, are far behind schedule. Most other nations have been complacent about the problem. The Third World simply cannot afford the expense, nor can the newly depressed countries of Asia, Latin America, and the former Soviet empire. In Mexico, the vast majority of companies have no inkling of the gravity of the situation.

Since the United States is the best-prepared nation to face the virus, it is likely to become more competitive in 2000 than other countries. U.S. exports could get a much needed boost, and imports will suffer from this effect. While this is likely to have positive consequences for output and employment, it will aggravate things on the inflation front, since one reason consumer prices have been subdued in the late 1990s is the increasingly cheaper level of imports. As foreign goods now account for almost 15 percent of American consumption, if import costs go up substantially, the U.S. inflation rate will climb.

For the world as a whole, the computer glitch is likely to have worse effects than the oil price shock of 1973, because this time around there will be no beneficiaries, only losers. When the U.S. economy tumbles, the slump in Asian Tigers, Japan, Brazil, South America, and Russia will be exacerbated. They are already suffering from either stagflation or an inflationary depression, and the computer glitch will aggravate their crisis. Overall, though, the United States will come out ahead of other nations. The country will be hurt, but less than other nations.

THE FEAR OF THE Y2K GLITCH

Some people think that we have more to fear from fear of the computer bug than from the bug itself. Uncertainty about the prospective effects of the virus has already spawned an industry. Hundreds of articles and books have appeared on the subject, most of them alarmist in tone. They talk about the end of the world as we know it.

In Richard Lacayo's words: "Apocalyptic fantasies, which have always been freely available in an atomic-age Christian culture, are about to reach another climax. . . . Religious millennialism has once again found a real world problem on which to hang its visions of doom—the Y2K." But Lacayo goes on to write, "To the extent that there is some consensus among sensible experts, it is that the dire predictions of major social disruptions are overblown."[26]

However, Y2K apocalypse is not the sole preserve of the religious faithful. Secular alarmists are growing in numbers and their clout is likely to expand with the proximity of January 1, 2000. The Internet is full of ominous Y2K web sites, which recommend a variety of steps to prepare for the coming disaster. Their advice ranges from the practical to the surreal: stocking up at least a month's supply of food, buying a gas-fired generator, storing enough water, maybe moving away from the bustle of the cities, getting some guns and ammunition for self-defense, withdrawing all or a large part of our money from our banks, selling our stocks and bonds and waiting for bargains to turn up in the new millennium, and so on. Some of this advice may indeed be sound, but not for the reasons they have mentioned. I will return to the subject of advice in chapter 10.

Some experts fear that growing public anxiety itself could trigger a financial panic. If people make a run on the banks, begin to withdraw cash from ATM machines, start selling their stocks and bonds, or even stockpile essentials, the economy could be seriously disrupted. I personally think that such fears are mostly unfounded.

The American economy is being fueled by tons of foreign money and until that distribution chain is disrupted, the U.S. locomotive will keep humming and generate vast financial gains for stock and bond investors. Nothing since April 1991 has been able to bring this engine to a halt, not even the post-NAFTA Mexican meltdown of 1994; the federal government shutdown of 1995; the economic turbulence of Asia, Russia, and Latin America; or the impeachment of a U.S. president. The U.S. behemoth keeps chugging along, oblivious to all the opposing crosscurrents inside and outside the country. The Y2K bug itself is unlikely to derail the engine, but it could aggravate the malady erupting toward the end of 1999. In the meantime, I recommend taking a few practical precautions, but nothing more.

8

THE MILLENNIUM BUBBLE

There must be something in human nature—call it irrationality, frailty, or good old greed—that occasionally drives us to gamble away our hard-earned money. Why else would speculative bubbles keep recurring in history? Ordinarily shoppers would do anything to get a bargain—brave long lines and even drive several miles to find merchandise on sale. Such is the law of demand that you buy more when the price tumbles. However, once in a while the law turns upside down, and folks buy things simply because they have become pricey. This is the stuff of which bubbles are made, and of late you can find one in almost every region of the world: globalization and irrationality seem to go hand in hand.

Speculative bubbles are as old as recorded history: reports of profit gains of 1,000 to 2,000 percent in Buddhist India around 500 B.C., of megafortunes made and lost in ancient Rome, of millionaires emerging and disappearing almost overnight in Europe in the Middle Ages. In the postmedieval world, the first bubble sprouted in Holland when thousands of people took a sudden fancy to tulips. Who could have imagined that a fragile flower would actually spark a buying frenzy not for its aroma but for its potential capital gains? The mania began in 1633 and lasted for four years. Well-educated people paid hundreds of dollars to buy one bulb. Some made quick fortunes, and the craze lasted into 1637, when the house of cards collapsed and sanity returned. The Dutch were not enchanted by tulips again.

Something similar transpired in England and in the North American colonies in the early eighteenth century. The British had a love affair with the South Sea Company, Americans with the Mississippi Company, both of which were engaged in the rather innocuous activity of trading. Even great intellects were trapped in the lure of quick money. Ever heard of Sir Isaac Newton, the father of science? In 1720 he made a killing of seven thousand pounds trading South Sea stock (not by selling apples that had fallen from a tree) and then lost twenty thousand pounds the very next year. He himself had observed that it was easier to calculate "the motions of heavenly bodies, but not the madness of people."[27] Yet his genius could not prevent his huge loss.

A century later another bubble developed in the United States during the 1830s, as speculators paid unheard of prices for land and cotton. Banks loaned money as though it was worthless paper, and people treated crops and real estate like diamonds. Inevitably, the balloon punctured, but not before bankrupting many banks, individuals, and companies.

What is a speculative bubble or mania? When the value of anything—land, commodities, flowers, shares, real estate, gold, silver, diamonds, currencies—skyrockets relative to the rest of the economy, then a bubble is said to develop. It is a pejorative term for an investment that keeps appreciating until it collapses. Historically, this appreciation has to last at least four to five years for it to qualify as a speculative binge.

BUBBLES IN THE TWENTIETH CENTURY

While bubbles have been reported throughout history, they were infrequent until the dawn of the twentieth century. Perhaps the lack of cheap and easy credit kept them on a leash. People were also more religious, and their faith may have helped rein in their avarice. From the start of the twentieth century, bubbles became more frequent, larger, and deadlier. They also became more durable, yet each and every one burst in the end. Some lasted more than a decade, others less, but every balloon was eventually punctured either by an unexpected global event or by the internal dynamics of the market.

Like wars, bubbles recur in history in spite of their deadly consequences. There must be something in human nature and institutions that makes them inevitable. Some were even caused by government policies. If the bursting of a bubble were not painful, one could ignore its formation and consequences. But few bubbles have been benign; when they rupture, they leave behind a sorry trail of bankruptcies, unemployment, broken homes, crime, and starvation. Not just the speculators, but society as a whole then suffers and grieves. For this reason, speculative manias should be nipped in the bud, before they get out of hand. Governments should never encourage their formation and expansion.

The capitalist world today is known as an information society, where the flow of ideas, news, and data is swift and voluminous. Computers, facsimile, telephones, jets, and satellites have linked the planet in a vast chain of communications constantly on the move. One wonders why bubbles are born at all in a milieu where information is so readily available. The marvels of cable and satellite TV are such that even distant wars can be seen live on your screen. With so much wisdom and information around, why should there be any buying frenzy at all? Don't people know that, without exception, every bubble has burst in the past? Perhaps developing technology is easier than restraining our own nature, or perhaps misinformation can now be spread just as easily as information. Whatever the cause, from time to time the law of demand is suspended and people buy more and more of increasingly expensive things.

THE BUBBLE OF THE 1920S

For some reason, bubbles in our century have grown in frequency and virulence. As early as 1907, a credit bubble was in the making in the United States. It was cut short by a banking panic that led to a quick recession, so the buying fever didn't get out of hand. However, it didn't take long before the first speculative binge of this century materialized in the 1920s. An inflationary boom in one asset normally sparks a similar boom in other assets as well. When stock markets jump, the value of real estate, and sometimes art objects, also climbs. During the 1920s, share prices soared along with residential real estate in some parts of the United States, especially Florida, cheap credit from unscrupulous banks feeding the frenzy.

The property bubble burst open in 1926, but the share bubble continued until October 1929, when it too collapsed to start an unprecedented global depression. The Dow jumped from 72 in 1920 to 360 by October 1929, and then began to crash. Within four years, it had plummeted to sixty, a drop of more than 80 percent, back to just about where it had started in 1920. The stock bubble of the 1920s lasted, with a few minor interruptions, the whole decade.

THE JAPANESE BUBBLE

The depression of the 1930s, global in its tentacles, was so long and traumatic that it completely transformed U.S. politics, mores, and the economy. The rest of the world also learned an enduring lesson about the perils of uncontrolled speculation and greed. As a result, a bubble with planetary consequences did not erupt for another fifty years, but when it finally did, it eclipsed all its precursors.

A speculative fever took hold in Japan in the mid-1970s and lasted for a full fifteen years before it collapsed. The bubble began rather innocuously with land speculation, which had been a profitable activity for banks, corporations, and individuals ever since the end of the war. In a land-scarce economy, the banks were always eager to lend money against property as collateral. To control such speculation, a huge capital gains tax was imposed on the transfer or sale of land in 1974. The idea worked for one year. Property prices fell in 1975 but then resumed their upward march.

The capital gains tax had the intended consequences, discouraging the sale of land, but with few sellers around, land prices could not be contained for long. The tax also sparked stock speculation. Instead of selling land, landowners poured money into company shares while borrowing copiously against their valuable holdings. For gamblers and profiteers, the capital gains tax took the charm out of land, so they turned to stocks.

The Nikkei index stood at 4,350 at the end of 1975. By the end of 1980 it had climbed to 7,110. The huge rise in oil prices in 1979 did nothing to cool the stock fever. By the end of 1985 the Nikkei had jumped to 13,110. In ten years share prices had tripled. This was an era of quick profits, easy money, multimillionaires emerging overnight, endless greed, and ambition.

More drama was yet to come. Under pressure from the United States, Japan deregulated its financial markets. The cost of deposits increased for banks, which increasingly turned to the stock market in search of a higher return. Thus the relaxation of controls over interest rates partially inflated the share bubble, just as it had done in America in the 1920s.

Deregulation of financial markets had, in fact, triggered a global bubble. It was in this go-go milieu that my *Great Depression of 1990* made its appearance. I warned about a stock market debacle, possibly at the end of 1987 and then during 1990. On October 19, 1987, shares crashed around the world, stunning everybody in the process. In Japan, however, the panic faded quickly.

By the end of 1989, the Nikkei galloped to 38,916. In the decade after 1975, the stock index had tripled. After 1985 it tripled again in just four years. By mid-1989, however, it was clear that the bubble party would soon be over. The Bank of Japan, anxious over zooming asset prices, had begun to boost the discount rate. Yet no one took it seriously. The bank tried again. Inebriated with quick profits, again no one noticed.

At the end of 1989, an unusually sharp cold spell suddenly raised the price of oil. This, along with rising interest rates, pricked the market bubble, and share prices began to sink from the first trading day in 1990. Japan's bubble economy has been limping ever since.

Interestingly, as with the United States in the 1920s, the Japanese frenzy of the 1970s and the 1980s combined stock inflation with property inflation. The two fed on each other, as the world first watched with amazement and then denounced what was the longest and the fattest bubble heretofore, which began to burst at the start of 1990. Both share prices and real estate values crashed at that time, and fell intermittently for two years, before they became more or less stable and recovered. In 1997 Japan's share prices began their free fall again, and the Nikkei index plunged more than 20 percent during the year. In 1998 the index sank as low as thirteen thousand. All in all, the share market plunged almost 70 percent between 1990 and 1998, with perhaps more to come in the near future.

BUBBLES IN ASIA, EUROPE, AND LATIN AMERICA

Since the 1970s, the pace and breadth of speculation has picked up all over the world. Globalization of the world economy has linked the markets for goods, services, and assets. After 1982, when the worst postwar recession came to an end, bubbles sprang up all across the planet. The 1987 market crash reverberated throughout the world, but didn't have lasting effects. Within a year, share bubbles resumed in the economies of the Little Tigers—South Korea, Hong Kong, Singapore, and Taiwan—as well as the Baby Tigers such as Indonesia, the Philippines, Malaysia, and Thailand. Latin America and Western Europe followed suit, and so did Eastern Europe and Russia after 1989, when the Berlin Wall fell. Former Soviet lands, with economies sinking into joblessness and inflation, became havens for foreign investors. Russia has yet to develop the elementary rules for business contracts and a market economy, but such is the feeding frenzy of speculation today that its share markets managed to attract billions from abroad.

It is ironic as well as amusing that as soon as the satellite states were free from Soviet dominance, speculative activity took off. In Poland, share prices soared 470 percent in terms of the dollar in just four years between 1992 and 1996; in Russia, with the economy in depression, the corresponding jump was 100 percent, whereas in Hungary, the jump was 64 percent between 1992 and 1996. One would think that these countries would be sizzling with mammoth rates of economic growth to generate such extraordinary returns on investment. In reality, Eastern Europe was a hotbed of inflation and inefficiency. In Russia, output and wages collapsed after the fall of communism, while joblessness soared.

The inevitable followed. From July 1997 on, share markets in the Asian Tigers, Japan, Russia, and finally Brazil tumbled like dominoes. It all started with Thailand, one of the leaders among the Baby Tigers, which had enjoyed a high, steady growth rate approximating 8 percent since 1955. In 1989 it had a tiny external debt totaling $12 billion. Its neighbor Malaysia was also prosperous and relatively debt free. Thanks to financial deregulation governing the flow of speculative capital, both countries ended up with a giant debt load by mid-1997—$50 billion for Malaysia and a hefty $100 billion for Thailand.

In fact, all the Baby Tigers were now burdened with overseas debt and thus an easy prey to currency speculators.

Sizzling growth and financial liberalization endeared the cub economies to foreign investors and speculators after 1992. European banks and U.S. mutual funds poured billions into the shares of what came to be known as emerging markets. Asia, with a supposedly limitless future, became the scene of the action. Investment advisers, believing their horoscopes, fervently preached the gospel of global diversification. Japanese banks lent money at give-away interest rates, which in turn ignited a speculative binge in shares and real estate in the cubs of Asia.

In 1996 Thailand had a trade shortfall of $14 billion, a deficit that grew the next year. In order to attract overseas investment to finance the growing import surplus, Thailand had pegged its currency at the rate of about twenty-five bahts per dollar. But as the trade deficit soared in 1997, it was increasingly clear that the exchange rate could no longer be maintained. Sensing vulnerability, currency speculators unloaded the baht in foreign exchange markets; foreign capital fled in panic, and the value of the currency plummeted in July.

Overseas investors were caught off guard, even though similar events had rocked Mexico just two years before. But that country had been bailed out and foreign investors recompensed by an aid package arranged by the United States and the IMF. Investors expected the same type of aid for Thailand, and aid did come, but only after the crisis erupted. The IMF offered a quick loan of $17 billion in return for austerity measures that included a rise in taxes and interest rates, and a cut in the government deficit and in the growth of credit. However, because of political instability and popular unrest, the baht continued to sink.

Currency depreciations normally tend to escalate gradually among competing nations. This time, however, the Thai devaluation spread like a brushfire among the Baby Tigers, because they were all in the same boat of high debt and trade shortfalls. Foreign money fled overnight. East Asian currencies shriveled in a chain reaction: first in Thailand, then Malaysia, followed by Indonesia and the Philippines. As *Time* magazine put it in its November 3, 1997, issue, "On July 2 the baht plunged more than 12% in value against the greenback. Then it crashed into the Philippines, Malaysia and

Indonesia, where government officials were forced to devalue their currencies. That triggered a region-wide crisis, in which stock markets gave up as much as 35 % of their value, inflated real estate prices fell through the floor, banks collapsed, and hundreds of thousands of Southeast Asians, rich and poor, lost their jobs and fortunes."[28] On the same page, *Time* quotes a lament from a World Bank official: "There were no obvious warning signals of the kind of catastrophe that was about to hit Indonesia." Growth was lofty, inflation puny, and exports projected to soar. In a sense, the United States is just a giant Thailand. Like Thailand, America also has spectacular growth, low unemployment, a mountain of foreign debt, and a big trade deficit.

International efforts to douse the currency fires proved abortive. From the Baby Tigers, the share blight quickly rushed to the Little Tigers. Hong Kong, Korea, Singapore, and South Korea were caught in the whirlwind. The IMF bailed out Korea, but the country's economy slipped into a slump anyway. In 1998, the doldrums hit Russia, Brazil, and Latin America. Russia even defaulted on its foreign debt, and many U.S. and European banks and brokerages suffered huge losses. By early 1999, entire regions had sunk into steep recessions.

U.S. MANIA: THE BUBBLE OF THE MILLENNIUM

Finally we come to the U.S. bubble, which I have left until last, because nothing like it has ever happened before. Recent American speculative frenzy has no parallel. Even the Japanese mania of the 1970s and 1980s pales before it. The U.S. bubble began in August 1982 and was punctured in October 1987, only to resume its growth the next year. It suffered a short-lived correction in 1990, regained its footing in early 1991, and did not look back for the next seven years, when it deflated briefly again in August 1998. By mid-1999 the bubble was bigger than ever, beating all historical precedents.

In the recession of the early 1980s, the Dow fell especially hard. It hit a low of 780 in August 1982 and then began to climb, as Federal Reserve chairman Paul Volcker began to trim interest rates in order to fight the economic slump. Falling rates of interest stimulate stock prices for a variety of reasons. First, other financial instruments such as corporate and government bonds become less attractive because of lower yield. Second, business investment and hence the economy and profits grow faster because of the reduced cost of borrowed money. Third, declining bond yields induce people to purchase new homes and appliances that most buy on credit, again stimulating the economy and eventually corporate profits. Finally, low borrowing costs may ignite speculation as people invest borrowed sums into share or property markets. Speculation flourishes especially when a host of new instruments, such as options and other derivatives, mushroom in asset markets. (After all, without casinos, there will be very little gambling.)

Starting in 1982, the U.S. bubble swelled slowly until 1986. At the beginning of 1987, it began to balloon, the Dow soaring from around 1900 to a peak of 2,722 reached on August 25, or a hefty 43 percent in barely eight months. Compare this with the long-term gain in the Dow of about 12 percent per year. Then, during one week in October 1987, the share-price index declined nearly 10 percent, and the following Monday, on October 19, it plunged 508 points, or 23 percent, all the way down to 1,738. This was the largest single-day drop since October 1929, in both absolute and percentage terms.

The reverberations of Black Monday were felt around the world. The following day in Tokyo, which had the hottest share market at the time, the Nikkei index plummeted 15 percent. That was the worst-ever stock market crash. Did it cool the speculative fever? Yes, but only for a few months. In 1988 speculative bubbles made a comeback, tentatively in the United States but vigorously in Japan. Central banks around the world trimmed their interest rates, and as the cost of borrowing sank, stock markets sizzled again. Wall Street experts and scholars criticized Japanese financial institutions, fearing a repeat of the October massacre in 1987. But pundits in Tokyo, annoyed by U.S. lecturing, declared the 1987 debacle a minor anomaly in a country that had been growing strong ever since 1950.

In the United States, share prices continued their positive trend until August 1990, when oil prices rose sharply because of Iraq's invasion of the oil-rich kingdom of Kuwait. Following Iraq's crushing defeat in the Gulf War in January next year, the Dow resumed its climb, this time all out of proportion. From around 2,600 at the beginning of 1991, the stock index hit a high of 8,260 by August 7,

1997, rocketing by more than ten times the low of 780 reached fifteen years ago in August 1982. In Japan the Nikkei had climbed from 4,350 in 1975 to 38,916 on the last day of 1989, a jump of 793 percent. The U.S. bubble dwarfed even the Tokyo bubble. From trough to peak, the Dow had soared 958 percent. No wonder, financial analysts now fondly call the New York Stock Exchange—the home of the Dow—the market of the millennium.

At the beginning of October 1997, share prices, as mentioned above, began to collapse in the economies of the Asian Tigers. By the end of the month, the rout was on, afflicting many nations. History was made on October 27, 1997, when trading was halted twice on the New York Stock Exchange, with the Dow plummeting a record 554 points. In percentage terms, the Dow fell only 7 percent and recouped much of the loss through a big rise of 337 points the very next day. Nevertheless, U.S. share markets had been jolted, while markets in Asia and Latin America were in a free fall.

The aftershocks of the Asian eruption were short lived. Profits of American companies continued to rise, and so did their share values. By July 1998 the Dow reached another high point, ascending to 9,337. In *Stock Market Crashes of 1998 and 1999,* I wrote: "If nature continues to follow its laws of history, the current global bubble will burst by August 1998. . . . Alan Greenspan will reassure the public and possibly lower the interest rates. Experts will sing the glories of long-term investing to the public. As a result, after each downturn, stock markets will recover somewhat"[29] This is precisely what happened, as in the month of August, the Dow sank about 20 percent from its peak reached in July. Other market indexes were hit even harder. The Nasdaq composite index shrank 25 percent, while half of the over-the-counter stocks plunged more than 50 percent. A similar blight also struck the small-cap stocks traded on the New York exchange.

The world of speculators and Wall Street was shaken. The bubble had clearly burst into pieces. As *Time* magazine wrote about the street panic in February 1999, by which time the markets had recovered again: "It sounds silly unless you understand how close we came to economic meltdown last year. . . . Famed financier George Soros lost $2 billion in Russia last summer; a hedge fund blessed with two Nobel prizewinners blew up in an after-noon, nearly taking Wall

Street with it."[30] In fact, the Fed, an assiduous champion of free markets, had to arrange a $4 billion bailout of Long-Term Capital Management, a hedge fund that had placed option bets on as much as $1.25 trillion of government bonds and was on the verge of collapse. The panic was worldwide, as confirmed by Kenneth Klee and Rich Thomas in *Newsweek:* "Make no mistake: the world's overachieving markets were so shocked by Russia's late-summer default that they nearly stopped working."[31]

As anticipated, Alan Greenspan repeatedly cut short-term interest rates in order to reassure global markets, and the world dutifully returned to the task of speculation. In March 1999 the Dow crossed its July peak and broke the ten thousand mark, whereas the Nasdaq went into a tizzy, soaring 40 percent from the low reached last October. The balloon that had been punctured in August 1998 was patched up by the end of the year. The patch held up even when Brazil depreciated its currency in mid-January in 1999, but it was apparent by then that something was fundamentally wrong with the world economy, a subject that we will explore in subsequent chapters. The IMF had tried yet another bailout, this time in advance, and failed yet again.

The current U.S. bubble is now the biggest in the human chronicle. By its April 1999 peak, the Dow had surged more than 1,150 percent above the 1982 trough. The Dow index, first computed in 1885, took about a hundred years before breaking one thousand for good in November 1982. Even with the help of the Roaring Twenties, the Dow needed almost a full century to cross the thousand-point milestone, yet in the next sixteen years, it surpassed ten thousand. Unless the eternal laws of nature concerning supply and demand have turned topsy-turvy, the situation is unsustainable, just like that in many other nations.

Share values are now totally detached from reality. Something unprecedented is cluttering the vision of investors. Consider the prices of some stocks that have yet to show a dime in profit. Amazon.com, an Internet bookstore, surged more than 1,500 percent in just one year. If someone invested $10,000 in Amazon.com in January 1998, it would be worth $160,000 in January 1999. The reason for the investor euphoria a year later: a lower estimate for its profit loss.

There is more. Theglobe.com climbed a record 606 percent on its first day of trading. This stock, with no profit history whatsoever, is not an exception. Another called Marketwatch.com climbed 665 percent at its peak on the first trading day, closing with a relatively modest gain of 474 percent. Nor is the market madness limited to just the Internet shares. A thousand dollars invested in Wal-Mart in 1982 was worth more than $3 million in early 1999. The majority owner and chairman of Microsoft, Bill Gates, according to *Forbes,* was worth a paltry $58 billion after the bubble burst in August 1998. The EMC corporation had gained more than 35,000 percent during the 1990s and Dell Computer over 70,000 percent. The total stock market value was about $12 trillion in early 1999. This is better than finding money growing on trees.

With stock returns routinely breaking records year after year, the average investor is understandably giddy about the future. A survey by Montgomery Asset Management in San Francisco in October 1997 found that its shareholders expected an annual average return of 34 percent over the next decade, as compared with a bond yield of just 6 percent at the time, or the historical stock return average of 12 percent. Why not? Each time share prices plunged, they came back in a hurry and scaled new heights. Only a highly disciplined investor, out of concern for principle or history, could keep himself away from such glittering temptation. When geniuses like Newton could not resist the lure of easy money, what chance do other mortals have of conquering the quick-buck mentality?

MIT economist Paul Krugman, writing in *Fortune,* aptly describes market behavior during the 1990s.[32]

> It was a time of unprecedented prosperity. And it was also a time of soaring stock prices, a time when the market became a national obsession. As more and more ordinary Americans began buying stocks, there was a sense, almost a consensus, among sober heads that this was *a classic bubble.* [my italics]

No question about it. We are trapped in the bubble of the millennium. The only query left is what caused it all.

The strongest explanation lies in a combination of the rise in productivity and the wage gap, which spurs a ceaseless rise in profits, and hence the markets. Since 1982, U.S. productivity has been on a relentless increase, whereas real wages have been sinking for the vast majority of workers. Only after 1996 was there a slight rise in worker earnings, but even then the wage gap, because of galloping productivity, continued to zoom.

Once market fever heats up, it is fueled by cheap credit or low interest rates. The Fed has not adopted an easy money policy since 1982; nevertheless, interest rates have steadily declined since that year, mostly because of the cheap money policies of Japan and Germany. In a global economy, interest rates in other advanced economies also affect U.S. interest rates.

Wealth concentration also exerts a strong influence on market mania. As a person grows rich, he or she is less fearful of risky investments. Furthermore, to a millionaire a small return offers little satisfaction. Someone who already has millions is not going to be satisfied with a few thousand dollars of extra income. He or she seeks large yields, which spring only from speculation. That is why speculative fevers cannot last without growing wealth concentration. It is now an open secret that the current level of wealth disparity is the highest ever in U.S. history. Barely 1 percent of Americans own more than 43 percent of national wealth and over 90 percent of nonresidential wealth. This is a staggering state unmatched in American, and perhaps world, history. In 1982, when stock mania first began, the overall wealth disparity was at the 36 percent level.

Another factor inflating the millennial bubble was a drastic overhaul of the tax system in the early eighties. Income tax rates were cut sharply, while Social Security and sales tax levies jumped. This transferred the tax burden from the rich to the poor and the middle class, which exacerbated income and wealth inequalities and further fueled the share market frenzy.

Another reason stems from the perennial presence of the U.S. trade deficit or the rest of the world's surplus. As the planet accumulates more and more dollars, it does not know what to do, except to send them back into U.S. treasury bonds or stocks. Both factors are bullish for shares. Foreign bond purchases bring down our interest rates and indirectly stimulate American stocks, whereas foreign stock buys provide a direct stimulus. Never before in world history has a nation benefited so much from its trade shortfall.

Still another factor inflating the bubble is NAFTA and the globalization of the world economy, both brainchildren of the U.S. government. Both are responsible for the mushrooming trade deficit, as well as a low level of inflation, which keeps interest rates low. They also keep a lid on U.S. wages, spurring the wage gap and profits. NAFTA came into being in 1994. American and Mexican experts were convinced that the treaty would pay dividends to both trading partners. Instead, the trade agreement created a peso crisis that rocked the financial systems in the emerging markets of the Tigers and Latin America.

Measured in terms of the dollar, the Mexican stock index, the Bolsa, climbed 1,642 percent in barely six years from 1987 to 1993—a speculative bubble by anyone's definition. In 1994, however, the index crashed and plunged 44 percent in one year; the next year, it fell another 23 percent, as Mexico moved into a full-fledged depression. Factories closed, unemployment shot up, and real wages tumbled, but American economists touted the gains the country had made under NAFTA.

President Clinton, alarmed that the peso crisis could infect other emerging markets and finally the United States, possibly hurting his chances of reelection, quickly arranged for an aid package to bail out Mexico and to keep it from defaulting on its foreign debt. A $50 billion loan from the United States and the IMF stabilized the faltering southern economy, and share prices began to recover at the end of 1995. But so strong is the human need for quick money today that the painful lessons of the Bolsa crash were soon forgotten by speculators. In 1996 the dollar value of Mexican shares jumped 16 percent and another 30 percent by September 1997, only to tumble again the following year.

The Mexican bailout, however, had an unintended effect. It convinced the speculating community of bankers and mutual funds that they could invest in risky markets with impunity. Thus billions more poured into the share markets of the Tigers, Latin America, Eastern Europe, and Russia, and when they all collapsed after July 1997, the IMF arranged new bailouts worth $200 billion.

Even though the IMF efforts failed to revive the rescued economies, their stock markets did stabilize and partially recover, thus reassuring the American public that the U.S. government will try its level best to protect American share markets. This is not an unreasonable judgment either. What else are the people supposed to think? If the administration can constantly bail out troubled foreign markets, it should certainly go all out in preserving share prices at home. The American investor is now fearless in the chase for ever-growing returns, as was demonstrated by the meteoric rise of the Internet stocks in January 1999. Some people have used their home equity loans to purchase company shares; others have borrowed on their credit cards, paying double-digit interest rates, to gamble in markets. This is a replay of the Japanese frenzy in the 1980s. As columnist Louis Uchitelle points out, "More than 24% of the nation's household wealth is now invested in stocks, up from 10% in the 1987 crash."[33] Excluding housing, as much as half of the nation's financial wealth is now trapped in the share markets.

Also contributing to the unprecedented market bubble is the U.S. administration's antitrust policy, which winks at megamergers among large and profitable companies. Such industrial marriages spur the Dow, and when unchallenged by the government, generate expectations of more to come and new highs in stock indexes. At the end of 1998, two highly profitable firms, Exxon and Mobil, announced their intent to merge. Exxon had earned $5 billion and Mobil $3 billion that year. Few politicians and economists complained, even though the two behemoths had been once carved out of a monopoly called the Standard Oil Trust. Neither company was hurting for profits. The antitrust policy that was supposed to create healthy competition in 1911 was no longer deemed necessary in the go-go 1990s. In an article titled as "From Trust Busters to Trust Trusters," columnist David Sanger remarked that "in 1998, monopoly players do not go to jail."[34] They are treated as celebrities instead.

These then are the causes underlying the millennium bubble. Any one or two of them could trigger a speculative fever, but when all work together the end result is a share market that comes along once in a thousand years. Most of the market movers are attributable to the American government. The administration trio of Bill Clinton, Alan Greenspan, and Robert Rubin seemed to believe that ever-rising share prices reflect a vigorous economy. They were like three bartenders serving drink after drink of capital gains to the American investor; now they have even grannies and grandpas hooked to the habit. Alas, soon the entire nation will wake up and shriek from the hangover. Of course, this administration's follies are nothing new; they have been rooted in laws adopted since the early eighties. Presidents came and went, congressional majority changed parties, but the government policy of enriching the rich did not budge. So the bubble kept inflating, and now our fates are intimately linked to the world's largest casino ever: the New York Stock Exchange.

9

THE FUTURE

Here we are in the middle of 1999, and thanks to our technology and our governments, we are saddled with the likes of the millennium bubble and the millennium bug; both are potential nightmares. The one has always burst in the past; the other, a mystery, could be as lethal as the first. Our chances of escaping a calamity are extremely low. If the computer virus doesn't get us, the puncture of the bubble will. If we are lucky, only one will hit us. My worst fear is that they will explode in tandem to create an unprecedented trauma around the world. We're now, after all, in the last year of a decade. Remember the final-year syndrome, discussed in chapter 2.

Ever since the 1920s, the syndrome has produced a nightmare somewhere on earth. All but one, in 1989, traumatized the U.S. economy or society. Some spawned bloody revolutions, others a world war, market crashes, or roaring inflation. What are we in for now? Sadly, my forecast calls for an inflationary depression, potentially the worst type of economic disaster. Is this a figment of my overheated imagination? Hopefully yes. But all my forecasts have appeared fantastic at first.

The decade's final year is a climactic point. In the 1920s it was continuous growth in stock prices that peaked in 1929; in the 1930s it was the rise of Hitler and the gradual German militarization that culminated in the Second World War; throughout the 1940s China was convulsed by the communist rebellion before Mao's revolution occurred in 1949. The Cuban Revolution of 1959 came at the end of many years of official repression and Castro's rebellion, starting as early as 1953. The U.S. inflation of 1969 capped a decade of slow but steady climb in consumer prices. Seeds of the Iranian Revolution of 1979 were sown years before in the exile of Ayatollah Khomeini from his homeland. The fall of the Berlin Wall in 1989 was similarly rooted in the Soviet invasion of Afghanistan beginning a decade earlier. The final-year syndrome is the climactic point of a significant trend developing through the decade.

What are the prominent events of the 1990s? The bubble of the millennium is the most momentous development of the decade, even more so than the president's impeachment. The bubble saved Bill Clinton from removal from office; in the absence of America's share market euphoria, and the resulting paper prosperity, the public would have turned against him. He would have either resigned or been forced out of office. Over 80 percent of Americans believed that he was guilty of the impeachment charges, but most did not want to risk the nation's prosperity by ousting him. The American market mania comes along once in a thousand years, and it will peak by the end of 1999. Such is the dictum of the final-year syndrome.

The bubble is likely to explode all of a sudden, at the height of business and consumer optimism. It will rupture with few advance warnings, just like in August 1998, barely a month after the Dow's peak in July, except this time the damage will be far greater and uncontainable. Alan Greenspan along with the rest of the world will react again by lowering interest rates, but the positive effects will be brief and ineffectual. The bubble has been already patched up once and is all the more fragile for it.

We already have an inkling of how our financial system could come tumbling down. Thanks to the near collapse of the hedge fund Long-Term Capital Management in October 1998, it is now clear that share markets today are perched atop a precipice, supported by expanding debt and the growing inflow of foreign money. Their foundation rests on quicksand, which could swallow the entire structure in a hurry. We have seen this happen in the economies of the Asian Tigers, Japan, Russia, Mexico, and Brazil. Thus the mechanism by which seeming prosperity can vanish overnight, in spite of frantic and frequent bailouts, is no longer a mystery. It is not something that transpired in the distant 1930s.

What will trigger the stock market crash, or a whole series of crashes over three to six months? When a speculative bubble has reached its zenith, even a pinprick can burst it open. Anything could bring it down, including the Y2K woes starting as early as September. But the likely scenario is one we've seen before. In August 1998 it was the financial meltdown in Russia and its default on foreign debt that sparked a crisis. This time it could be default by Brazil or other debtors in Latin America. Building our prosperity on borrowing and calling it free enterprise is very much the fashion sport among our economists, politicians, and financiers.

At the end of February 1999, Brazil needed some $53 billion to service its foreign obligations coming up during the year. Thanks to the flight of capital, it had only $26 billion left in reserve, which was eroding at the rate of $1 billion per week. At this rate of accretion, Brazil will definitely run out of foreign exchange by the end of 1999, even if an already depleted IMF opens all its money spigots to expand its Brazilian bailout.

But Brazil is not the only headache. Its January 1999 devaluation is already tormenting its neighbors. Exports from Argentina, Uruguay, Venezuela, Peru, and Chile are hurting; these countries also have big debts that must be serviced every year. What transpired in Asia in 1997 is now brewing in Latin America, and just as the other Tigers slowly crumbled under the assault of Thai devaluation, the financial systems of Brazil's neighbors are likely to follow suit. Will the IMF be able to bail out all of Latin America?

It took about six months before the Thai virus infected the other Tigers, suggesting that by July or August, certainly by the end of 1999, Brazil's flu could afflict its neighbors. And that would dovetail neatly with the final-year syndrome. Also, the syndrome usually struck in the last four months of the year. The 1929 crash erupted in October, the Second World War in September, the Chinese Revolution in October, the Berlin Wall in November. The Cuban and Iranian revolutions occurred during January but did not afflict the United States until the fall. Similarly in 1969 inflation surged toward the end of the year. If the past is any guide, then the 1999 eruption will also wait until the fall.

Once the Dow begins to crash, the so-called hedge funds will collapse quickly. Some of these funds gamble on variations in interest rates, some on the direction of share price indexes, others on international currency movements. Whatever their specialty, they all make bets by borrowing vast sums of money, involving trillions of dollars in bonds and stocks. When panic strikes, even the best brains behind speculative funds become powerless. Long-Term Capital Management, after all, was run by two Nobel prize–winning economists, who won laurels, of all the things, for properly managing risk. If the high priests of economics couldn't preserve their own capital, what chance do the rest of us have in surviving the assault of market crashes?

The collapse of the hedge funds, with their international reach, will precipitate a financial meltdown not just in the United States but around the globe. Governments, with all their debts and special interests, will be powerless to stop it. It won't matter if a stock market crashed recently, because its prices could and will sink even deeper. Global share markets from Tokyo to London, Toronto to Sydney, and Moscow to Milan will tumble as the financial tornado unleashed in the United States swallows the whole planet.

Fall 1999 will bring back memories of fall 1929, except that the thunderbolt this time will be far louder, and its aftershocks over the coming decade will set off an inflationary, not a deflationary, depression. In the first half of the 1930s, prices tumbled; this time around they will soar. Why the difference? In the 1920s the United States was a lender to the world; now it is a debtor. Back then the country had a perennial trade surplus; now it has a perennial and mushrooming deficit.

The millennium bug could also sting us as early as fall 1999. Computers will read September 9 as 9-9-99. Many are designed to shut down automatically or stop processing the data once they encounter four nines. That month will offer a big test of the Y2K compliance, which many businesses are now touting. If the glitch turns out to be bad, a global financial panic could ignite in any important economy in the world.

If we are lucky enough to escape financial disaster in the fall, we could get it sometime in the next six months. But the final-year syndrome is very likely to bring about another nightmare, if not a stock market crash then something else, such as a war or natural disaster. NATO's aerial bombardment of Serbia, followed by Slobodan

Milosevic's genocide in Kosovo and the worst refugee crisis in Europe since World War II is a reminder of what can suddenly happen in the last year of a decade. However, the overwhelming likelihood is for inflationary depression, encompassing a sharp rise in both inflation and unemployment.

EVIDENCE OF THE CYCLE

Let's first reexamine the three-decade cycle of inflation. I used this cycle in the early eighties to predict falling inflation over two consecutive decades. Once you know the likely behavior of inflation, you can be fairly accurate in forecasting several trends in the economy. Inflation is the key that holds the secrets of what the future will be, since price behavior determines the demeanor of interest rates, which in turn set the course of bond and share prices. Low interest rates stimulate business investment, home ownership, consumer demand, profits, and stock markets as well as growth in the economy. High interest rates do the opposite.

Once I concluded that inflation would tumble in the 1980s, I was certain that interest rates would also sink and, along with the prevailing high wealth disparity, create a share market bubble. All this did come to pass, thanks to the inexorable cycle of inflation that travels as far back as the 1750s, peaking every third decade, except in the aftermath of the Civil War, which, let's assume, is not likely to recur. However, contrary to my expectation, the share bubble burst only in Japan in 1990, but not in the United States. The vast flow of Japanese money into American assets, as explained in chapter 4, kept the 1990 slump from turning into a depression. Perhaps the stabilizing institutional changes since the 1930s mean that the balloon has to be far bigger than the one in the 1920s before it would puncture. The Japanese bubble was certainly large and old enough to rupture, and the U.S. bubble is now the biggest and the oldest ever. So its time has come.

The 1990s turned out to be even more speculative than the 1980s, yet the inflation cycle continued to hold. The rate of inflation sank even more; so did interest rates, and the result was an ever magnifying bubble. The cycle now tells us that inflation is around the corner, starting with the year 2000. The first decade of the coming century should be all inflationary.

The trend of the money cycle has been upward, as you can see from figure 9.1. The trend line indicates that the coming decade will be at least as inflationary as the 1970s, when the annual rates of inflation varied between 3.5 percent and 13 percent. The ethos of that decade had, of course, been foreseen by 1969, when prices surged 6.2 percent. In 1970 the inflation rate fell somewhat, and kept falling until 1973 when the rate soared and plagued the nation for the next eight years. This time, however, a different process will unfold. The coming decade indeed will be inflationary, in line with the cycle, but the price spark could come primarily from the stock market crash. Here is why.

THE EXPERIENCE OF EMERGING MARKETS

The recent experience of all the emerging markets—the Tigers, Russia, Mexico, Brazil—is that when foreign capital flees, currencies collapse and output declines while prices and unemployment soar. Among the Tigers, Thailand was the first casualty of capital flight, and in 1997 its baht fell about 90 percent between July and December; the currency recovered somewhat by the end of the next year but was still down 50 percent. The Thai inflation rate surged from 5.8 percent in 1997 to over 9 percent in 1998, even though its output and employment tumbled during the year. The other Tigers followed suit. Malaysian inflation and unemployment both doubled in the same period; Korea behaved no differently, its inflation surging from 4.5 percent in 1997 to 7 percent in 1998, and joblessness soaring from 2.5 percent to 6.5 percent. In Taiwan, inflation doubled to 2 percent, although unemployment held steady in the same period, and in the Philippines the inflation rate was 10 percent in both 1997 and 1998, while GDP growth became slightly negative. Indonesia was the ringleader among the Tigers, with an inflation rate of over 50 percent along with an output decline in excess of 15 percent in 1998. The nation was rocked not just by currency depreciation but also by a revolution that toppled the thirty-three-year regime of President Suharto. So it is not surprising that Indonesia suffered so badly among the Tigers. Its currency and employment tumbled dras-

FIGURE 9.1

The trend in the long-run rate of inflation in the United States, 1750s–1990s (in percent)

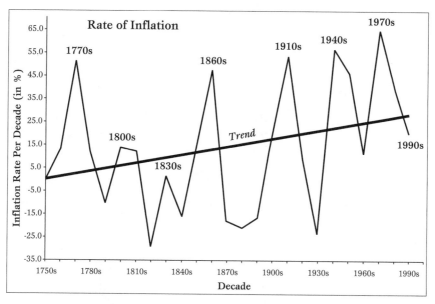

SOURCE: Data from Ravi Batra, *The Great Depression of 1990* (New York: Simon & Schuster, 1987), 188; and *Economic Report of the President* (Washington, D.C.: U.S. Council of Economic Advisers, 1999), 401.

Note: Except for the aftermath of the Civil War of the 1860s, the rate of inflation peaked every third decade in the United States. Every peak in the twentieth century is higher than the previous peak.

tically, and inflation surged accordingly. The behavior of inflation, unemployment, or GDP growth of all these nations is captured by figures 9.2, 9.3, and 9.4.

The agony of the Tigers was actually a replay of Mexico's just two years before. In 1995 the peso lost half its value, and Mexican prices surged over 50 percent that year, followed by another jump of 30 percent the next year. By 1998 Mexican inflation had cooled to 19 percent, still a worrisome rate. However, Russia was the worst hit of all, suffering an inflation rate of over 90 percent in 1998, as its currency fell from six rubles per dollar to twenty-three per dollar, a vast devaluation. Brazil's recent devaluation has not hit home yet, but its history in the 1980s confirms that inflation and unemployment are inevitable by-products of devalued money in a debt-ridden economy.

FIGURE 9.2
Unemployment and inflation in Thailand and Korea, 1997–1998

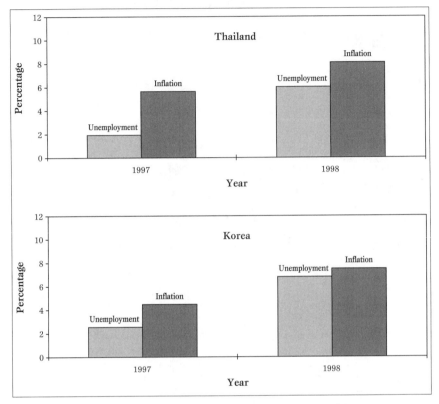

SOURCE: Data from *International Financial Statistics* (Washington, D.C.: International Monetary Fund, April 1999), 420 and 708.

How does currency depreciation, which means a nation's money buying fewer units of foreign currencies, translate into surging prices? For instance, the dollar bought 360 yen in 1970; in 1998 it bought only 125. The dollar had lost a lot of value in terms of the Japanese currency over twenty-eight years. Devaluation raises the prices of foreign products in terms of the home currency; at the same time home goods become less expensive in foreign countries.

Currency depreciation causes inflation because foreign goods become costly, especially if imports are a significant proportion of national consumption. It all depends on how open or globalized an economy is. With increasing trade liberalization, imports loom large in our consumption. So even minor devaluations can be inflationary.

FIGURE 9.3

Unemployment and inflation in Taiwan and Malaysia, 1997–1998

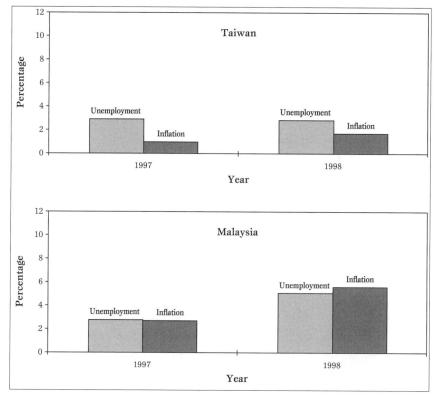

SOURCE: Data from *International Financial Statistics* (Washington, D.C.: International Monetary Fund, April 1999), 470.

The level of competition at home also matters. When industries are dominated by regional monopolies, as is the case in Mexico, Indonesia, Brazil, and Russia, devaluations become ultrainflationary, because these companies can then raise prices at will; in highly monopolized economies, inflation is very hard to control. However, in more competitive economies such as Korea, Thailand, and Malaysia, inflation cools down fast as output falls, unless, of course, the country fights the crisis by printing money. Most of the Tigers have not made this mistake, so their inflation rates were plunging at the start of 1999.

Why should the U.S. stock market crash by itself be inflationary? The reason is that it will cause a collapse of the dollar. As mentioned

FIGURE 9.4
Inflation and GDP growth in the Philippines and Indonesia, 1997–1998

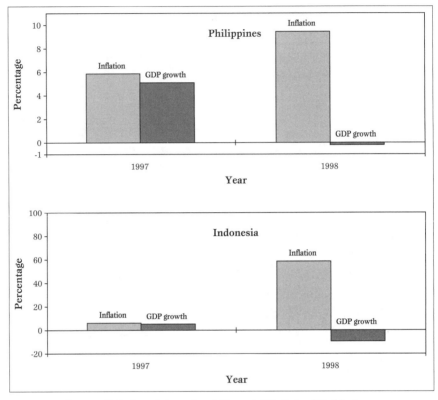

SOURCE: Data from *International Financial Statistics* (Washington, D.C.: International Monetary Fund, April 1999), 371 and 584. Directorate General of Budget and Statistics, Taipei, Taiwan, 1999, tables 1–5.

before, the United States is a giant version of Thailand, a country with huge foreign debt and a surging trade deficit in 1997. The dollar should be in trouble already, but in a strange and unprecedented quirk of nature, the mounting trade deficit has been a boon to the U.S. economy. The deficit is one reason for the inflow of international capital into American assets, and the continuing inflow has kept the value of the dollar high since 1995. U.S. currency has depreciated sharply with respect to its 1970 value, but relative to its low point in 1995 it was much higher at the end of 1998.

When the Dow plunges, the dollar will fall almost immediately. The Thai scenario of 1997 will be reenacted toward the end of 1999, this time in the United States. First the Dow tumbles and then the dollar, followed by a rise in interest rates and plunging bond prices. The interest rate rise would invite a response from Alan Greenspan, but this time he will be powerless to contain the crash. Share prices will resume their plunge, and the vicious circle will begin again. U.S. markets will then taste the bitter medicine that until now has been limited to emerging markets.

Brazil's default over external debt would destroy confidence in the U.S. economy and administration, because America has invested copious amounts of investment and intellectual capital in the preservation of this South American giant. Again the Fed would want to reduce interest rates, but for fear of the plunging dollar, it won't. The G-7 countries could, and perhaps will, coordinate an international interest rate cut to stimulate share markets but will be unable to contain the shock of the Brazilian default for long. Other nations could also default. Mexico, like Brazil, has a huge foreign debt. It could also renege on its obligations as the fever of currency depreciation spreads through South America, which absorbs significant levels of Mexican exports.

It is worth noting that capital flight away from U.S. assets need not be huge for the crisis to materialize. Data collected in a recent study by two *New York Times* correspondents, Nicholas Kristof and David Sanger, reveal what a little outflow can do to the economies hooked to the drug of foreign money.[35] Between 1992 and 1994, Mexico enjoyed an inflow of $69 billion, or an annual average of $23 billion. In 1995 it lost a relatively small $11 billion, and its economy collapsed into an orgy of soaring inflation and unemployment.

Between 1994 and 1996, five Asian Tigers—Indonesia, Malaysia, the Philippines, Korea, and Thailand—received $211 billion, a relatively large sum, from abroad. In 1997 an outflow of $12 billion, a mere 5.7 percent of their inflow, sent their economies into a tailspin. This is not all. Between 1979 and 1982, the developing world took in $137 billion, but then lost just $9 billion in 1983. That year many developing countries suffered sizzling inflation, some even hyperinflation. Of course, none of these illustrations includes an industrial giant like the United States, but then never before has a giant been buried under such a mountain of international debt. What is remarkable is that even a smallish outflow of foreign capital can spark megacrashes in share markets, currencies, and the economies that are addicted to external aid.

THE EURO

Where would the foreign money go from the United States? Some of it would go back home, and some would go into the euro, the new currency of western Europe that came into being on New Year's Day in 1999. Eleven countries—Germany, Belgium, Italy, Spain, the Netherlands, Austria, Portugal, France, Ireland, Luxembourg, and Finland—have successfully begun using that single currency. They have merged their currencies into one unit, which is initially being used in bank transactions and for trading financial assets such as stocks and bonds. Euro notes and coins won't be issued till 2002, by which time the members of the monetary union, also known as Euroland, will be comfortable with the new system. Notable absences from the membership were Britain and Sweden, which are waiting on the sidelines to see how the experiment unfolds.

The euro made a successful debut, and immediately attracted some money from Australia and Japan. It has not yet offered a serious challenge to the global hegemony of the dollar, but potentially it is a bigger challenger than any other national currency, such as the yen and the Swiss franc. The euro also supports a major bond market, rivaling the size of the U.S. government bond program. The stock markets of the eleven members have been essentially unified with the formation of the monetary union. As a result, Europe could attract big chunks of the foreign money that has been parked in the United States.

Thus far the U.S. economy has remained a raging dynamo, and few countries seem eager to abandon the American haven. The euro has slightly depreciated relative to the dollar, falling from its opening value of $1.16 to about $1.05 in April. But when a crisis strikes sometime around the fall, the dollar will be severely tested. Until the birth of the euro, individual European currencies were not strong enough to challenge the greenback, but the situation has drastically altered now. The dollar's collapse becomes more likely than before.

What is more interesting is that some countries, such as Sweden, that have not joined the monetary union, have already issued euro bonds, making the European bond market even larger than the combined market of eleven countries. Euroland itself has a bond portfolio worth $2 trillion, about four-fifths of the U.S. Treasury market. Combined with other nations, the euro bond market can easily absorb a few hundred billion dollars of foreign money without suffering the hangover of excess liquidity. That is all it would take to bring the U.S. financial system down to its knees. As we have seen, less than 6 percent of foreign money left five Asian Tigers and their economies disintegrated overnight. The birth of the euro, together with the other factors we've seen, makes the dollar's collapse all but inevitable.

The euro has not appreciated since its birth. But when the dollar fell sharply in the second half of 1998, especially with respect to the yen, some Japanese institutions switched part of their funds from dollar-denominated assets to euro bonds. The result was a depreciation of the dollar relative to other important currencies, including those of Europe. Not a single currency unit of Euroland buys more than one dollar, but the euro does. The reason lies in the dollar depreciation occurring in late 1998. So the euro's fall soon after its successful debut was just a market correction.

When share markets collapse in New York, they would also crash in London, Frankfurt, Paris, and Rome. Why would foreign money move at all from the United States to Europe? Simply because Euroland does not have much foreign debt. In any case, if Europe does not enjoy the inflow, foreign capital will simply go back home. The dollar, after all, sank to eighty yen in April 1995 even before the euro was born. That happened as a small portion of Japanese money went home. True, at the turn of 1999, the dollar was worth 115 yen, but the point is that a collapse of the dollar is not out of the realm of probability.

FUTURE BANKING CRISIS

The collapse of the dollar, and resulting inflation, will lead to a serious banking crisis in the United States, much worse than the savings and loan (S&L) debacle of the mid-1980s. Surging prices normally spark a rise in interest rates. Inflation lowers the purchasing power of money over time, so that the lender expects to get depreciated dollars back in the future. If inflation heats up, a banker, seeking a certain inflation-adjusted return from his loan, automatically adds a premium to the fees he was charging before. Thus high price-growth and high interest rates go together.

During the 1970s, the last peak decade of inflation, federal laws regulated the interest fees, which did not keep pace with market conditions. As a result, many banks and S&Ls made long-term mortgage loans at low interest rates. As prices continued to surge, the public woke up and began to transfer its savings into unregulated money market mutual funds that offered much higher yields. The S&Ls were then forced to pay higher interest rates as well to retain their funds. The end result was that their prior loans offered a return much lower than their current costs. Many went bankrupt and had to be bailed out by the government in the 1980s. All in all, the crisis cost American taxpayers some $200 billion.

A similar crisis, though on a vaster scale, will occur in the coming decade. The banking industry has loaned huge sums to home owners during the 1990s at very low interest rates, which will surge with inflation in 2000 and beyond. Hundreds, if not thousands, of banks will then have to be bailed out.

Financial institutions are also busy speculating heavily like hedge funds. When the stock market crashes, they will lose billions and cause a credit crunch, which means that many businesses will not be able to get loans at any cost, much less the attractive rates they have enjoyed. Banks are in for some rough weather soon.

THE UNFOLDING SCENARIO

If past patterns repeat themselves, the U.S. economy will begin to unravel by fall 1999; if not, the debacle will start three to six months later. But come it must. The millennium bubble has violated all the laws of nature that I know of, and it will not be able to sustain itself for long. What will come first, the market crash or the bite of the Y2K bug? I think the crash will precede the bite by a few months, but in the final analysis, it won't matter.

Suppose Brazil and other Latin American countries including Mexico manage to hang on with the help of the IMF. Since the U.S. market bubble has to burst through an inexorable dictum of supply and demand, then the computer virus could turn out to be just as deadly as some experts suggest. If the economy is severely disrupted, that in itself will trigger a share price debacle around the world. The dollar will collapse and spark a major jump in prices. The computer bite will also be inflationary, as we have already seen in chapter 7, further fueling a big jump in prices and hence interest rates. Rising interest fees will spark further market crashes.

How long will inflation last? It all depends on the sting of the computer virus. The rupture of the bubble will indeed spark a price surge, but it will be a one-shot deal, unlikely to last more than one or two years. If the Y2K bite is mild, the fever of inflation will be over by 2002, provided the administration does not repeat the mistakes made in the 1970s of printing excessive money to deal with various crises. Historic economic cycles suggest that money growth will also soar, in which case all bets are off, and the entire coming decade could be inflationary, dwarfing even the sizzle of the seventies. Hopefully, we have learned our history lessons well and will resist monetary temptation.

If the computer bite is sharp and the Y2K problems take a few years to resolve, then the first half of the decade could be inflationary even if money growth is controlled within reason. It will be easier to deal with this issue in the new century, although the cycle of inflation tells us that unless fundamental reforms are introduced, the entire coming decade is likely to suffer a price boom.

THE REST OF THE ECONOMY

The market boom thus far has been a blessing to the economy. It has created prosperity for a vast number of Americans. As foreign money poured in, first bond yields fell, then business investment and home buying soared, and productivity and the economy enjoyed their growth. With wages leashed by the growth of monopolies, foreign competition, and downsizing resulting from mergers, profits surged. So did share prices, whose profits financed new bond issues and investments, and interest rates fell further. This was the virtuous circle starting as early as the mid-1980s; it received a shot in the arm in 1990 and a further boost after 1996.

When the New York Stock Exchange collapses, the explosion will be heard around the globe. Nearly half of Americans have their fortunes directly tied with the market, and the other half are linked indirectly. Although 1 percent of the public has enjoyed nearly 90 percent of the market growth, 40 percent owns company shares or stock mutual funds. They will lose in a big way from the crash of the millennium, crimping their spending in the process.

The falling dollar will help exporters and hurt importers, and since we import a lot more than we export, the net effect on business profits will be negative. Furthermore, profits will also succumb to the sharp rise in interest rates. The market crash itself will destroy business and consumer confidence. None of this is good for business investment.

Soaring interest charges will cripple the financial institutions not only because of rising deposit costs but also because of a huge fall in the value of their bond holdings, whose prices move inversely with interest rates. A credit crunch will follow, further hurting investment in the process. In short, the virtuous spiral since 1982 will turn into a vicious spiral.

Trigger-happy American companies will immediately resort to layoffs. Even in the best of times, our corporations are only too glad to get rid of their highly paid senior employees. In their view, only the executives, especially the CEOs, need to be rewarded regardless of their performance. What an irony of turbo-charged capitalism. The worst case of downsizing, reflected in the largest number of industrial layoffs, occurred in 1998 at the height of the speculative boom. It will not take long before the stock market crash, or a series of crashes, induces massive unemployment.

Inflationary syndromes from the bites of the millennium bubble and the bug could be contained within a few years, but not their employment effects. Once the economy goes into a tailspin, it will take many years before recovery starts. The reforms offered subsequently in this work will jump-start our factories, but they will be resisted by senior management. The employment depression is likely to endure, unless wages fall drastically. When national spending sinks, either employment or wages have to give. In either case, the nation as a whole will have to endure years of growing poverty. Such is the eventual by-product of debt-deluded prosperity and speculative manias. Having begun in the final year of the 1990s, the market crash could ripple through the entire next decade.

The U.S. bubble is now a patched-up behemoth, and its rupture could spark something that has never plagued the nation before—falling real wages as well as employment. Even during the thirties, real wages for the employed rose because of tumbling prices, but the great inflationary depression, itself a U.S. first, could spur layoffs as well as a loss in real earnings.

INDIVIDUAL INDUSTRIES

Many industries will tumble from a nearly simultaneous outburst of the bubble and the bug. The first victims will be the financial institutions. Brokers, financial planners, merger specialists, investment bankers, and the like will be laid off as soon as panic overcomes Wall Street. Theirs have been the most lucrative industries and positions since 1982, and they would be the first to collapse.

Real estate will be next. The housing and construction boom in the 1990s has been so potent that it has neutralized the harm done by surging imports. As interest rates zoom, this boom will come to a grinding halt, generating an unprecedented glut in real estate. Most construction companies will go bankrupt as will real estate brokers. Office and shopping mall rents will drop sharply.

With housing in decline, durable goods industries will be affected as well. Soaring interest rates will also cripple machine tools, autos, furniture, appliances, computers, airplanes, and so on. Linked to these are the fortunes of firms producing raw materials or semiprocessed goods such as copper, aluminum, iron, steel, lumber, and plastics. Their demand will also shrink, leading to several rounds of layoffs. Next in line will be services—hotels, restaurants, airlines, truckers, attorneys, accountants, day-care centers, and so on.

Among the least affected will be physicians, nurses, and other health care personnel. However, because people won't be able to afford their expensive services, their incomes will decline. Dentists and cosmetic surgeons perhaps won't be as lucky as other doctors, because their services are not as indispensable. The education industry also will not suffer as much as manufacturing and some services.

As jobs become scarce, the demand for higher education could actually rise. Employers will be able to pick and choose from the available pool of skilled workers.

Some, though very few, could actually benefit from the coming depression. As new goods become unaffordable, businesses geared to their repair will flourish. All sorts of repair services could prosper. The need to fight the Y2K bug itself will generate vacancies for thousands of computer experts. However, such jobs will be only temporary, as there will be little need for bug fighters once the virus is killed by or about the end of 2000.

As crime climbs amidst poverty and joblessness, the security and crime prevention industry could also flourish. Business and individual bankruptcies would soar, so resale stores, pawnshops, legal services, and auction firms would be much in demand. The need for inexpensive transportation could help companies producing bicycles, mopeds, and minicars.

DEFLATIONARY DEPRESSION: EUROLAND, JAPAN, AND CHINA

The crisis will plague the whole world, but some might not suffer inflation. Countries with little or no foreign debt will perhaps not see their prices rise. They could in fact see a price decline or deflation. Among the Tigers, Hong Kong and Singapore have already witnessed declining inflation, because they have little foreign debt and their foreign exchange reserve is large enough to defend their currency. The Thai crisis had little effect on their currencies, so they suffered only increased joblessness but not a surge in prices. This much is clear from an examination of figure 9.5.

Euroland as a whole also has little foreign debt, although some of its members do have large obligations to other nations. The collapse of the dollar will likely raise the value of the euro, the British pound, and the yen. Euroland, Britain, and Japan need not suffer from inflation. They will be afflicted only with layoffs and perhaps falling real wages, depending on how severe the U.S. depression is. They too will pay a harsh price for the speculative bubble but not as much as the United States and the rest of the world.

However, if Euroland, Britain, and Japan choose to pump money

FIGURE 9.5
Unemployment and inflation in Hong Kong and Singapore,
1997–1998

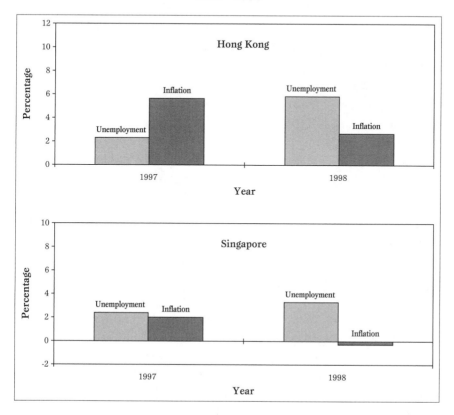

SOURCE: Data from *International Financial Statistics* (Washington,
D.C.: International Monetary Fund, April 1999), 210 and 642.

into the economy the way they did during the 1970s, or the Y2K bug
stings them hard, then they could also invite inflation along with
high unemployment. Given the leftist tendencies of the current governments in Britain, Germany, Italy, and France, pump priming cannot be entirely ruled out.

Let's now take a look at China, which has enjoyed phenomenal
growth since the early eighties and is now undergoing deflation.
Aided by foreign investment and the multinational firms, the
Chinese GDP expansion routinely exceeded 10 percent per year. As
with Thailand, China emphasized showcases of development rather

than balanced growth in which wages keep pace with productivity. Office centers, shopping malls, high-tech factories, and so on were added by the hundreds, but real wages failed to rise. Like Japan, China looked to the United States for expanding demand and by 1998 had a nearly $60 billion surplus in its American trade. Since wages failed to keep pace with hourly output, now domestic demand is insufficient to absorb domestic supply, and the economy is poised for a fall. Hong Kong is facing the same peril, because history shows that deflation is far more devastating to an economy than inflation.

The currency debacle afflicting most Tigers has bypassed both China and Hong Kong, which have become the victims of shrinking demand in the neighboring nations. If their currencies remain stable or appreciate relative to the greenback—a likely prospect—then they both would continue to experience deflation.

CANADA AND LATIN AMERICA

Canada, living in the shadow of its southern giant, quickly gets infected by what transpires in America. Over three-fourths of Canadian exports go to the United States. As a part of NAFTA, the two nations are interlinked through trade and investment. So strong is their linkage that, as the saying goes, when America sneezes, Canada catches a cold. When U.S. share prices sank in August 1998, so did Canada's; when they rebounded in the south, they also did in the north.

If the U.S. depression turns out to be inflationary, so will the Canadian. The rupture of the millennium bubble will also puncture the bubble up north. The stock market debacle itself will create a downturn in Canada; however, the Canadian dollar will collapse not with respect to the greenback but rather relative to other currencies. The Y2K virus will also be inflationary for both trading partners.

Canada's main exports are farm goods, raw materials, and oil, all of which have already suffered price declines because of the falling world demand resulting from the Asian tumult. Unlike the 1970s, oil prices would continue to fall this time around. So the Canadian depression could be just as bad as that in the United States, even though interest rates in Canada won't rise as much as those in America.

The continuing fall in oil prices spells trouble for all oil-exporting countries, including Mexico and Venezuela. When the United States goes into depression, those nations in Latin America will not stay far behind. Some could see political upheaval as well. To sum up, not all countries will experience an inflationary depression; only those with large foreign debts and trade deficits will. Others could face a deflationary depression or one associated with stable prices.

THE FALL OF CRONY CAPITALISM

Every cloud has a silver lining, and the coming thunderstorm will be no exception. The global economic cataclysm will induce the collapse of crony or monopoly capitalism that now masquerades as free enterprise. Crony capitalism manifests itself in a variety of ways. In the United States it takes the form of the rule of money in economic policy and politics, especially elections.

When President Clinton appointed Robert Rubin, formerly the head of an investment banking firm, Goldman Sachs, as U.S. Treasury secretary, it was a classic case of crony capitalism at work. When in the name of free markets they both pushed for financial deregulation around the world, they gave into the self-interest of their patrons, particularly bankers.

It is crony capitalism that induced President Reagan and Congress to cut income taxes—allegedly to stimulate saving, investment, and growth—and then turn around and impose the heaviest-ever tax burden on the poor in the form of what they called Social Security fees. Alan Greenspan, an investment banker in 1983, presided over the commission that recommended the hefty rise in Social Security taxes and was later rewarded with the chairmanship of the Fed. How could the income-tax cut favoring the affluent combined with the largest tax rise on the poor and the middle class ever promote savings, investment, and growth? Such policies reflect nothing but crony capitalism. Not surprisingly, the growth record of the 1980s and the 1990s pales before that of all other periods except the depression decade of the 1930s.[36]

When the IMF and the U.S. administration bailed out Mexico to save investments of American bankers such as Goldman Sachs, it reflected the influence of money over politics. What else were professional bankers like Rubin and Greenspan expected to do when American banking institutions were saddled with huge speculative losses? When bailouts were extended to the Asian Tigers that had borrowed copious amounts from U.S. bankers and mutual funds, it was simply crony capitalism. When Congress routinely grants last-minute tax breaks to its patrons in the annual budget, it is nothing but money dominating politics.

Crony capitalism is not the sole preserve of the Third World and emerging markets. It may be more pervasive and virulent there, but it plagues the American economy and society as well. In the ultimate analysis, it is crony capitalism that is responsible for the bubble of the millennium and the resulting global collapse that is knocking on our doorstep.

Fortunately, crony capitalism is seeding its own destruction, having lost all sense of decency and common sense. Why else would American CEOs reward themselves with huge raises and bonuses while downsizing millions of their subordinates? At the height of the current U.S. boom, half of Americans have less than $1,000 in the bank. Most live from paycheck to paycheck. Thousands are still being downsized. Poverty and homelessness, especially child poverty, coexist with plenitude. Wealth disparity grew fast under Reagan and Bush, but even faster under Clinton. In the coming inflationary depression, crony capitalism will collapse, and the poor, the children, the handicapped, and all minorities will have a cause to celebrate, because true free enterprise will come into place.

I have examined this subject in detail in a previous work, *The Downfall of Capitalism and Communism,* and will briefly present the argument here again. Capitalism and communism are creeds that have globally competed for the heart and soul of people ever since Karl Marx wrote his *Das Kapital* in 1867. The two systems have had a checkered career. During the thirties, capitalism tottered because of the Great Depression, while communism offered hope to the starving masses. Now communism has all but vanished, while capitalism seems to be shining brighter. Isn't this the finest hour for the United

States? Seemingly yes, but not in reality. Crony capitalism will go the same way as Soviet communism.

A close look at any society reveals that there are three possible sources of political power—military might, intellect, and money. Religion may also bring social supremacy, but because priests sway society through their mastery of scriptures and rituals, their power may be properly categorized as intellectual. Thus political leadership stems from only three sources. As a result, through the paeans of history we find that society is sometimes dominated by warriors, sometimes by intellectuals (including priests), and sometimes by the wealthy.

What's more interesting is that a pattern exists in political evolution as well. Specifically, the age of the military, in which the army rules, is followed by the age of intellectuals, wherein the educated bureaucracy reigns, and then by the age of the affluent or acquisitors, in which money reigns supreme. During the age of the wealthy, the acquisitors eventually acquire so much wealth that other groups of people have to spend most of their time at work just to earn a living. That is when people get fed up with the rich and overthrow the rule of money and the institutions associated with it. In other words, a swift and unprecedented rise in wealth disparity is the surest sign that the age of acquisitors is about to end. After that, warriors come back to power again and the cycle of social evolution starts all over. In other words, warriors are followed by intellectuals, then acquisitors, and so on.

This law of social cycles was expanded by my late teacher, Prabhat Ranjan Sarkar, in *Human Society*.[37] The Western world and Japan have passed through two such cycles since the birth of Christ. In Western society, the Roman empire was an age of warriors, the rule of the Catholic Church an age of intellectuals, and feudalism an age of the wealthy. This completed one rotation of the social cycle. Another rotation began when feudalism was replaced by the dominance of army generals who founded kingdoms and dynasties; this was followed by the rule of prime ministers and diplomats, or another age of intellectuals. Today, and since about 1860, the capitalistic West is in another age of acquisitors. The preeminence of U.S. business around the globe suggests that much of the world today is in the era of the wealthy.

I wrote *Downfall* in 1978, explaining the law of social cycles and predicting that both monopoly capitalism and Soviet communism would collapse around the dawn of the new millennium. At the time I had no inkling that a computer bug or a gargantuan speculative bubble were simmering. I also had no idea that the Soviets would invade Afghanistan, cripple their own economy in the process, and look for Western-style cures that ultimately spelled the demise of their system. All I knew was that, in accordance with the law of social cycles, Russia and its satellites would move from the age of warriors to the era of intellectuals, whereas the West would move into another age of warriors.

After the fall of the Berlin Wall in 1989, the Soviet empire collapsed right before our eyes and split up into smaller states. In some former satellites, intellectuals are clearly dominant. Vaclav Havel, the first president of Czechoslovakia, is a novelist, for example, and Hungary was initially headed by a professor. But the most prominent symbol of the new age of intellectuals is that the army no longer dominates the former Soviet protectorates of Poland, Romania, Hungary, Czechoslovakia, the Ukraine, and so on; nor does money play a strong role in their elections. Educators and technocrats now top the social hierarchy in ex-Soviet satellites.

With respect to Russia, the country is in an utter state of confusion economically as well as politically. In 1990 I wrote that the prime minister would eventually be the effective ruler of the forthcoming semidemocracy in Russia. With President Boris Yeltsin so often ill, that has been happening for some time, as the recent prime ministers have been truly in charge of the administration. This is likely to be the case for some time to come; in other words, Russian presidents will be ineffective rulers. Similarly, Russia's oligarchs or men of wealth will only exercise token power. It will perhaps take another decade before the dust settles on the Russian political landscape, and the country emerges from the dark shadows of instability and economic turmoil. National mores and ideas formed during four hundred years of autocracy cannot be washed away just by the collapse of the Berlin Wall.

The eclipse of communism and the current wobbly state of crony capitalism speak volumes about the brilliance of the law of social cycles. How prophetic has the idea been? The millennium bug and the bubble, coupled with an extreme concentration of wealth, fore-shadow the demise of the age of money in the near future. The United States and the West are about to be catapulted into a new age of warriors. The future era of the military would be one where army officers are democratically elected as top political leaders without any help from the wealthy.

At the end of the era of acquisitors, there is extreme debt and poverty, because the rich elite have acquired much of the nation's wealth. That is the point where feudalism met its death knell and that is where we stand today. In the early eighties, my teacher used to say, "Communism will die a premature death, and capitalism will explode like a firecracker." He didn't put dates on the collapse of the two systems, but communism is already dead, and I believe the demise of capitalism will start at the end of 1999, in line with the final-year syndrome. It will be a fitting climax to the 1990s, a mira-cle decade that has already produced at least one major event per year somewhere on earth.

The main form of government in the past was monarchy. Today it is democracy, which is also the government of the future. But the former Soviet bloc will develop an intellectual's democracy, and the West a warrior's democracy, replacing the acquisitor's democracy that is now prevalent. The U.S. republic began as a temporary war-rior's democracy, as George Washington, the first American presi-dent, was an exceptional soldier. Soon after Washington's departure, however, wealth began to play a dominant role in elections, and the nation came under the sway of acquisitors to join the acquisitive age of Western Europe.[38] This will change as a series of army officers are elected presidents in the near future to start an age of warriors in the United States and elsewhere in the world. Money's rule will then end to the relief of all. The new age will be a warrior's democracy, not a militaristic or despotic state, respecting the free press and human rights. The warrior presidents will be just as answerable to voters as their precursors. All that will change are the perks and privileges of the current elite.

Soon after the stock market crash, a democratic revolution at the ballot box will catapult the United States into a golden age that will eclipse the reign of wealth in politics, establish a truly free-enterprise economy, end permissiveness, and bring now discarded spiritual values back into fashion. Then will dawn a brilliant day, quickly sweeping across the world, the beginning of a thousand years of righteousness, compassion, and innate goodness on earth. The darker moments in human history will finally succumb to the nobility inherent in each and everyone of us. It could take another thirty-year cycle before the new age sprouts in its all-encompassing effulgence, but come it will.

10

INVESTMENT STRATEGY AND BUSINESS PLANNING

n its long march to prosperity, the U.S. economy has been through a variety of convulsions, including frequent recessions, deep slumps, and rarely, deflationary depressions. Never before has it encountered an inflationary depression, during which both prices and unemployment surge for, say, three to five years. The preceding analysis implies that following the market crash of the millennium, the United States will suffer a hefty jump in the cost of living as well as joblessness. We will then be navigating through completely uncharted waters.

The only precedent for what we are about to face occurred in the 1970s, when, for nearly two years, both joblessness and inflation surged. Interest rates soared, and profits, along with bond and stock prices, tumbled. This took place between 1973 and 1975, and again between 1979 and 1980. But even then unemployment did not exceed 10 percent. Now I believe our job losses will be the worst since the 1930s.

How do we tread on uncharted territory? With extreme caution. I cannot provide a strategy that will make you rich in the coming decade; all I can offer is a self-defense mechanism designed to minimize your losses and earn no more than a low, risk-free return. I am sure some speculators will indeed profit from the coming double jeopardy of inflation and unemployment, but they will be exceptional. A vast majority of bettors will knock at the door of insolvency.

Furthermore, my advice relies on trends, not short-term fluctuations that may temporarily contradict those trends. For instance, the trend may be for shares to drop over the coming decade, but periodically they will rise, since nothing moves in a straight line. So you shouldn't follow my advice if you intend to make quick moves in your portfolio. Similarly, you should adopt my strategy only if it makes sense to you, because ultimately only you are responsible and liable for your actions. I can only guarantee that I have offered you what I honestly believe and that I practice much of what I preach.

In spite of the overall inflationary surge, some product prices will tumble. When the depression comes, high-ticket items, along with oil, raw materials, and farm products could experience a serious deflation, while the cost of services and imported goods will keep rising. Luxury items and real estate, being expensive, are likely to depreciate. These considerations have an important bearing on any steps we can now take to meet the imminent crisis. It is essential to know what prices and interest rates are likely to do in the future.

Of course, your personal investment strategy will vary according to your income, assets, and appetite for risk, how much you have in savings and liquid assets that can be quickly sold without a loss, and so on. Some of you may be wealthy, others comfortably middle class, and still others struggling to stay afloat. Some may hope to profit from the coming crisis, while others will be happy just to survive it without undue pain. But regardless of your income and wealth, some investments should be shunned by everybody; others are in everyone's interest, and still others are not for the fainthearted.

A bewildering variety of investment vehicles is available these days, from money market funds to commodity futures and options. I am not going to lead you to the latter, because even in good times many experts suffer losses in these volatile instruments. Of course, there are always a lucky few who become rich in a hurry, but the likelihood of you and me joining their ranks is negligible. A safe investment strategy, then, is one that yields a reasonable return without unduly endangering the investment itself. A number of options are available in this regard.

I try to avoid risky investments, but you may have different preferences. In the pages ahead I will simply give you the pros and cons of various options and conclude by designing a conservative, defensive strategy. It won't make you a millionaire, but it could protect you from a very real threat during a depression—that of insolvency and starvation. History tells us that to be forewarned is to be forearmed. Even in this the age of information, few people are aware of the terror pervading a depression.

STOCKS

With stock markets expected to tumble toward the end of 1999, and then to continue in a depressed mode through at least 2000 and 2001, it would be only prudent to get rid of your shares and related investments. When a crash comes, stocks of all stripes and colors sink; some drop faster than others, but most of them fall. The question is, should we try to pick and choose among the losing stocks and ride out the intensely bearish market?

Since the U.S. speculative bubble is the world's biggest ever, its rupture, along with likely damage from the Y2K computer bug, could flatten our economy for the entire decade. Share prices could remain in the tank for a very long time. In Japan the Nikkei index toppled in 1990 and is still in the doldrums. At bottom it lost more than 65 percent of its value from its zenith. When the Dow crashed in October 1929, it sank almost 80 percent over four years, and then failed to regain its previous peak until 1952. Similarly, the Standard and Poor's index of common stocks did not return to its 1929 crest until 1953. If you have that much patience, then by all means hang on to your stocks. Otherwise sell, especially if you have purchased shares with borrowed money from credit cards, home-equity loans, or brokerage accounts.

Among the various industries, those that have appreciated the fastest will likely go down the fastest as well. Thus high-flying Internet and high-tech stocks, Wal-Mart, and so on could be the biggest losers. The Nasdaq over-the-counter market is riddled with speculative shares. In the market correction of August 1998, such stocks were the biggest victims. They pose the largest risk, and should be sold right away.

In recent years, most people have purchased stock shares through mutual funds, which are usually run by savvy managers. These funds have generally appreciated as fast as the market. Some of them are riskier than others, depending on their investment philosophy. Some specialize in speculative stocks, some in blue chips, and still others in corporate and government bonds. My advice for stock mutual funds is the same as that for the individual stocks underlying them; namely, they should be sold as soon as possible.

Having seen share values rise and rise and rise ever since 1982, with only temporary and short-lived dips, most investors are unprepared to accept that this time share prices will not make a quick comeback. In fact, a new mantra, "Buy the dip," which was coined during the 1990s, indicates that the public regards every market decline as a buying opportunity. This is one reason the bull market has been alive for so long. However, this time around, buying the dip could prove lethal. Remember that every bull market turns into a bear someday. One law of nature is that nothing moves in a straight line forever, as illustrated by the recent experience of the Tigers and Japan. U.S. share prices have been moving upward almost linearly for a long time, seeming to violate this simple but fundamental law of nature. But there are no exceptions. American markets are now poised for a dramatic fall to restore market balance.

However, most people are psychologically unprepared to sell. Wall Street brokers and experts have sold them on an elegant slogan: "Stay in the market for the long haul." This is normally sane advice except around the time of a giant bubble. Few Wall Street professionals follow their own counsel. Why else would major dips occur at all? If the experts stayed in the market over the long haul, why would there be any serious, though short-term, drops? You would need to overcome the current popular mind-set against selling shares and taking profits or minimizing losses.

You may also be worried about the capital gains tax that applies to earnings from the sale of shares. The tax rate has sharply declined in recent years, and in any case it's better to be in a position to face the tax bill than to have no such bill at all. At least you get to keep a large fraction, about 80 percent, of your profit. Many mutual funds have been passing their annual capital gains on to their shareholders, who then are required to pay a tax whether or not they sell their share of the fund. For such investors there will be little tax liability from the sale of their shares, because they have already paid the IRS.

Suppose you are among those who bought stocks at the height of the market. Or perhaps the market has already plummeted before you come across this information. An amateur investor finds it doubly difficult to sell at a loss. Indeed, most investors don't want to unload shares if they have depreciated in value. They prefer to ride out the bear, which may be usually fine, but not this time. Sensing long-term trouble, a savvy investor sells and salvages whatever he or she can.

The new mantra for investors should be "Sell the recovery"; that is, sell the shares, in one batch or in installments, whenever there is a short-term recovery in the market. Nothing moves in a straight line for long. There are dips in bull markets, and upswings in bear markets. A long and brutal bearish sentiment will unfold toward the end of 1999, punctuated by short-lived spurts. Those moments are when a prudent investor will sell and cut his or her losses.

When would be the right time to get back into the market? This is a difficult question to tackle today. The answer depends on so many imponderables. How harshly will the Y2K computer bug bite? How much money will the Fed print to keep the economy buoyant? How soon will basic reforms be adopted? How will the rest of the world respond?

If the administration refrains from pump priming, and the sting of the computer bug is mild in accordance with current expectations, then inflation should cool by the end of 2002. Interest rates will then drop, and bullishness could return. That will be the right time to get into the market in an aggressive manner. Of course, you have to exercise your own judgment at that point. The key lies in waiting until the inflation monster is tamed, for surging prices are not healthy for any advanced economy. If the Dow is close to twenty-six hundred, the turning point when the current bull run started in 1991, then perhaps it is time to reenter the arena cautiously, via mutual funds.

BONDS

How do bonds respond to a slump? As business activity sinks, interest rates drop and debt instruments appreciate consistently. So an expected downturn presents a buying opportunity for bonds, especially those with long maturities. This is the advice I gave to my readers in *The Great Depression of 1990,* and since 1982 interest rates have steadily dropped, and conversely bond prices have appreciated manifold. In that case good quality bonds turned out to be a risk-free investment with a hefty appreciation.

However, even surefire bonds have some risk, although they should be a part of any diversified portfolio. A bond is essentially a debt instrument. Its buyer lends a sum of money to the borrower or seller for a specified period, at the end of which the principal is returned to the lender. In the interim, the bond buyer receives regular interest payments, called coupon charges, until the maturity of the loan.

There are two risks associated with bonds. One is that the seller could go bankrupt and default on its loans. The other is the possibility of a capital loss. The first risk can be avoided altogether by obtaining bonds issued by stable governments. U.S. Treasury securities, for instance, are considered to be default free. So are the debt instruments of some European governments. Bonds issued by corporations are riskier, but they pay a larger return. In general, the greater the default risk, the higher the coupon payment. There are agencies that rate the risk factor associated with debt instruments, starting with AAA as being the one with the least likelihood of default, followed by AA, and then simply A and so on.

Bonds are not as risky as stocks, but their potential for appreciation is limited. Bond prices decline when interest rates go up and rise when interest rates fall, and therein lies the second risk factor, capital loss. If bondholders can wait until maturity, this risk is zero, but if they need the money in the interim, then they have to sell at a loss if market rates of interest have risen or bond prices have declined. Conversely, they can also enjoy a capital gain, if market rates have sunk following their purchase of the bond.

Most people purchase bonds for income and safety. Obviously, U.S. Treasury bonds are the safest, but their return is commensurately low. Next in safety are the AAA corporate bonds, with slightly higher interest rates. In general, the lower the rating, the higher the return. A good mix of safety and return is in A-rated corporate bonds, which are reasonably safe and yield modest interest as well.

Municipal bonds with a rating of A or better are also relatively safe; they are tax free as well. However, we should remember that in a depression many municipalities also default. Only U.S. Treasury bonds and AAA municipals may be worth keeping at that time. There is one type of government instrument that is virtually free from the risk of capital loss—the Treasury bill, or the T-bill. This is a short-term note that matures within a year; it is highly liquid and very popular among investors, because it can be bought and sold at any time without much risk of a loss.

Then there is another category called convertible bonds. They have a lower yield than the nonconvertible issues discussed above, but their potential for appreciation is greater because they are exchangeable into a fixed amount of the borrower's common stock. They offer a guaranteed return, and price appreciation as well if the underlying stock value goes up. For those who dislike the low dividends generally paid by common stocks and yet would like to participate in a market boom, convertible bonds offer an excellent option. They are a hybrid between a stock and a bond, and have the best risk-reward combination of any security.

Bonds are generally good investments during deflationary depressions, but the one looming in the near future will be inflationary in nature. Bond values are likely to fall sharply in 2000 and 2001, and perhaps beyond. So, like stocks, long-term bonds are also very risky at this point. Their prices could plummet until 2002, though not in a straight line. Bonds are risky instruments in all countries that have a huge foreign debt and a trade deficit. In areas like Euroland, perhaps they offer a slight potential for capital gains. They are also risky in Japan, where interest rates are so low that they can go nowhere but up.

Bonds were a poor investment during the 1970s, which was the last peak decade of the long-run cycle of inflation. As a result, interest rates rose to the stratosphere, and bond prices fell into a bottomless pit. The coming decade could be a replica of the 1970s, perhaps on a larger scale, especially in terms of unemployment. Though not as risky as stocks, even bonds should be avoided at this time. A prudent investor would sell them before the end of 1999. However, a bond market crash might not be as calamitous as the stock market debacle, because a bondholder won't be wiped out immediately (unless he or she has invested borrowed money, anticipating capital gains). A failure to sell bonds could simply be a lost opportunity, but not a disaster, because a bondholder could wait to receive the principal at maturity, earning a meager but positive return in the interim—assuming the seller does not default. The likelihood of default will grow as the slump deepens, in which case you should definitely consider selling your corporate and other bonds rated below AAA.

REAL ESTATE

Real estate was the darling of investors in the 1970s as speculation and double-digit inflation dramatically raised the prices of houses, apartments, and office buildings. The public was afraid to touch stocks and bonds, so the bulk of national savings went into other areas. Some people made a killing from property, and a few became millionaires overnight. Can that success be duplicated in the coming decade? I have my doubts.

During the 1970s, the interest rates that banks and S&Ls, also known as thrifts, could pay on savings deposits were regulated to be no higher than 5 percent per year. These deposit rates, too low to be compatible with raging inflation, enabled financial institutions to make long-term mortgage loans at very low rates. Thirty-year mortgage charges at the time varied between 8 percent to 9 percent, not far above the 7 percent fixed rate generally available in 1998, even though the rate of inflation routinely exceeded 8 percent during the seventies. This was a great anomaly inconsistent with a market economy, because it led to what we call a negative real rate of interest.

The real rate of interest is the difference between the interest fee actually received by a lender and the current rate of inflation. The idea is that lending enhances the value of money by the amount of interest income, whereas rising prices trim the value of money by decreasing its purchasing power. Therefore the net or the real return from lending activity is the difference between the actual interest rate and the rate of inflation. With mortgage rates tied to low savings deposit rates, the real rate of interest on mortgages was negative or close to zero during the seventies. With home buyers and builders able to obtain such cheap loans, there was naturally a great housing and construction boom in the economy, even though unemployment tended to be high.

During the 1980s, interest rates were deregulated. Now they shoot up anytime there is a whiff of inflation. Therefore in spite of high expected inflation, the coming decade is unlikely to see another boom in real estate. The boom has come and gone, and you should not expect the dramatic rise in value we saw in the 1970s.

Plainly speaking, real estate will be a bad investment in the near future. With a record inflow of foreign money and the stock market bubble, the 1990s have enjoyed an unprecedented construction boom. Millions of new homes and apartments have been added to residential inventory. Thousands of office and shopping malls have been constructed. In fact, the share market frenzy has also spawned a real estate bubble in terms of square footage though not in terms of value. The U.S. real estate bubble is more reminiscent of Thailand than Japan, where home prices went through the roof. That is scant consolation, however, because home values will still plummet.

When the share market bubbles burst open, both Asian countries saw their real estate values shrivel. Now offices, motels, and shopping centers stand nearly empty, inhabited by bats and pigeons. Another victim of puny real rates of interest was Hong Kong, which also passed through a giant property boom between 1990 and 1997. When the real rate surged in sympathy with the Thai debacle, overnight Hong Kong's property market collapsed. Thus real rates too low to be compatible with a free market usually end up victimizing an economy.

Real estate used to be a great tax shelter. But the tax reform of 1986 has changed all that, greatly reducing depreciation expense and limiting the ability to write off losses against other income. Even owning your own home has fewer tax advantages, because of the reduction in income tax rates and the reduced deductibility of interest expense.

Even though interest charges are now the lowest in two decades, this is not a good time to buy a house. If you own one already, it is a good time to refinance it, especially if you have a variable mortgage. Interest rates are about to rise, and variable mortgages will sharply increase your housing costs. If possible, convert your mortgage into a fixed-rate one with a loan maturity of fifteen years. Such loans cost less than the more popular thirty-year mortgage.

If you live in an apartment, stay there. Renting today is more prudent than buying for two reasons. First, rents in many areas are less than monthly mortgage payments; second, there is a great risk of job losses in the near future. Who knows which one of us will retain our job in the depression? If you insist on owning rather than renting, then buy an inexpensive residence and finance it through a fixed-rate mortgage. Your down payment should be as low as possible, *because staying liquid with cash is the key to surviving a depression.*

In spite of the inflationary nature of the coming depression, property values will tumble in most parts of the United States. In the long run, home prices will probably continue to climb. In the short run, however, they could sink and sink hard. During depressions, home values shrink in most areas, especially in small- to medium-sized cities. In large cities, where choice locations have been already settled, real estate may drop no more than 10 percent, but in small towns they can lose as much as half their value.

Even in crowded metropolises, expensive homes will depreciate substantially. Rental property will also take a beating. If you own rental property, you should plan on selling between now and 2000, take your profits, and then be well positioned to buy properties after 2002. Of course, once you sell out and become liquid, you have to exercise great caution and examine contemporary market conditions before jumping into any new venture. Right now, the year 2002 appears to be a turning point for inflation, but official policy, as mentioned earlier, could easily change all that.

GOLD AND PRECIOUS METALS

At this stage you perhaps wonder if I am an iconoclast bent on challenging all your cherished beliefs. If stocks, bonds, and real estate are currently bad investments, is there anything worth buying in the current milieu? There is: gold. Precious metals such as gold, silver, and platinum are among the riskiest investments, but they often do well in an inflationary economy. The world is mostly worrying about deflation today; few believe inflation will accelerate in the future, so there is hardly any interest left in precious metals. But some hardy experts, especially the disciples of the computer bug peril, still suggest that we should be putting more trust in them. "Go with the glitter," they say.

Gold experienced two great bull markets in the 1970s, increasing dramatically from $35 per ounce in 1971 to $200 in 1974. It then dropped to a low of $103 in 1976, after which it soared to an astonishing high of $886 in 1980. In early 1999, it had settled around $270. But aside from professionals who make a living touting the virtues of gold (known as the "hard-money" gang), few advisers foresee gold as a major growth area.

Gold as an investment is not a good choice for us ordinary folks. Those who have strong stomachs or a lot of money to burn may gamble with precious metals, but unless you can spend every day charting their performance, don't get involved. Gold can rise and fall so fast that the timing of buying and selling makes a big difference between profit and loss, and there are few with the requisite sense of timing.

By gold I am referring specifically to bullion or coins. I don't recommend them as an investment for the common person. But gold as a hedge against calamity is something else. Whenever times are tumultuous, people turn to precious metals. This is the dictum of ten thousand years of human history and has been true in every society after people turned from barter to gold as a medium of exchange. Currencies may come and go, but gold retains its eternal luster.

Precious metals tend to appreciate during inflation and depreciate during disinflation or outright deflation. Ordinarily, I would not recommend the purchase of gold, in spite of the impending threat of inflation. But the coming decade is going to be far from normal. Although historically, people have turned to gold during times of uncertainty, that uncertainty has to be dire. It has to persist and create chaos before people will abandon their currency and turn to precious metals. Something like this could happen in the next decade as the age of acquisitors comes to an end.

I wish to make it clear that I don't recommend gold for speculation. It is worth considering only as insurance against a financial meltdown. As the dollar collapses, or if the government attempts to stimulate the economy by pumping copious amounts of new money into circulation, gold will hold its value. The metal by itself does not yield any return. No one pays interest when you park your funds in precious metals. Gold, of course, can appreciate fast; but it can depreciate just as quickly.

When choosing between gold bullion and coins, I prefer coins. They do cost a bit more than bullion, but they have higher liquidity and some of them are also legal tender; that is, you can use them as currency in the country issuing them. There are many countries offering such coins today. Mexico, Canada, South Africa, Austria, and Hungary have minted them for years. In addition, the United States, Australia, and Japan have introduced their own coins in recent years.

For U.S. investors, the best coin may be the American Eagle, which is available in four sizes: one ounce, half ounce, quarter-ounce, and one-tenth ounce. Like the South African Krugerrand, it is 91.67 percent pure gold; it has a lower gold content than the Canadian Maple Leaf, which is 99.99 percent pure. Some people prefer the Canadian coin because of its purity, others the Krugerrand because of its longevity, but the American coin is as good as any other.

You can buy gold coins from a number of dealers. Pay cash only upon delivery. If you are ordering by mail, use a "sight draft" through a bank. The coins are then shipped to that bank, and the bank simultaneously releases them to you and the money to the dealer. If convenient, you should store your holdings in a safe-deposit box at the same bank. Many jewelry stores also deal in coins.

Another way to participate in the glitter of gold is to buy shares of companies involved in gold-mining operations. Many such companies such as Anglo Gold are located in South Africa; there are also non-African gold companies in the United States, Australia, and Canada, such as Meridian Gold, Homestake, and Dome Mining, traded on the New York Stock Exchange, or Echo Bay traded on the American Exchange. Other good companies are American Barric, Newmont Mining, and Euro Nevada. Initially, when share prices crash in general, even gold stocks are likely to fall. Gold is unlikely to lure many experts until the monster of inflation becomes visible. The metal may remain lackluster for a while even after the markets keep sinking. In time, however, as the dollar continues to shrivel, and deflationary expectations are reversed, it will make a move. That may be the right time to get into gold stocks. The best strategy may be to keep an eye on the price of gold and related stocks as the market begins to crumble. If the bullion and company stocks respond immediately, then it is time to start buying. For those who like to take action in anticipation of an event, right now is the time to go with the glitter of the coins but not the related shares.

Normally prices of all precious metals move together. When gold goes up, so does silver, and vice versa. Deflation is bad for both silver and gold, whereas uncertainty and social unrest benefit both. Silver, however, is much more affordable than gold, and may have a larger market. It is also bulkier and harder to store. In my view gold is preferable to silver as a hedge against calamity, especially in an inflationary depression, when national output of goods and services is likely to plunge. A big chunk of demand for silver comes from its use in industry, which will shrivel, cutting into its price.

Silver bullion or coins can be bought from the same dealers handling gold coins. Here again, the same caution should be exercised as in the purchase and storage of gold. Just as silver is more affordable than gold, so are silver mining shares. But silver mines are not as financially strong as gold mines. And in a bear market they may have great trouble staying in business or maintaining their dividends.

Silver is mostly a by-product in the extraction of other metals, especially copper. During recessions and depressions, prices of non-precious metals fall drastically. For that reason alone silver shares should be avoided, since commodity prices have been falling recently, and in the future could fall even more. For companies that produce both silver and other metals, the rise in the price of silver may not be enough to offset the falling price of their other products, so that their profits and shares could still sink.

What about platinum, another precious metal? It has the same features as silver, as its demand is proportional to industrial prosperity. It is generally used in autos and jewelry, both of which see shrinking demand in a depression. Among gold, silver, and platinum, I am most impressed with the potential of gold to ride out an inflationary depression.

There are also some mutual funds that concentrate on precious metals; because of their focus on mining stocks they tend to be more volatile than gold and silver themselves. Still their diversification makes them an attractive way of participation in the potential appreciation of gold. If gold starts to make a move soon after the stock market crash, you should consider slowly getting into a fund that specializes in this area.

PENSIONS AND SOCIAL SECURITY

One of our most cherished goals since ancient time is financial independence upon retirement. An increasing portion of the population is turning gray in advanced economies, and before long baby boomers will start retiring in large numbers. Retirees, who live mostly on incomes from Social Security and pensions, face special risks. The Clinton administration and various economists are discussing how to spend the huge budget bonanza coming our way over the next decade. These are the same people who once worried about trillion dollar deficits far into the new century. They are now building great castles in the air, expecting a budget surplus of as much as $4.5 trillion over the next fifteen years. A surplus in 1998, the first since 1969, has turned their head. Columnist Louis Uchitelle makes an interesting observation: "Having declared an era of budget surpluses, Democrats and the Republicans are busy parceling out money that is not yet in hand. But they are twins in their confidence that a surplus, having finally materialized in 1998, will continue to do so for a decade. What goes unmentioned is Wall Street. Bluntly put, if stock prices fall sharply, the budget surplus disappears."[39] For all we know, the surplus could also be connected to the three-decade cycle of inflation. After all, inflation is the key to the performance of an advanced economy.

Just as in the 1970s, three decades later we are likely to see huge budget deficits, not surpluses over the coming years. As tax receipts shrink with the economy, and the government raises its spending levels to combat unemployment, the budget deficit will rise to dizzying heights. Although Congress will try its best to maintain the Social Security system, it may have no choice but to trim payments or to dilute the formula linking the payment with the soaring cost of living. Government pensions could meet a similar fate. For these reasons retirees face a special peril.

What about private pensions that have been invested in a variety of financial instruments such as stocks, bonds, and real estate, among others? As I noted earlier, all three of these instruments are now vulnerable to a stock market crash. Thousands of businesses are going to fail in the coming depression; thousands will also survive, but we don't know which ones. In an extended depression, some pension funds, depending on the health of the industries in which they are invested, could also go bankrupt. You could then be left with a worthless piece of paper. If you are about to retire and have the choice to take out your pension in a lump sum or in the form of an annuity spread out over several years, you should take it all, or as much as possible.

Some private pensions are insured by the government. When businesses fail, these pension liabilities become a federal responsibility. But don't count on it. How many problems can the government tackle at the same time? It insures bank deposits of up to $100,000, residential mortgages, pensions, and farm loans. Its liabilities run into trillions of dollars. We can't depend on the government to cure all our ills. Clearly, we have to take action on our own, and withdrawing as much of our money from pension funds as possible is the action to take.

The same goes for Keogh plans, 401(k) programs, and the IRAs. A few years ago Congress created three new tax-deferred devices: the Keogh plan for the self-employed, the 401(k) for those working for corporations, and the individual retirement account (IRA) for others. With these vehicles a qualified person can reduce his taxable income by certain amounts, which must be set aside with an approved trustee. This tax-deferred fund can grow until you are fifty-nine and a half, when you can withdraw your money either in a lump sum or in the form of a yearly annuity. Of course, you have to pay tax at the time of withdrawal.

If you are fifty-nine and a half by now, then the decision about your Keogh or IRA plan is very simple. Just take it all out in a lump sum. The tax consequences are minor with this decision, because with the Tax Reform Act of 1986 most of you will be either in the 15 percent or 28 percent income-tax bracket. However, if you have not reached the required age, then the decision becomes complicated, because there are penalties for premature withdrawal. (The tax penalty is 10 percent of the amount withdrawn.) In addition, the trustee of the plan may impose a minor penalty of its own.

The decision ultimately depends on the safety of the vehicles in which the Keogh and other funds are invested. Banks are safer than many brokerage houses, because bank deposits as well as these plans are each insured for up to $100,000 by the government. In any coming crisis, the government's first priority will be the solvency of financial institutions. The Federal Deposit Insurance Corporation (FDIC) will try its best to keep the banks afloat and protect up to $100,000 of each deposit, even if billions of dollars of new money have to be printed. That would raise the threat of hyperinflation resulting from inordinate monetary expansion. In a crunch, the government may decide to honor only its commitment to bank depositors.

Fortunately, the IRAs can be shifted from one institution to another. The best course for such funds is to transfer them to banking institutions. With Keogh and 401(k) plans, premature withdrawal, if permissible, may be the best option in spite of various penalties, unless you can persuade the plan's trustee to shift funds out of stocks and corporate bonds into short-term Treasury debt. Financial expert and best-selling author Suze Orman suggests a number of ways in which such penalties can be avoided altogether. With 401(k)s, for instance, she writes, "If you're fifty-five or older in the year of retirement from a particular company, you can withdraw whatever you like from what's known as a *qualified employer retirement account* without any penalty whatever."[40]

If you are not at the permissible age for 401(k) withdrawals or your money is in an IRA, then there is another way of averting penalties—a technique called substantially equal periodic payments (SEPP). All you have to do is to withdraw a certain predetermined sum of money annually for five years or until you are 59.5, whichever is longer. "So if you are 57," says Suze Orman, "and you start to take money out of your IRA account under SEPP, you will have to do so until you are 62. If you're 52 when you start, you'll have to continue withdrawing the money until you're 59.5—again the rule is whichever time period is longer."[41] For more information on this, you should consult the IRS code 72(t)(2)(A)(IV). This could be a very important piece of information in the near future, something crucial to your family's survival, especially if you're handicapped, retiring, or laid off and need emergency funds that you could draw from your retirement plans.

Whatever you take out, keep it in a money market or a negotiated order of withdrawal (NOW) account in a bank or thrift. Despite the many safeguards provided by the government, hundreds of banks and S&Ls failed in the 1980s, and thousands more will fail in the coming decade. In fact, there were more bank failures in 1985 and 1986 than at any time since the 1930s. Yet depositors have been fully protected so far. They have faced no more than minor inconvenience.

Even if the government takes good care of the bank customers, there are bound to be delays and inconvenience in the case of a major crisis. Remember what happened to the troubled savings institutions in Ohio and Maryland in 1985, where for a while depositors were allowed to withdraw only $1,000 from their accounts. A reasonable strategy for such possibilities is to keep some cash in a safe-deposit box. This may also be a good bet in case the Y2K bug temporary wipes out your bank records, and your money becomes inaccessible for a while. All cash in your safe-deposit box is yours, and even a bankrupt bank can't legally deny you access to it.

What about annuities? Some people fear that they will outlive their savings and pensions after retirement. Given our increasing life expectancy, such apprehension is well founded. One way out is to buy an annuity from a life insurance company or a bank. The instrument guarantees an annual income, fixed or linked to the cost of living, to a retiree until his or her death. This is the main attraction of an annuity, which, like most pension devices, also has a tax-deferred feature.

Insurance companies rarely fold, but two large concerns, Executive Life and Mutual Benefit Life, went bankrupt in the early 1990s. That is why it's important to know how a company is rated by various agencies. There are five independent firms that examine the insurance industry and evaluate its members. They are A. M. Best, Duff & Phelps, Moody's Investors Service, Standard and Poor Corporation, and Weiss Research. These companies rank insurance firms every year. Make sure your annuity is with one of the top-rated concerns, which over the years have included Prudential, Metropolitan Life, Equitable Life, Aetna, New York Life, TIAA, John Hancock, and others. But ratings can change, and before selecting an insurance firm you should inquire about its ranking. Needless to say you should stick with only those that have received top billing from several agencies.

Some major banks such as Bank of America and Bank One also offer annuities either by themselves or through another insurance company. Such programs are not federally insured, but banks often provide added protection to their customers. Note that you can't completely eliminate risk from your investments; all you can do is to minimize it, and that's what my advice is designed to do. If the coming inflationary depression turns out to be as bad as I fear, then even the best of companies could go bankrupt, with millions on the verge of hunger and starvation. In that case, our only recourse will be to launch a vigorous campaign for fundamental economic reforms— discussed in the final two chapters—and quickly change the system that produced the debacle.

CERTIFICATES OF DEPOSIT

Banks and thrifts offer a financial instrument called a certificate of deposit, or a CD, which enables you to obtain slightly higher interest rates than checking or savings accounts. CDs in banks and S&Ls will be among the safest places to park your money, provided each deposit is no larger than $100,000. If there is one lesson to be learned from the 1930s, it is that banks should not be allowed to fail. If a government wants to stay in power today, it cannot afford to neglect its banking system.

CDs are highly flexible and are usually issued in maturities of six months to two years, but many banks will tailor them to suit your needs. CDs with longer duration generally yield a higher return than the short-term ones. Large denomination CDs in excess of $100,000 are also available, but the excess amount is not federally insured. They do pay higher returns, but they are also riskier. Large corporations and brokerages are the main buyers of such CDs.

Although CDs generally have higher yields than other bank accounts, they have a penalty for premature withdrawal, varying from a month to half year's interest. To remain liquid and still earn the higher rates, I suggest that you go for one- or two-year maturity, offered by any bank and thrift. If you prefer large-denomination CDs, then go with a big multinational bank with assets exceeding $100 billion. The size of such banks offers an extra degree of safety.

MONEY MARKET MUTUAL FUNDS

While banks and thrifts offer a variety of deposits, so do brokerages such as Merrill Lynch and Prudential, and so on. Their accounts are known as money market mutual funds, which work like bank deposits and may pay slightly higher interest but lack the insurance offered by the FDIC. Some brokerages permit the investor to write checks against such funds. They are highly liquid and are generally invested in short-term instruments such as T-bills and large-denomination CDs, but they are not as safe as money market accounts offered by banks and thrifts. The banking institutions also offer NOW accounts, which pay a slightly higher return than the regular money market account. But NOW accounts permit only limited checking privileges: no more than three checks per month. Because of their insurance feature, the money market and NOW accounts are superior to the money market mutual funds offered by brokerages. This could make a crucial difference in the near future, when the economy falls apart and many financial companies go bankrupt.

OPTIONS

An option, also known as a derivative, is an investment that enables you to gain from the fluctuating value of connected securities. A bewildering variety of such instruments—options for stocks, bonds, currencies, and so forth—is now available. For instance, a stock option gives an investor the right to buy or sell shares at a given price on or before some future date. A smart investor can use it to increase his income and at the same time limit his risk from the purchase of shares. His maximum loss is the price he paid for the option, but his gain can be several times the purchase price.

Options are listed on the business pages of most major newspapers as well as in the *Wall Street Journal*. The right to buy a number of shares on or before a certain date at a certain price is called a call option, and the right to sell a number of shares on or before a certain date at a certain price is called a put option. If you expect a stock to appreciate, you buy a call option, and if you expect it to depreciate, you buy a put option. In either case, your maximum loss is the price you pay for the option.

However, the option price itself is determined by the market. It moves much more rapidly than the price of the stock it represents. Some people simply bet on the option price itself, hoping it will go up. They have no desire to buy or sell the stock at the specified price.

Most of the hedge funds, including the ones betting only on bond price movements, are primarily involved with derivatives. That is what has made the millennium bubble so potentially explosive, because many options are simply very long odds bets made by investors.

Margin buying and short selling basically follow the same underlying principle except they involve borrowed money, while options do not. Margin trading is simply buying stocks on credit; the buyer has to pay a fraction, usually half, of the price of the stock, and for the rest he borrows money from his broker at a certain interest rate. This way, with a limited level of investment, the buyer can make big money in a generally bullish market.

Short selling, like the put option, relies on the gamble that stock prices will sink. The idea is to borrow shares from someone, sell them at the current price, buy them back later at a cheaper price, and finally return them to the original owner. The short seller then pockets the difference between stock prices at two points in time. If your bet is right, you gain; on the other hand, if the stock value jumps, you lose.

The principles behind options, margin buying, and short selling are quite simple, and in fact many have profited from them in the biggest bull market in history. The trouble comes when the bubble bursts, because the markets then not only crash, they also become very volatile, which sometimes devastates the best of investors. Thus Newton first gained and then lost in a big way; so did George Soros in the Russian debacle, followed by two Nobel prize–winning economists, Robert Merton and Myron Scholes, who managed the Long-Term Capital Management Fund.[42]

CURRENCY TRADING

The most popular vehicle for speculation among banks and some hedge funds is currency trading. Some $1 to $1.5 trillion dollars of international currencies—dollars, yen, marks, pounds, francs, lira, euros—change hands every day. Yes, you read that number correctly. So much trading occurs daily, not monthly nor weekly. It is this type of speculation that has brought many economies down to their knees.

An interesting question arises. If the dollar is expected to collapse, doesn't it make sense to get into foreign currencies at this time? It certainly does, especially for about two years—2000 and 2001. But currency trading is not for the fainthearted, and that will be truer than ever in the near future; in the coming financial upheaval currencies will undergo violent fluctuations, possibly on a daily basis. But it is something worth looking into, bearing in mind that the activity can also generate losses. There are some banks in the United States that have engaged in this business for some time; one of them is Mercantile Bancorporation in St. Louis; Nations Bank, recently acquired by Bank of America, is also a good source for getting into currency trading. You can buy foreign exchange and then have the bank invest the funds into a government bond maturing over, say, three months. If the dollar has collapsed in the meanwhile, you can sell your bond and take the profit by buying back the greenback. If not, then reinvest your funds in the same instrument, and wait until the currency value has depreciated.

You may also adopt a long-term program of buying the euro or the pound. British interest rates are higher than the U.S. and European rates. If you buy the pound, you can park your money into a two-year government bond and stay with it until the dollars falls sharply. On the other hand, the greenback could tumble initially for about a year and make a comeback. Whatever you do, it is essential to stay on top of your foreign currency venture. That is why you should get involved only if you can stay fully informed, and completely understand the risk of this adventure.

EMERGING MARKETS

While there may be some merit in purchasing foreign currencies such as the euro, mark, pound, or yen, I don't see any point in getting entangled with the so-called emerging markets of the Third World, Asian Tigers, Russia, and Eastern Europe. They were very popular with savvy money managers as late as 1997 but no longer. Even the Mexican currency debacle in 1995 failed to enlighten the financial experts, who, in fact, were emboldened by that year's bailout engineered by the IMF. Since then billions of dollars have been lost in the share-price bloodbath in the emerging markets. Many global funds that specialize in international investing have lost money since the Thai crisis. As a review article in *Business Week* aptly describes it, "It's the same story throughout Asia and much of the rest of the developing world. The winds that blew hundreds of billions of dollars into emerging markets with hurricane force in the early 1990s have gone deathly still. Now, these economies must struggle their way out of recession with much less Western investment."[43]

A SAFE STRATEGY

By now you have some idea of what happens to various investments under differing market conditions. Now I can suggest a step-by-step strategy for the coming catastrophe. Again, please remember my goal here is to help you safeguard your assets, not to help you get rich quickly. No low-risk program can accomplish that.

Step 1

If you come across this information prior to the market crash of the millennium, sell your stocks and related instruments, like mutual funds, and pull out of call options. (Puts, on the other hand, may be all right in a bear market, but even they can be treacherous in a volatile arena.) Then deposit that money into a money market or a NOW account with a bank or thrift; don't let it sit with a brokerage house or mutual fund, even if they offer their own money market mutual funds. It is not that the money market mutual funds are not safe vehicles (most of them are invested in T-bills), but if the company that manages the mutual fund declares insolvency because of its losses from some other source, your money, though safe, may be tied up in bankruptcy court for a while. In any case, the bank and thrift accounts have the added protection of FDIC insurance up to $100,000.

Whatever you do, don't park more than the insured amount in any one account. Banks and S&Ls can offer a variety of accounts under different names so that your money may be insured up to $500,000 or more. You could make use of this legal provision, or, preferably, open accounts in more than one bank or thrift, leaving no more than $100,000 with any single institution.

If the Dow has already crashed before this information reaches you, then sell your shares during any recovery, but don't wait too long. The bullishness will be short lived, enabling you to cut your losses, but perhaps not make any profit. A long bear market is about to set in, and taking profits or minimizing losses is the best strategy at this time.

Step 2

If you are involved in pension plans, such as a Keogh, 401(k), or an IRA, ask the trustee to sell your portion of the stocks and put the money into a NOW account. Let the money stay there for a while, and monitor the behavior of interest rates. Initially, as the market crashes, bond yields could actually fall as panic-stricken investors seek the safety of U.S. government debt. But soon the dollar will start to plunge, and interest rates will rise. That may be the time to move your pension money into short-term government bonds for one to two years. The emphasis is again on the short term, because we don't know if the administration will respond to the crisis by printing tons of new money, exacerbating the danger of continued inflation. If prices keep surging, so will interest rates, and long-term bonds will then depreciate. Alternately, you may stay put in the NOW accounts, because money parked there will earn higher yields with soaring inflation.

Step 3

If you own long-term corporate, municipal, and government bonds, a variety of steps is desirable. Corporate debt should be sold right away, unless it is rated AAA and offers a decent return, 8 percent or above. You should be prepared to hold the bond until its maturity to avoid the real possibility of capital loss. The same consideration applies to municipal bonds, unless they are also rated AAA and provide a yield of 7 percent or more. The yield factor may be ignored if you are prepared to hold them until maturity.

With U.S. government bonds, the yield is the only important consideration, because such instruments are very safe. If you bought them a long time ago, when they offered a high return of, say, 7.5 percent or above, then keep them and wait till the debt expires. Otherwise sell. With bond mutual funds, since most offer puny returns nowadays, a safe strategy is to sell them now.

If your pensions are tied up in bonds, then the safest strategy is to trade them, and wait for interest rates to rise. In the interim, you may keep your funds in the NOW or money market account, whichever offers a higher return. Of course, you may not have the flexibility to alter the program of the pension fund or plan. In that case, let your trustees read my book; perhaps they will change their mind.

Step 4

Even before you get rid of shares and bonds, buy some gold coins; you may want to put as much as 10 percent of your portfolio into the precious metal. In early 1999, gold bullion was selling for $270 per ounce, and a coin for about $290. These are not bad prices, considering that at one point the metal sold for more than $885 per ounce. But don't overdo it. Gold, after all, is highly volatile, but I recommend it as a hedge against uncertainty and calamity. If you don't have the resources to buy gold now, then use some of the funds from the sale of stocks and bonds.

Step 5

If the sale of assets gives you the necessary funds, consider paying off your credit card debt. Many employees will be laid off in the near future; Congress will provide unemployment compensation of up to a year, but perhaps no longer than that because of the swollen budget deficit. In any case, you can't count on government largesse for sure. Conserving cash could be the key to survival. I fervently believe in clearing up debts, but in a crunch the survival of your family comes first. If your job situation is wobbly, you should hold on to your resources rather than pay off your loans. You can attend to your debts later, once the crisis has passed. But if your job is safe, or if there is no shortage of funds to take care of your minimum needs, then by all means pay off your credit card bill in entirety.

Step 6

If you are retired or about to do so, then take your pension in a lump sum, or as much of it as possible, and deposit the money in money market accounts in different banks. I am not sure if all insurance companies will survive the coming decade; some will, some won't. Let me emphasize again that bank and thrift deposits are the safest assets for two reasons. First, they are all insured by the government; second the Fed is committed to their safety and will print oodles of money, if necessary, to protect them. We all know what happened in the 1930s when the banks were left unprotected. Note that the president and his cabinet have no power to create money, but the Fed does. The government will have to borrow from the bond market to meet its obligations, but not the Fed, which is empowered to start the money pumps if it sees fit. Thus bank deposits are the safest assets in the United States today. They are also protected against inflation, which will raise interest rates and benefit your bank accounts.

Step 7

The six steps suggested above are designed to create a safety net around your assets in the short run. Once you have protected your wealth from the possibility of market crashes and soaring interest rates, then just sit tight and wait. If inflation continues to rage, and the government has to borrow much to finance its deficit, then interest rates will keep rising. By 2002, however, inflation may be ready to cool, provided nothing else goes wrong. That may be the year to get into long-term government bonds and bank CDs, and lock in the high rates. In case inflation continues to rage, then stick with the short-term strategy.

With respect to company shares, I don't have the slightest clue today when it would be right to get back into the market, because stocks are far more volatile than debt instruments. They depend on many short-term factors that cannot all be foreseen at present. With high inflation will also come high joblessness that could persist for a while. The twin punch of the bursting bubble and the computer bug could really devastate the economy for a long period, and the share markets would simply have no way to go but down. Of course, if interest rates begin to fall, then the markets will move up slightly, though not in the same way as in the eighties and the nineties. We perhaps will not see another market of the millennium for centuries.

Step 8

By the middle of 2000, gold stocks will likely make an upward move. Whenever they do, start buying these shares, or get into the surviving mutual funds that handle precious metals. Again, don't overdo it. No more than 20 percent of your portfolio should be in such companies. The rest could be in government bonds, money market accounts, and bank CDs. If high inflation is accompanied by official confusion and uncertainty in 2002, then five-year CDs and government bonds will be preferable at the time to those of longer duration, provided they offer a substantially larger return than the two- to three-year debt instruments.

Step 9

What about the investment strategy for countries facing a deflationary depression? Japan, Euroland, and other areas such as Hong Kong and Taiwan could encounter a deep slump with falling or stable prices, provided they refrain from dramatic monetary expansion. In these regions, stock markets could revive faster than elsewhere. After 2002, provided the depression shows signs of ending, investors in those countries may consider buying their version of blue-chip shares again. Speculative or growth stocks should still be avoided. Europe and Japan could then become a good place for American investors. The best way to participate in their prosperity would be to go through some no-load global funds specializing in advanced economies.

These then are my nine steps to crisis investing. They are not designed to help you choose between various investment vehicles but to protect your assets from the devastation ahead. Once the global cataclysm is over, then you may consult books on financial planning and chose a conservative strategy offered by them. Two of my favorites are the investment guides by Suze Orman and by Charles Schwab. Another informative, comprehensive work is *Everyone's Money Book* by Jordan Goodman.[44] The advice I have just given holds good for all people, rich and poor, young and old, married and unmarried.

BUSINESS PLANNING

For businesses some additional steps can be taken. During the first four years of the Great Depression, national output plummeted more than a third, and joblessness hit 25 percent. Thousands of companies closed their doors, and many more shrank. But seven out of ten businesses survived. Whether or not a company makes it through the coming disaster will depend on timely action and proper planning.

There are thousands of industries, businesses, vocations, and jobs in the vast industrial landscape of America, and many of these didn't even exist during the 1930s. Personal computers, fax machines, motor homes, VCRs, video cameras, and many other gadgets are all products that came into being after the Second World War. However, the factors that enabled some companies to survive the 1930s, while others folded, are still the same.

The least-hit sectors in the 1930s were the postal industry, newspapers, some services, communications, variety stores, department stores, general merchandise and drug stores, life insurance, health care, secondhand stores, and education. Among those that were all but crippled were radio, music, automobiles, furniture, tires, farm equipment, florists, banking, and advertising. In a few businesses such as the health care industry, repair services, and bicycles, sales actually went up, while some others like book publishing survived by slanting the product mix toward cheaper goods such as the paperbacks. In general, luxury sales collapsed first, followed by goods and services linked to them. The following businesses are likely to weather the coming onslaught.

Computer software, especially that linked to Y2K problems
Home health care
Day-care centers for the elderly
Education
Repair shops
Bicycle stores
Bus and rail transportation
Gasoline stations
Drug stores
Grocery stores
Export business

If your business made this list, then you don't have much to worry about; you'll have plenty of work, although your earnings could still decline. You will prosper relative to companies that could suffer huge losses and go bankrupt. But even if your current business falls outside the purview of the above mentioned list of survivors, the best within each industry will make it. To make sure that your company is one of them, you have to take some steps now.

Bank Diversification

Perhaps the single most crucial step that you can now take is to diversify your bank accounts. Most companies have their funds parked in just one or two banks, with deposits far in excess of the maximum insurance limit of $100,000. Their payroll, capital, and taxes usually sit in a single bank account. Hundreds of banks will fail in the near future, and the Fed would be under no obligation to protect sums exceeding the limit of FDIC insurance. Your company could be wiped out overnight. Just like individuals, companies should also diversify their financial base, and open deposits in as many different banks and thrifts as possible. Bank diversification is inconvenient and time consuming, but in a crunch could be a lifesaver.

Your company can also open a variety of interlinked accounts in the same bank. You can have a checking account linked to a savings account, thus increasing your interest income. Whenever the checking deposit runs out of funds, it will automatically tap into the savings account. You may also open accounts in the names of trustworthy company officers, each insured up to the limit. If all this is too much for you, then stick to a very large multinational bank, which will be among the last to fail.

Cost Reduction

You should make a detailed plan of how to react quickly in case your sales sink. Plan on reducing costs right now, while the economy is sizzling. In prosperous times, companies have a tendency to be lax about expenses; wherever possible, cut corners and eliminate wasteful and duplicate operations.

Some costs are related to the scale of your business and cannot be trimmed in a booming economy; nevertheless, you should adopt a contingency plan today for cutting back. If possible, don't augment your payroll; hire temporary help instead. The key to surviving a financial crisis is the ability to cut overhead and operating expenses rapidly. In the future, you may have to lay off some people, or cut salaries, so planning is required now. Wherever possible, you should trim costs not through layoffs but through reduction in wages and working hours. This way you can do your part in easing the agony of unemployment, because those laid off would be hard pressed to find another job.

Low overhead costs and inventory control are the keys to success in a small business. A large concern can afford to ignore these savings, but not a venture of modest size. Inventory control will be especially important in 2000 and thereafter. It is crucial that you not get stuck with excessive levels of unsold goods, which could lead to insolvency.

Business Diversification

In addition to spreading your assets across diverse banks, you should look into strategic diversification. Branching out into another business, especially those listed above, is another way to increase the likelihood of survival. Diversification pays dividends only when it occurs in a related line of business, however. Venturing into an entirely new area can be risky in the best of times, and especially when great peril is around the corner.

Retail stores are the best candidates for diversification; they can readily add repair facilities, for example. Thus computer and video shops, appliance businesses, and furniture stores can easily expand into fixing whatever they sell. An upholstery business, for instance, can be easily added to a furniture shop. Another promising prospect is adding a consignment branch to the sale of new products. Coming back to furniture again, you can sell both the new and the old furniture from the same facility. The old product can be taken on consignment or as a trade-in. Even if you wouldn't like to do this now, you could prepare a contingency plan in case the worst does happen. There is no stigma attached to selling old and new brands simultaneously. Car dealers do this all the time, with rich reward in terms of expanded sales. According to entrepreneur and author James Cook, "The ideal diversification would be totally recession-proof and impervious to the business cycle. Such a company probably doesn't exist. Next best would be a venture that offsets the cyclical nature of your main business."[45]

The diversification imperative should be balanced by the need for cost reduction. It is essential that the new venture not be very expensive, so it won't interfere with the efficient running of the current venture. You don't have time to waste, and if you do decide to branch out, entrust the job to trusted employees already on the payroll instead of hiring new people. Remember that there are two sides to profits—sales revenue and cost reduction. Both need to be emphasized today to survive a chancy tomorrow.

Retrenchment

Some companies are overextended or overdiversified. What they need is retrenchment. In good times, some firms expand faster than prudence dictates. They build new factories or buy out other firms. A tremendous wave of mergers erupted in the 1980s and the 1990s. Many mergers don't work. Such has been the experience of some companies in the past. Sears, for instance, acquired several companies in the early eighties and then divested them a few years later. If some of your companies are currently unprofitable, just breaking even, or marginally profitable, get rid of them now. It will be very difficult to sell them in the near future.

Many companies are also saddled with large debt acquired in the process of mergers and acquisitions. This debt ought to be trimmed as soon as possible, even if you have to sell profitable concerns. It is true that an inflationary arena is friendly to debtors, so you may be tempted to take on even more debt anticipating surging prices in the near future. But depressions are very hard on debtors. Sales can evaporate overnight, leaving you insolvent. Regardless of the inflationary nature of the coming depression, it is better to be free from debt. Retrench now while there is still time, and concentrate on your own niche where you have the best chance of survival. Thus for those companies stretched enough to be saddled with unprofitable concerns, retrenchment is desirable, whereas for those too specialized and small, diversification may be useful.

If your debt burden is too large to be eased quickly, then try to convert short-term loans into long-term debt. Instead of borrowing from your bank and thrift, float corporate bonds and sell them in the bond market. Use the bond proceeds to pay off the short-term borrowings. The long-term interest rate will perhaps be a notch higher than your short-term loan costs, but it could really pay off in an inflationary economy. If you have issued long-term debt now, you will pay the same rate way into the future, when bond yields could skyrocket. The idea is that, like a home owner with a fixed mortgage, a business with a fixed rate bond issue will save a lot in interest expenses if yields heat up in an inflationary environment.

Efficient Cash Management

Cash management is another area that deserves your attention, because in good times companies tend to neglect the cost savings or increased earnings made possible by efficient utilization of their cash flow. However, proper cash management can be crucial to corporate survival even in a booming economy. In the absence of enough cash, a company can go bankrupt even if its assets far exceed its liabilities. During depressions, proper cash management can be the lifeblood of business.

A company should always keep enough cash on hand to pay operating expenses and cover unforeseen problems. Bills have to be paid with balances in a checking account, not with goods produced or sold, or with property that isn't liquid. Nor do capital equipment and accounts receivables help much in this matter. Only cash can do the job. Cash is king in bad times. Banks and thrifts become extra cautious during depressions and demand high collateral. In depressed times, your capital equipment and inventory may not be sufficiently reassuring for a financial institution.

Business economist Leon Wortman argues that there are two types of cash needed by a company—working cash and capital cash. Money needed to meet expenses for wages, inventory, rent, utilities, travel, and daily operations are part of working cash, whereas funds needed to pay for worn-out machines or new technology are included in capital cash. The difference between the two is that a business needs to generate enough working cash to pay for operating expenses, whereas the money for capital improvements can be borrowed from banks or the bond market. Given what lies ahead, if you don't have enough working cash, then it would be better to shut down rather than take on a lot of debt.

In a slumping economy, cash should be conserved, not expended on long-term projects requiring new technology and equipment. Survival is more immediate than progress. The temptation to expand your business and take on rivals should be resisted as much as possible. You just don't know what is lurking behind the financial storms. Anticipating a major cataclysm, you should conserve on cash now and shelve all your capital projects. Don't borrow money unless it is for wrestling with the Y2K bug or for diversification into a repair service or a secondhand product.

To stay afloat, you will need a bigger cushion of cash in an inflationary rather than deflationary depression. If prices fall or remain stable, you don't have to set aside extra funds for inventory; but when prices rise, inventory consumes more money at a time when banks become extra cautious in their dealings. You need to generate bigger sales now by offering cash discounts, increased advertising, or simply selling some assets. And the extra cash, of course, should be parked in a variety of banks, not just one and the same bank.

A manufacturing operation has to be particularly careful now, especially in seeking and taking new orders, because the order backlog can quickly disappear in a deep slump. If possible, insist that your customers offer a large down payment at least equaling your operating expenses for the project, including the cost of wages and raw materials. Tighten your credit terms as well. If orders vanish in a sharp downturn, you will be left with expenses but little revenue to match them. If credit tightening costs you some customers, you should be prepared to accept it. It is better to lose some sales than risk the extra indebtedness incurred in meeting too many orders. Instead of giving your customers sixty or ninety days to pay your bill, you should offer them thirty days, along with a generous cash discount of as much as 3 percent. When customers fall behind in their payments, don't hesitate to send them a timely but courteous reminder. Although this piece of advice should be followed all the time, it will be especially important in the near future.

Keep your cash in interest-bearing money market accounts with banks and thrifts. Very large banks hardly pay any interest on such deposits, especially when you have to write checks against them, but small banks and thrifts offer competitive rates. Of course, with a smaller institution you are taking an increased risk of a bank failure. You have to clearly weigh such risks and rewards and craft a proper cash management strategy. A large company requiring millions in working cash ought to stay with a large bank, whereas a small business with low fund requirements may do well by diversifying among smaller banks.

When a slump begins, often operating expenses stay the same, while sales decline. The business's cash needs then rise dramatically. You still have to pay wages, rent, interest, and utilities, even while the customer traffic plummets. For this and other reasons discussed before, cash management should be among your top priorities now.

You also need to look at your office lease. If it is up for renewal, take a short-term lease rather than a long-term one. Two benefits flow from this decision. First, if your business doesn't make it through the depression, then you won't be stuck with a long-term bill in case you shut down. Second, because of the construction boom during the nineties, office rents will plummet during the coming slump, enabling you to renew your lease at better terms. This could provide you with great cost savings.

Export Sales

The coming crisis is likely to cripple world trade, mostly because of the collapse of the dollar. Global commerce has soared in the nineties thanks to soaring U.S. trade deficits that have been generously financed by other countries. When the Dow crashes and the dollar tumbles, American imports will plummet; foreigners will no longer be eager to invest their funds into depreciating U.S. assets. The U.S. market will become inaccessible to many international businesses, but for many American corporations this could be the opportunity of a lifetime. American products will be dirt cheap abroad, easily out-competing foreign goods. Consequently, if you are not in the business of exporting now, you should carefully look into it, and make contingency plans to market your product or service abroad.

Exporting can be very lucrative, but it takes time to develop and nurture contacts abroad. There are, of course, businesses that will help you with foreign marketing, but they take a big cut from sales. Direct selling is far better than going through a middleman, but it is more time consuming and difficult. Now is the time to make advance preparation.

Some government agencies offer invaluable aid in locating foreign contacts. The Bureau of International Commerce of the U.S. Department of Commerce can help you find buyers in foreign countries. It has a list of foreign companies eager to be linked with U.S. concerns and assist you in getting in touch with foreign retailers and wholesalers. Many American companies sell directly to foreign retailers, eliminating the middlemen in the process. You can do the same, especially if you have a good product. The price of your product will be no problem with a sinking dollar.

The U.S. Department of Commerce also publishes many lists, directories, and magazines that can keep you up to date about the changing market conditions overseas. Prominent among them are *Export Market Digests, Global Market Surveys,* and *A Basic Guide to Exporting.* Of course, in a fast-changing world, the list of magazines expands or contracts each year, but the U.S. Department of Commerce can provide further information on their publications.

The Bureau of International Commerce, with its offices in many large cities, can help you develop a marketing plan for shipping overseas. As Leon Wortman advises: "It can be extremely valuable to contact them if you are (1) entering the field of export sales for the first time, (2) expanding your export sales, (3) trying to locate overseas sales agents or representatives or (4) licensing your product for manufacture in a foreign country."[46]

When the dollar collapses in the near future, the American market place will become a graveyard for many foreign corporations, but domestic firms will find it much easier to sell abroad. Even though international commerce will tumble in general, American companies could discover a bonanza in global markets, at least relative to their foreign counterparts. The downside is that foreign nations themselves will be in a huge slump and therefore won't be able to buy much from America. Nevertheless, U.S. companies will flourish relative to foreign concerns in their own lands. There will be depression everywhere in the world, but for American companies, foreign trade will offer one silver lining, whereas for others there might be none. Much of the world now has a trade surplus with the United States, and the collapse of the dollar will prove to be its worst nightmare.

Starting a Business

With a depression right around the corner, this is not a good time to start or acquire a new business. You should stay in your current job, where you may have earned some seniority. Don't make a move to another firm or occupation, where, because of the slump, you could be the first to be fired. Those who are hired the last are also fired first in a downturn.

Starting a business from your own home is something quite different, especially if it is a service business and won't eat up much capital. Any venture with high investment requirements should be avoided at present, because you could be faced with a killer slump even before you have a chance to stand on your feet. Depressions are hard even on established companies; new ventures are the first to fail in such a milieu.

Summary of Various Steps

Here is a list of steps that a businessperson should take now to prepare for the worst in the future.

1. Diversify your banks.
2. For now keep your business planning short term.
3. Avoid debt, but if you can't, then borrow using long-term bonds. Stay away from short-term loans from banks and thrifts.
4. Sign a short-term office lease.
5. Diversify into a repair business.
6. Conserve on cash, and tighten credit terms you may be offering your customers.
7. Consider exporting your product, because the dollar could sharply fall in the future, giving you a decided advantage in foreign markets.
8. Divest yourself of unprofitable or marginal concerns, and use the proceeds to build your cash reserve.
9. Finally, don't start or buy a new business now.

These then are the nine steps to crisis business management. They don't guarantee success, but maximize the chance for survival. This general advice applies especially to small businesses, which are often undercapitalized, pay more for bank loans, and lack the reserves to survive an extended depression.

11

PROUT

During the 1980s, Japan, then the land of the rising yen, was often denounced by American economists, politicians, and bankers for igniting a vast speculative frenzy, fearing that the mania could topple the Japanese financial system and with it the world. As it turned out, Japan's bubble economy did crash in 1990 and has been in the tank ever since, but the rest of the world continued to prosper, partly with the aid of Japanese money that found little worthy of investment at home. More manias sprang up in quick succession in the Asian Tigers, Mexico, South America, Euroland, Eastern Europe and, above all, the United States. In fact, America's economy, the world's behemoth, swelled into the millennium bubble.

In every book I have written since 1982, I have called for a variety of reforms to stabilize capitalism and enhance the general standard of living. In spite of my repeated warnings, the system is about to self-destruct and truly take the world down with it. Given the opportunity, the same American critics, who once castigated Japan for its excesses, created an even bigger frenzy at home. Clearly the system is fundamentally so flawed that, given congenial circumstances, it consistently sparks a bonfire of speculation and moves toward a cataclysm.

Monopoly capitalism is simply beyond repair. Bribery, corruption, and decadence pervade the capitalist world. Nepotism and graft are the order of the day. Crony capitalism is defiling the landscape of

America and every nook and cranny on earth. Even the International Olympic Committee is not beyond its reach. In March 1999 the entire executive branch of the European Union, facing scathing criticism over corruption and certain dismissal by the European parliament, resigned. Fifteen nations of Europe are members of the European Union, and not a single country's representative escaped the scandal. We must create a new framework that restores compassion and integrity, is inherently productive and stable, needs no bailouts for survival, and generates debt-free prosperity for all, not just for a privileged few. Is such a paradise possible or even conceivable? It doesn't exist yet, but it has been conceived by my late teacher, Prabhat Ranjan Sarkar, who, I might mention, was so brilliant that he never made an inaccurate forecast in his life. He is also the author of the law of social cycles that has proved invaluable in the precision of my forecasting. His system offers some fundamental economic reforms capable of creating a truly free enterprise framework, free from the defects we see today.

We have already seen that, according to a historical pattern we can trace back to the 1920s, the final year of each decade produced a dramatic change somewhere on earth and then convulsed parts of the world over the next ten years. Let us take advantage of such patterns to create a blueprint for reforms that could then guide the planet over the coming decade.

Not too long ago, we lived in the belief that if character is lost everything is lost, if health is lost something is lost, but if money is lost, nothing is lost. Today we think if character is lost, nothing is lost, if health is lost, something is lost, but if money is lost, everything is lost. Our society is obsessed with money and cares for little else. A great moral degradation has occurred in just fifty years, much of it as a by-product of crony capitalism.

The technological marvels of monopoly capitalism have certainly helped us in meeting the physical needs of a mushrooming population. They have enhanced our lives by providing comforts only royalty could attain in the past. Today machines heat and cool our homes, mop our floors, do the cooking, and provide luxuries that only a few decades ago required an army of servants.

However, with our single-minded devotion to things material, we have lapsed into a debilitating myopia about the nonmaterial side of our existence. In the process, morality has been shattered. People live in constant fear for their personal safety. Children gun down other children and their parents and teachers. The elderly are robbed and assaulted every day. Mothers abandon their babies. Is this what we call a civilized society? But for our living standard, which is about to vanish overnight, our age seems little different from the Dark Ages.

We need a system that preserves the technological excellence of capitalism, while returning us to old-fashioned virtues. We need to restore human dignity; compassion and honesty must be revered; leaders must pursue ethical goals, not extramarital affairs and money.

We need a new philosophy that reconciles our inner needs without sacrificing the material gains we have made through advanced technology and rapid industrialization. Prabhat Ranjan Sarkar, the discoverer of the infallible law of social cycles, offers a new system called Prout, which is designed to fulfil the needs, of humanity today.

Sarkar was a great linguist, philosopher, musician, historian, and economist. Because of his vast knowledge in many areas, he was able to devise a totally new philosophy that covers all aspects of life and is consistent with human psychology, needs, and aspirations. Sarkar was a renaissance man with a universal vision that combined rationality with an extraordinary sense of practicality. He was way ahead of his time and needed great courage to voice his ideas challenging the orthodoxy in many areas of life, and his ideas are proving timely today.

I met him on August 16, 1964, in an unostentatious room in Lucknow, a small town in the state of Uttar Pradesh, India. A month later I met him again in Jaipur, a city with a rich historical heritage in the state of Rajasthan. There I told him that I wanted to work to alleviate India's poverty. His response was: "Your goal should be to eliminate poverty not just from India but from the world. And in this goal you should not have a single thought of becoming a leader." As a result, I pursued that dream through scholarship and writing, and I hope my books deriving from his ideas will advance that objective. Such was the brilliance of my teacher.

Sarkar calls his concept for a new social framework progressive utilization theory: "pro" taken from progressive, "u" from utilization, and "t" from theory, together make up Prout. It is a socioeconomic philosophy that blends traditional values with productive efficiency and distributive justice, offering everyone an equality of opportunity along with a fair reward. The basic idea is that all our actions and institutions should be such as to produce progress.

Prout is not an esoteric theory but a set of principles for the administration of society in various spheres. One might call it a practical guide, because its emphasis is not on abstract concepts but rather on that which works in practice and does the maximum good for people. Sarkar regards his system not as a reaction to the intellectual bankruptcy of modern-day socioeconomic systems but as something that is universal and will be valid for a long time to come. He views capitalism and communism as passing phases of social cycles. Yet what is interesting is that the economic system of Prout does not do away with capitalism, technology, and industrialization; rather it ends up advocating what may be called mass capitalism, as will become clear from the policies and reforms explored in the next chapter. It offers a new and useful way to view and harness advanced technology.

I first introduced Prout to Western mainstream in 1985 in *The Great Depression of 1990*. Since then the idea has made a slow but steady progress, especially in Japan, and by now the new system offers a full-fledged alternative to monopoly capitalism. Its logic, simplicity, vision, and internal consistency will simply astound you.

BALANCE AMONG THREE FORCES

Prout touches on all aspects of our existence—the physical, the intellectual, and the spiritual. True progress occurs only when a balance occurs within each aspect and among all three of them. Our troubles have multiplied, because we have lost sight of this balance in our obsession with the material side of life. Our interest in money, and only money, is choking our thinking.

Prout is a vast philosophy with many fertile branches. My concern here is only with Proutist economic reforms insofar as they can stabilize and revive the world economy. If the United States, the world's financial leader, adopts the suggested reforms, it may still be possible to contain the aftershocks of the coming crash.

In the realm of economic policy, Prout contends that there should be a balance in the utilization of physical and intellectual resources.

On the face of it this statement appears simplistic, for everyone likes the idea of balance. However, as we saw in chapters 5 and 6, global economic ills have sprung from what may be called unbalancing economic policies. Specifically, poverty, hunger, recessions, inflation, depressions, and so on result when the government and private behavior create an imbalance in the labor market and in other sectors of the economy.

THE CONCEPT OF PROGRESS

To understand Prout, it is necessary to begin with its concept of progress. Humanity is said to have made tremendous progress today, which is commonly understood to mean an increase in living comforts through scientific inventions. All this, to Sarkar, is not progress. To be sure, it has resulted in a great change in lifestyle, but at the same time created problems that were nonexistent before. Faster travel today has increased the risk of accidents; industrialization has resulted in environmental pollution, cancer, and psychosomatic diseases unheard of in the past; modern medicine quickly cures the malady but generates side effects requiring further treatment.[47]

Sarkar views progress as a positive movement unaccompanied by a negative reaction, a step forward without a step back. Progress, according to him, is simply not possible in the physical arena of the world. Why? Why must any positive development in the physical aspect of our life be associated with a negative movement? The reason lies in the very nature of the universe, which Newton discovered it a long time ago. To every action there is an equal and opposite reaction. Therefore, if life becomes easier in some respects, it will become harder in others. Never will science and technology be an unmixed blessing.

Sarkar's view, as always, challenges our stereotypes. It is based on the notion that if you take some steps forward and then some back, it is difficult to be sure if you moved forward or backward. The overall effect, the sum of the positive and negative movements, may or may not be salutary. Only when there are no negative ripples from a discovery, is it clear that progress has really occurred.

Sarkar's claim that progress is not possible in the physical realm is very strong indeed. It seems incredible, but it has an internal logic of its own. Today, with the fruits of science visible all around us, this logic has become manifestly clear. Can you think of any invention that while reducing our boredom has not added to our danger at the same time? Repetitive work is drudgery; when machines do that work, life seems to be more pleasant than before. If dishwashers wash our dishes, air conditioners cool our rooms, laundries clean our clothes, automobiles do our walking, and so on, life certainly appears blissful relative to what our forefathers had to endure in a science-less world. But then they did not have to contend with electric shocks; fatal accidents; air, water, land, and noise pollution; noxious automobile fumes; urban congestion, smog, and so forth.

Indeed the harm done by an invention varies directly with its promise of comfort. Coal results in smoke pollution; so does oil. Nuclear power promises one vast reservoir of power but is many times deadlier than traditional sources of energy. You can move away from the pollution of oil and coal, but from nuclear radiation, because of its vast reach, there is no escape. The side effects of science and technology, long hidden from the naked eye, have abruptly come to the surface, with a ferocity that just cannot be overlooked. No longer can we ignore automobile fumes, noxious chemicals in urban air, congestion on the roads, rivers that spew fire or vomit dead fish, oil slicks that destroy beaches, smog that suffocates our lungs and spirits, airplanes that deafen our ears, nuclear plants and wastes that yield deadly radiation. Nor can we ignore the growing rate of cancer, heart failure, respiratory diseases, and deformed babies. These are the irrefutable by-products of our so-called progress.

Pollution of the environment is not partial to any country or ideology. Former communist nations are afflicted as much by it as the capitalist nations. Nor have the underdeveloped countries been spared, although there the pollution springs from poverty, not affluence. Environmental degradation is not a capitalistic disease, but a disease of unbridled materialism.

Today solar energy holds greater promise than nuclear plants, but its dangers are not yet known. Every scientific development contains invisible dangers that only become apparent much later. While developing a new technology, we don't expect any trouble from it. Sarkar corrects this faulty logic by saying that the side effects of every invention are inevitable, because a visible physical change producing comfort must be counterbalanced by an equivalent physical change producing pain.

Does this mean that science should be discarded? Not at all. With our overwhelming problems concerning energy, population, and pollution, a return to prescientific times is unthinkable. All it means is that we have to be more cautious about inventions. Before translating any new invention into industrial technology, its side effects should be thoroughly studied, and investments should be simultaneously made to control those effects.

Sarkar implies that an invention's harmful emissions are proportionally linked to its potential benefits. Need we say any more about this linkage in these days of the Y2K scare? Who can deny the vast benefits of the computer revolution? The discovery has totally transformed our lifestyle and sharply enhanced our productivity. The world as we know it today would come to a halt without the computer, and that is precisely our worry. Just one little mistake of representing the year by two digits instead of the usual four could bring the entire planet down to its knees. A microchip is now hidden in virtually every machine and appliance used by American businesses and households: manufacturing control systems, telecommunications, financial institutions, transportation, gas, water, and electric utilities, stock markets, national defense, heating and cooling, alarm systems, and so on.

The peril of the bug is not just confined to financial meltdown. It could also lead to a holocaust. The Pentagon is increasingly concerned about an accidental launch of missiles by Russian nuclear weapons that are unlikely to be Y2K compliant when the new year dawns. The United States has already allocated as much as $3 billion not for its own computer glitch, but Russia's. China faces the same dilemma and may have trouble fixing its computers in time, if at all.

TECHNOLOGY VERSUS COUNTER TECHNOLOGY

When economic development occurs, the environment should not suffer in the process. If it does, economic growth is not progressive in Sarkar's definition, for then a positive movement on the growth front has been accompanied by a negative movement in the quality of the environment. What is the point in enjoying the comfort of

modern conveniences while suffering the diseases of a polluted atmo-
sphere? Rising production alone cannot be called growth if air
becomes unbreathable and water undrinkable.

While there is general consensus today about the gravity of our
sickly environment, there is less agreement among scholars about
its causes and cures. Sarkar identifies the true culprit, namely science itself, which points him toward a proper solution. Diamond
cuts diamond. Let counter technology cut down the side effects of
new technology.

Prout calls for an international effort to clean up the environment. This is not a simple task, but it must be done for our own sake
and certainly for the sake of our children. Since every invention generates its own ills, the government should set up an agency to regu-
late the introduction of new technology. Every firm that seeks to
utilize a new invention or sell it to other businesses touts its benefits
and slights its dangers. But the possibility of harm should be explored
right away, and new technology should not be approved until counter
technology has been discovered.

Counter technology controls the harmful emissions of a new discovery. In the case of the auto industry, which produces massive air
pollution, catalytic converters control car fumes. Thus the catalytic
converter is counter technology to the invention of the automobile.
Similarly, for industries spewing tons of noxious gases into the atmo-
sphere by burning coal and oil, smokestacks are their countertech-
nology. When a company seeks to introduce a major new invention,
it should first get the approval of the government. It should establish
that the new technique will not have strong side effects, or the agency
should conduct its own tests to determine the harmlessness of the
invention. The firm should be asked to introduce counter technology
at the same time it uses the new technique.

This process, of course, will make scientific discoveries more
expensive, but it is the only way to control the inevitable side effects
of new inventions and reduce pollution. If the catalytic converter had
been introduced right at the time autos were invented, or smokestacks
installed just when iron and steel plants were first built, we would still
be able to inhale fresh air. The smog in metropolises like Los Angeles,
Paris, Moscow, Bombay, and Tokyo, among others, would not stifle
their denizens' lungs and spirits. The harm done by an invention may

not be clear immediately, unless we explore its other side. Prudence demands that we shouldn't wait until pollution becomes apparent, because by that time it is too late. Extensive testing is required, because counter technology itself could generate some pollution.

Something similar is done today in the United States, Europe, and Japan with respect to the use of new medicines. The U.S. Food and Drug Administration is the federal agency that approves new medicines by examining their side effects. A similar agency should be set up for new technology as well. No new discovery should be permitted industrial applications without government approval. Just as we don't approve new drugs without proper testing, we should not allow new technology without sufficient testing.

Today computers are increasingly used at businesses and in homes. Companies have rushed to introduce them because they sharply enhance productivity. Side effects (in addition to the Y2K glitch) are already emerging. Computers strain the eyes, create lower back pain, and generate swollen finger joints. We should immediately devise counter technology for their use, lest the coming generations suffer from poor vision, carpal tunnel syndrome, and poor posture— assuming some much more serious health threat does not emerge.

Computers already top the list of causes for workplace injuries, afflicting as many as twenty million Americans. Even more vulnerable are today's children. *New York Times* reporter Jane Gross warns: "There is a wide concern among physicians, physical therapists and ergonomists that a tide of injuries, mirroring those sustained by adults in certain professions, is inevitable as young people spend more time on computers."[48] She quotes Jane M. Healy, an educational psychologist and author of *Failure to Connect,* a seminal work on computer use by children, as saying, "What I saw, all over the country, was just appalling."[49] Even as American leaders, in the White House or at Capitol Hill, vocally call for a computer on the desk of every pupil at school, let's take a pause and ponder Sarkar's admonition that a major invention has major side effects. Our children could be courting disaster, if we rush them headlong into the use of burgeoning technology. The Internet is surely fascinating, but we know very little about its health risks. Let's explore the safety side thoroughly before exposing our offspring to the unknown but inevitable perils of computing.

The government should offer tax benefits to companies that discover and introduce counter technologies, while imposing hefty fines on polluters. One of the biggest polluters in the world today is international trade, which has risen sharply as tariffs have tumbled. The rise in world commerce has trashed the seas with cargo ships crisscrossing the oceans, burning fuel and dumping refuse. Oil tankers get into accidents and leak crude oil into water. There are countless ways in which growing commerce contaminates the world.

Prout proposes tariffs and export taxes. As they trim trade and transportation, they will also cut oceanic and air pollution and reduce energy use. When energy demand sinks, global oil prices will remain low. Instead of free trade, we should have free foreign investment. This way, factories can be located near population centers and mines, without sacrificing the benefits of commercial liberalization. Transportation of goods and raw materials among countries will then tumble, causing a major decline in pollution. I will have more to say on this later.[50]

Thus, while the problem of pollution around the world is horrendous, Prout offers many cures for this crisis. Counter technology, business tax incentives, fines on polluters, and foreign trade taxes can all be used to clean up our dirty environment.

REAL WAGE AND GDP

For most people, consumption is directly related to their earnings. According to Prout, a dynamic economy is one where incomes climb for everybody. When improving technology makes the rich richer without bettering the lot of the poor and the middle class, the economy is essentially static.

After Bill Clinton was reelected in 1996, GDP growth in America rose sharply. In the final quarter of 1998, the growth rate even exceeded 6 percent, the highest level in a decade. But what did it do to the lot of an average employee? Although American companies had introduced new technology at a furious pace, for much of the decade the real wage declined for almost 75 percent of the workforce, while the rate of poverty continued to rise. In 1989, just prior to the slump of 1990, real weekly earnings for the vast majority of

Americans, after inflation adjustment, were $264; they still had not caught up with that figure by the boom year of 1998.

With big business in complete command of the U.S. economy and many factories using cheap labor abroad, it should not come as a surprise that the wages of chief executives have skyrocketed; what is surprising is that the real wages of workers have steadily declined in an economy where productivity continues to rise.

The plight of the American worker is captured by figure 11.1, which plots the real wage index of chief executives and their employees. The real wage is the purchasing power of a person's salary. Both wage indexes start at one in 1976, but then the executives' index soars more than 200 percent by 1998, whereas that of the workers

FIGURE 11.1
Index of real wages of workers and executives, 1976–1998

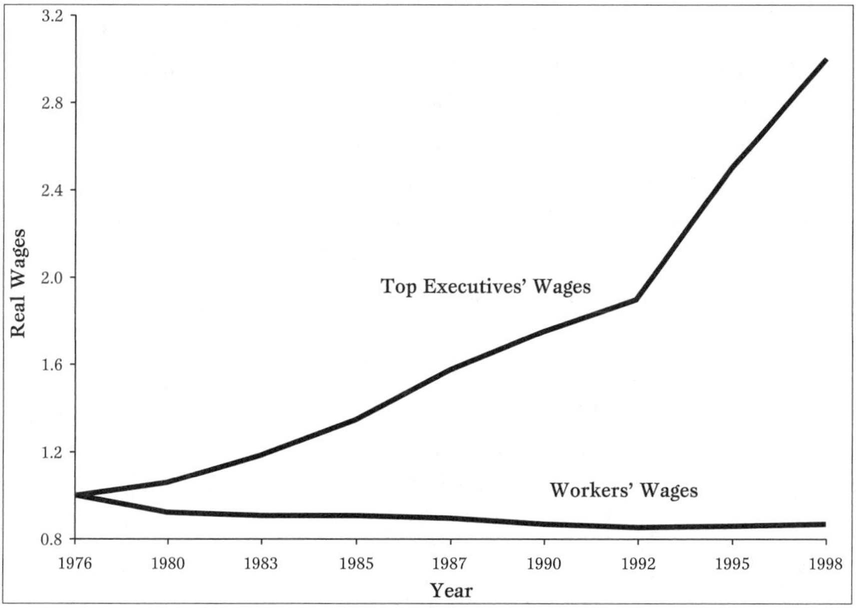

SOURCE: Data from Ravi Batra, *The Great American Deception* (New York: John Wiley and Sons, 1996), 263; Timothy O'brien, "Handsome Pay for the Co-Chairmen of Citigroup," *New York Times,* 9 March 1999, C1.
Note: Since 1976, inequality between the real wages of workers and executives has soared. The workers' wage index fell 14 percent by 1998 while that of executives jumped 200 percent.

falls 14 percent in the same period. On top of this, workers' tax burden has risen while that of the executives has plunged. Is there any doubt that monopoly capitalism rules America? Not in this graph.

The real wages of American employees have been sinking since 1972. According to the *Economic Report of the President,* an annual publication of the federal government, weekly earnings of production workers, measured in 1982 prices, were $315 in 1972 and $262 in 1998. This is a hefty decline of 17 percent, which does not take into account the tripling of the Social Security fees and state sales taxes, both of which fall disproportionately on the poor and the middle class. In view of such giant tax rises, real wages of production workers, who constitute at least 75 percent of the workforce, fell by a fourth.

Modern economists call this sad phenomenon technological dynamism. Prout calls it exploitation. In fact, it is a relic of medieval feudalism, where backbreaking work by the serfs was extracted by the feudal landlord. The only difference is that now the fruit of growing national productivity, stemming from the increased use of overtime and computers, is extorted by business executives and company chairmen. The poor and the middle class, husband and wife, strive day and night, master new technology, brave traffic jams, and toil up to sixty hours a week. What they get in return is a shrinking paycheck. Such is the tyranny of crony capitalism.

In order to evaluate an economy, traditional economics examines the level and growth of real GDP, which is the annual output of goods and services valued at retail market prices. After adjustment for inflation, if the GDP falls over two consecutive quarters, economists call it a recession. If the real GDP shrinks over several years, it becomes a depression. If the real GDP rises, the economy is said to be satisfactory, especially if growth exceeds 3 percent. By this definition, Japan's recession was over in 1992. Never mind how the public and workers feel. The government declared the recession over just because the real GDP no longer fell over two successive quarters.

The GDP lumps the incomes of the affluent with those of the destitute. In any economy, normally 5 percent of the households are opulent, 30 percent are poor, and the rest belong to the middle class. If the earnings of the top 5 percent soar, the GDP may rise while the incomes of the other 95 percent decline or remain constant. This has been happening in America since 1972 and has become worse since the election of Bill Clinton. Japan has been in the same boat since 1990.

In assessing economic performance, Prout examines the average real wage, which measures the purchasing power of people (i.e., salaries are adjusted for inflation). According to Prout, if real income falls for a majority of the public, then the economy is in recession, even if GDP growth is high. The economy is in depression if the average real wage and/or employment falls or stays low for more than three years. These concepts reflect common sense and how the general public feels. By this measure, Japan has been in a recession since 1991. Even though its real GDP has grown a bit, the majority has suffered a decline in real income because of record unemployment, plummeting overtime work, and thousands of bankruptcies. In the traditional view, the Great Depression was over in 1933, even though 17 percent of the American workforce was jobless as late as 1939. According to Prout, however, a vibrant economy is one where unemployment is low—less than 5 percent—and where both real wages and the GDP rise every year in proportion to national productivity. Thus the entire decade of the 1930s was a depression.

A BALANCED ECONOMY

Prout favors a balanced economy, which will enhance the living standard for everybody. We have already explored the most prominent feature of such an economy in chapter 5, namely, that real employee earnings grow in sync with productivity, so national demand keeps up with national supply without resorting to artificial spending created by domestic and foreign debt. We will now rejoin that discussion and extend it in many directions.

Another important feature of a balanced economy is diversification, as opposed to specialization. Diversification tends to mitigate labor market distortion, which is a measure of the chasm between real wages and labor productivity. As the saying goes, a prudent investor does not keep all his eggs in one basket, because if the basket were to fall, the eggs could all break at the same time. Instead, he or she diversifies by investing in a variety of assets or baskets: buying stocks, bonds, real estate, and gold; purchasing shares and bonds of different companies and entities; and so on. By diversifying portfolios, wise investors trims their risk. If one asset declines in value, the other could rise, thereby cutting investor losses and maximizing gains.

A balanced economy operates in much the same way and maximizes the living standard from the use of available resources. A diversified economy is far more stable and free from the scourge of speculative bubbles, market crashes, inflation, environmental decay, recessions, and depressions than a specialized economy.

Economic diversification occurs when a country allocates its resources to many important sectors, such as agriculture, forestry and fisheries, manufacturing, mining, construction (or housing), and a variety of services. When a country meets most of its needs for food, manufactured goods, finance and insurance, energy, construction materials, and services from its own production without reliance on foreign nations, then its economy is diversified or balanced.

For convenience, industries can be grouped into three categories: primary, secondary, and tertiary. The primary sector includes agriculture, forestry, fisheries, and mining; the secondary comprises construction and manufacturing; and the tertiary encompasses the remaining industries. In this classification the primary area has the lowest labor productivity, whereas the secondary sector has the highest productivity. The ideal case of diversification occurs when a nation or a region meets its consumption and investment needs mostly from its own production.

However, some nations (e.g., Japan, most Asian Tigers, Germany, and Britain) lack raw materials. Others have little arable or fertile land. Saudi Arabia, Egypt, Kuwait, and the United Arab Emirates provide cases in point. Such countries lack the ability to generate an adequate primary sector. In this case a diversified economy is one that exports goods and services mostly to meet the needs of its primary sector.

By contrast, when a nation concentrates its resources in certain sectors and relies excessively on foreign markets, its economy is unbalanced. It places most of its eggs in one basket and is vulnerable to external shocks such as the ones inflicted recently by currency speculators. It is subject to inflationary spasms, recessions, and depressions; that is to say, it may suffer rising prices and high unemployment, and its real wage may be stagnant or even decline, in spite of soaring worker productivity. Prout favors a balanced economy because the postwar history of America, Japan, Canada, and Australia shows that wage and productivity growth jumped when these nations were diversified, and sank with increased specialization. To be sure, the Asian Tigers developed rapidly by following the track of specialization, but their lofty growth depended crucially on capital from and exports to diversified economies. The economic history of the last two centuries reveals that economic diversification dwarfs export concentration as a long-term strategy.

Among various industries, manufacturing, mining, and construction have the highest productivity, whereas agriculture and services normally have the lowest productivity. For instance, housing has a large production value, which is the same thing as productivity, because house prices tend to be high in any economy, especially where land is scarce. Similarly, in manufacturing too the production value tends to be large. Productivity is not just output per hour; it is output value per hour divided by a common denominator such as an average price represented by a price index.

In mining, productivity is high in countries like Japan where raw materials are scarce and low in countries like India where industrialization is low and raw materials relatively abundant. It may be added that because of the way the government calculates it, production value depends not only on improved technology but also on the product price. That is why expensive things like autos, furniture, appliances, and so on have high productivity.

In agriculture and services the production value tends to be mediocre. The demand for food is limited by physical needs. How much extra bread or meat can you digest as your income rises? Not much. But there is no such constraint on construction and manufacturing. With growing affluence, you can switch to higher-priced homes, cars, computers, and so forth. That is why with rising prosperity farm prices normally decline relative to the price index, generating lower productivity in farming relative to other goods.

In services productivity tends to be especially low, because it is difficult to constantly improve technology in such industries. The scope for raising hourly output in hotels, restaurants, airlines, buses, railroads, insurance, banks, education, legal needs, retailing, and so on is rather limited. The production value in these areas trails that in construction and manufacturing, where productivity and its growth tend to be far higher. In brief, construction and manufacturing have the highest productivity, services and agriculture have the lowest, and mining falls somewhere in the middle.

A diversified economy has a good mix of both high- and low-productivity industries, whereas a specialized economy has excessive amounts of some and little of others. Among various areas, construction activity generates goods that are hard to export or import, because it is very difficult to transport finished houses, although construction materials—cement, bricks, lumber, prefabricated walls, structures—can be moved from one country to another.

The other four sectors—manufacturing, mining, services, and agriculture—are more amenable to economic and commercial policy. Until 1970 most countries had diversified economies but began to specialize increasingly thereafter. Canada and Australia concentrated on mining and agriculture, the United States on agriculture and services, and Germany and Japan on manufacturing. Thus Japan specialized in the high-productivity sector, whereas the United States, Canada, and Australia focused on industries with mediocre values. Not surprisingly, Japan continued to grow faster than other advanced economies. After 1972 real wages began to fall in Australia and the United States, whereas in Japan they rose a bit before taxes and stagnated after taxes were deducted.

The precious lesson of this whole argument is that specialization hurts workers, even if a country focuses on high-priced products. After the early 1970s, rising productivity failed to raise after-tax wages, even in Japan, while in North America and Australia real wages actually fell. And in Germany, where real wages continued to rise, workers suffered through growing unemployment. In most Tigers, which preferred specialization in exports, growth was fast, but wages rose gingerly. This is not Prout's idea of development and industrialization.

Another factor in support of diversification is the global competition for the production of manufactured goods. Most countries covet manufacturing, because it tends to have a higher production value than agriculture and services. That is why the United States wants Japan to import U.S. cars, even though American cars tend to be inferior. Now it is impossible for all countries to specialize in manufacturing. There is not enough global demand to support excess production of manufactured goods in every country.

The auto industry is a case in point. In Japan the production capacity for cars is at ten million autos per year. In the United States it is at twenty-five million. But the combined auto demand in the United States and Japan is for only twenty-three million. There is then extra capacity for twelve million cars in the two countries. Manufacturing glut is one reason for wage stagnation in both nations, generating a huge waste of capital, which could have been productively used elsewhere. To eliminate poverty from the world, it is necessary that, as far as possible, every country produce some manufactured goods, which have a higher production value and pay higher wages. The high-wage sector then generates the need for high-quality housing as well as services. Thus healthy manufacturing nurtures other sectors.

Without adequate manufacturing an economy tends to stagnate, because the high-wage sector is small. This tends to dampen the demand for housing and services, so total output and real wages stagnate throughout the economy. Thus, if feasible, every nation should produce as many manufactured goods as it can to meet its domestic needs, even if its productivity and quality are no match for those in other countries. Manufacturing is essential for a healthy and dynamic economy.

The experience of the United States, Japan, and Canada shows that until the early seventies their real wage growth was at its peak, when about 25 to 30 percent of their workforce was employed in manufacturing. In the late 1970s and 1980s, the proportion of manufacturing employment plummeted in Canada and America, whereas it rose a bit in Japan.

At present, just 16 percent of the labor force is employed in North American manufacturing, which is about where Canada and the United States were in the nineteenth century. The continent has lost its dynamism and therefore turned into a citadel of labor exploitation, so much so that real wages for twenty-five million retail workers trail even those prevailing before the First World War. Such has been the effect of industrial erosion on America and Canada since the early 1970s.

Another unfortunate example of the industrial erosion is Australia, where less than 18 percent of the workforce is now employed in manufacturing, which has been shrinking since 1974. Not surprisingly, its real wages have also been sinking since that year. Australia has vast natural resources. So do Canada and the United States, but that has not prevented a decline in their real wages. Such is the harm done by a shriveling employment share in manufacturing.

A diversified economy in today's high-tech and information age has about 30 percent of labor employed in manufacturing, 8 to 10 percent in construction, 10 percent in mining and agriculture, and the remaining 50 percent or more in services. These are, of course, approximations and may vary a bit from place to place. Japan, with practically no mining, imports much of its raw materials from abroad. Therefore a large mining sector, as stated earlier, is not essential for a diversified or balanced economy, but its presence helps the nation raise the living standard for everyone, as it once did in Canada, Australia, and America. Germany is another case of a diversified economy, even though the mining industry is small there as well.

A curious puzzle now presents itself. If Japan is diversified and America is not, why is the Japanese economy now crumbling while America's is sizzling? Two reasons account for this discrepancy. First, Japan is not as diversified and balanced as it has been in the past; in fact, in 1998 it had the highest trade surplus in its history, which is the mark of a terribly unbalanced economy. Second, though it has adequate manufacturing, its housing sector is among the worst in the world. The U.S. lead in the construction industry, because of abundant land, is decisive. However, it is worth noting that American prosperity depends crucially on Japan's savings, which have been pouring into the United States. Japan is America's money-lender. The debtor has little cause for self-congratulations, because a debt-supported structure is inherently unstable.

BALANCE BETWEEN SUPPLY AND DEMAND

Another feature of a diversified economy is free enterprise, with supply and demand equal in most industries and at affordable prices. Similarly, at the national level, supply and demand are close to each other. The idea is to emphasize the laws of internal markets. Few nations can suppress their own markets for long. The Soviet Union tried to do it with disastrous effects for its financial system.

In a diversified economy, international trade plays a minor role, so it is principally domestic supply and demand for most goods that should be close to each other at affordable prices. Price affordability is crucial, because, in theory, every market can be in balance at some exorbitantly high price. In addition, demand and supply always appear to be equal to the amount of goods exchanged. If a thousand cars are sold, then demand and supply must be equal to one thousand. In this sense, supply and demand are equal by definition to the quantity exchanged.

How can then supply and demand ever differ? They are certainly equal at some price, but at all other prices they will be unequal. For example, suppose IBM slashes the price of its computers without increasing production. At that low price there is great demand for IBM PCs and not enough supply. In this case, demand exceeds supply at the lower price. Thus the supply-demand balance always refers to a certain price. If price at the point of balance is generally affordable, we say that the supply and demand are in equilibrium in a market, but not otherwise.

Take, for instance, the property market in Tokyo and Bombay during the 1980s, when the demand for land far exceeded its supply. As a result, the demand equaled supply at an unbelievably high price. Clearly, the land market was unbalanced at that time, because the resulting market price was far from normal. The same was true for the Tokyo stock exchange as the Nikkei index rose above thirty-eight thousand at the end of 1989. Demand for stocks far exceeded their supply, so share prices kept rising and became unaffordable to the general public. Clearly, the stock market was then in an imbalance. Affordable prices usually approximate their recent average. If the price that equates supply with demand is far above its recent average, then that market is unbalanced. European and U.S. stock exchanges are clearly out of kilter today.

For prices to be affordable, regional monopolies and mergers among large firms should not be permitted. Monopolies generate shoddy products at high prices. Similarly, the market price should not be too far below the recent average. Take, for instance, the labor market, where the demand for labor comes from companies and the supply from households and workers. The price in this market is the real wage (i.e., the inflation-adjusted salary), including the bonus. If there is unemployment in the economy, then labor demand falls short of supply at the prevailing real wage. If salaries fall enough, labor demand will rise as employers can afford to hire more workers. At the same time, some people will be discouraged by lower wages and drop out of the market. As the real wage continues to shrink, labor supply will slide to the level of rising labor demand, and unemployment will vanish. Will this market then be in balance? Not necessarily.

If the real wage falls sharply below the recent average, then the supply and demand for labor is equal only because of so many discouraged workers who quit the labor force. And if the real wage sinks in spite of rising productivity, then clearly this market is imbalanced, because common sense dictates that individuals should earn more as they become more productive. If they earn less, then evidently there is something amiss. The laws of economics must all conform to common sense.

There are two types of goods—traded and nontraded. Normally, goods and services that cannot be physically moved cannot enter into foreign trade. Land, houses, education, and haircuts are all examples of nontraded goods. Most other products can be exported or imported. They are called traded goods and services. For nontraded goods, market balance occurs when domestic supply and demand are equal at an affordable price, approximating the recent average. For traded goods, by contrast, domestic demand differs from domestic supply at a price determined in the world market. For an exported product, domestic supply exceeds local demand, so the surplus is exported. For an imported product, local supply is less than demand, so the shortfall is met through imports.

The demand for oil exceeds its supply in the United States, and the difference is imported from abroad. On the other hand, the domestic demand for airplanes is lower than production; hence, surplus planes are exported. However, at the national level the supply and demand for all goods and services are equal in a balanced economy. In a totally self-sufficient economy with no trade, national supply and demand are always equal. When trade exists, domestic demand and supply diverge for some industries, but even then overall national supply and demand are equal in a balanced economy.

National demand is the total spending on goods and services by consumers, businesses, and the government. National supply, on the other hand, is the GDP. Therefore economic balance requires that GDP equals national demand or spending. When spending and production are equal at the national level, the country's trade is in balance, that is, its exports are no less or greater than its imports. Thus a balanced economy also has balanced trade; in other words, it has neither a trade deficit nor a trade surplus in what is known as the current account. In reality, exports and imports can rarely be exactly equal. In that case, balanced trade means that exports and imports are close enough that the trade deficit or surplus is small.

TIGHT REGULATION OF THE FINANCIAL SECTOR

A balanced economy requires tight regulations on the financial sector, including banks, thrifts, brokerages, and mutual funds, so there is very little speculation in the system. Employees and officers of these industries work with other people's money, and it is easy to be reckless when your own funds are not involved. Speculation also wastes capital that is used up in creating paper profits, not real goods. Similarly, stock markets should offer vehicles only for business investment but not for gambling. Thus a balanced economy does not permit loans for any kind of speculation.

We should remember the lessons of the 1920s, when deregulation of the financial sector created a speculative bubble, which then burst open and plunged the world into a catastrophic depression. Regulations on banking and stock markets were introduced in the 1930s but were then gradually removed during the 1970s. The painful lessons of the Great Depression, under crony capitalism, were brushed aside by the generation of baby boomers. Prodded by their patrons, politicians began to dismantle financial controls in 1977 and accelerated the pace in 1979 and thereafter. In the process, many new paper assets were created to lure savings into banks and the stock and bond markets. Some of these were designed to increase thrift. Others, such as options, currency, and interest rate futures, and stock index–related investments, tempted people to gamble their savings with risky investments where the potential for profit or loss was high. This marked a return to the 1920s, where investing became synonymous with betting.

Through financial deregulation inspired by American brokers and bankers, money and credit have exploded around the planet. This, not the so-called fundamentals, spawned the global bubbles in which many countries are now trapped. Multimillionaires in America wanted to become billionaires, and they did not care if they sank the world's boat in the process. Even the S&L crisis of the mid-1980s, which came on the heels of financial deregulation, did not faze them.

America went on a deregulating spree after Ronald Reagan became president in 1981. No longer were interest rates set by the government. Banks were permitted to pay fees on checking accounts, a practice that had been outlawed in the mid-1930s. The relaxation of controls permitted fraud in the thrift industry. Many S&Ls went bankrupt, and the taxpayer was saddled with the bill that came due, since the defunct corporations were insured by the government. All in all, the country paid a hefty $200 billion for its misadventure in financial deregulation.

The acolytes of such deregulation forgot the precious lessons of the 1930s and more recently of the 1980s. They continued to peddle their own self-interest as sound economic policy, and now the global economy stands perilously on the brink of a precipice, ready to collapse any moment.

There are two types of deregulation—industrial and financial. With industrial deregulation comes the removal of controls over businesses producing goods and service. In the late seventies and early eighties, restrictions were also removed from natural gas companies and the trucking and airlines industries, raising competition in these areas. This type of deregulation sparks national productivity and is healthy for an economy. Monetary deregulation, by contrast, ignites a speculative frenzy and then a financial meltdown, culminating in a great depression.

AMERICA AND JAPAN, 1950–1998

History speaks volumes in favor of balanced economies. Both the United States and Japan were diversified from 1950 to 1970 but have become greatly unbalanced since. In the first period, they had balanced trade and balanced budgets. Foreign trade, especially in America, was small relative to other sectors. Banks and thrifts were tightly regulated to keep interest rates affordable for housing. Share markets were also restrained to avoid wild speculation.

In these circumstances, both countries enjoyed a fast rise in living standards, as real wages rose in proportion to productivity for the vast majority of workers. However, in the early 1970s, crony capitalism began to flex its muscle. The bitter and painful lessons of the 1930s were brushed aside. Obsolete ideas made a comeback in the guise of helping the poor and the middle class. Under the influence of economists and politicians patronized by megacorporations, economic policies changed. Gradually, real wages trailed productivity, budgets went into deficits, and trade became unbalanced: Japan began to develop a surplus and the United States a deficit in the balance of payment, while banks and other financial institutions were deregulated.

As policies changed in the second period, speculation grew. Real wages stagnated in Japan and sank in America, while corporate profits and executive earnings soared. Wage stagnation gave rise to two-earner families, with both husband and wife toiling to eke out a comfortable living. Consequently, children were neglected. Because harried parents had little time to instill moral values in their offspring, social degeneration abounded.

In the United States the tax burden was transferred from the rich to the rest. Thus after-tax real wages slid even more, and the rich got richer. In other words, when economies were balanced, everyone prospered, but when they became unbalanced because of rising trade, tolerance for mergers, financial deregulation, and speculation, the living standard plummeted or stagnated for the vast majority of people in both America and Japan, even though productivity continued to rise. With so much money in the hands of so few, political power gravitated even more into the hands of an oligarchy of the affluent. Under their prodding, U.S. administrations pressed foreign governments to open up their financial markets so that rich bankers and financiers could make even more money. Thus crony capitalism grew even cronier, culminating in a mountain of debt at home and abroad. Finally, the debt burden was too much for the Asian Tigers, Russia, and Latin America to handle, and the dominoes started to topple. By early 1999 these countries as well as Japan were mired in a deep slump, whereas America had become a giant casino, with gamblers throwing away their money for quick but illusory gains.

COMPENDIUM OF A BALANCED ECONOMY

We can now summarize the features of a balanced economy envisioned by Prout.

1. The economy is diversified into the three main areas—the primary, secondary, and tertiary sectors. Ideally, in an advanced economy, about 10 percent of all employees are engaged in the primary sector, 40 percent in the secondary sector, and the remaining 50 percent in the service sector, which also includes public utilities, transportation, and communications. At the very least, economic diversification requires that no less than one-third of the labor force be employed in construction and manufacturing.

2. As far as possible, the economy is guided by the laws of nature. This means that in all markets, including those for stocks, bonds, land, and real estate, supply and demand are equal at affordable prices, which flourish only under free enterprise. In other words, there should be no big jump or fall in retail prices compared to their recent average. A truly free enterprise economy is the only way to correct a market imbalance.

3. The labor market is such that real wages rise in sync with worker productivity.

4. At the societal level, the supply-demand balance requires that national spending on final goods and services equal the GDP. This means that the country's exports roughly equal its imports so that trade in the current account is neither in surplus nor in deficit.

5. The government budget is balanced annually, except during emergencies.

6. Economic growth preserves, not destroys, the quality of life. A balanced economy requires a balanced environment as

well. In other words, the country invests money in counter technologies to maintain the purity of air, water, and land.

These, then, are the features of a balanced economy. Few countries today meet these requirements, and most suffer from vast imbalances. But some are more unbalanced than others. They are all unstable, some more so than others. Until the early seventies, the world economies were much more balanced than they are today. Most of them largely satisfied the first five features of a balanced economy. Even though their environment was polluted, at least their real wages were rising. But now most countries in the G-7, Euroland, China, the Asian Tigers, Australia, Israel, South Africa, Latin America, Russia, India, and so on suffer from giant imbalances, and their living standard is either stagnant or sinking. Yes, some still enjoy positive growth in the GDP, but not in real wages. How this sorry state can be corrected is our next subject for discussion.

12

POLICIES AND REFORMS FOR A BALANCED ECONOMY

W ell-known economist Michael Kalecki writes:

The period which preceded the present economic crisis abounded in capitalist utopias. American economists in particular excelled in forecasting an everlasting era of prosperity and—what is most astonishing—themselves believed in these horoscopes. Meanwhile . . . the financial crisis had already reached its climax in the raw-materials-producing countries of South America and in Australia: a sharp fall in export prices for their products made it impossible for them to pay both the installments and the interest on their loans. This checked the inflow of new capital and even caused the outflow of old capital. . . . These storms on the peripheries of the capitalist world were only faintly felt in its center. The losses incurred in the raw-materials-producing countries were offset by gains derived from the cheapness of raw materials.[51]

This passage, which could have been written yesterday, appeared in 1931. Kalecki, a Polish titan, and a contemporary of John Maynard Keynes, the most famous economist of this century, offers blunt and concise words, but they capture the essence of the world economy today. Ever since July 1997, when the Thai baht began to crumble, commodity prices have been sinking. Oil, copper, wheat, and so on are fetching no more than what they did twenty-five years ago during the seventies. The primary producing countries of Asia and South America are feeling the heat not only from sinking prices of their exports but also from capital flight. Kalecki went on to write that "only when, after some time, the fall in raw-material prices was followed by a fall in finished-product prices did the financial crisis spread to Europe and the USA."[52]

History is repeating itself. Today we are where the world was in mid-1929, racing blissfully toward a major catastrophe. Some can feel the advance chill of the coming tornado. *Time* magazine speaks of a financial meltdown; a *New York Times* editorial worries about our confused financial experts; *The Economist* openly muses, "Could it happen again? For the past 25 years the biggest economic enemy in most countries has been inflation. Today, in most of the world, a greater danger may be deflation."[53] MIT Professor Robert Solow, a Nobel laureate, is anxious about the current state of the economy. Even Warren Buffett, one of the gurus of stock speculation, laments about today's share mania.[54]

In my mind the question is not *if,* but *when.* A stock market debacle seems to be imminent, most likely by the end of this year, though possibly delayed until 2000. It will be followed by deflationary or inflationary depression in different countries, depending on the performance of their currencies. Politicians, bankers, and economists have ignored the voices of sanity for too long. It is too late now to stop the looming cataclysm. All we can do is to minimize its aftershocks and shorten its life span. The last depression lingered in the 1930s; let's hope that this time around we can do better. We need fundamental economic reforms. Last time, a world war ended the depression. Today only fundamental reforms will be able to do the job. Financial disaster usually mirrors a vast imbalance in the economies of many nations, especially in an interdependent world. We need to abandon crony capitalism and adopt the Proutist prescription of a truly free enterprise and balanced economy. To restore global economic balance, monopolies must go.

Ever since the Second World War, governments have actively participated in the growth process, not just in socialist countries but also in capitalist democracies. The ideas needed to create a balanced economy are quite different from those currently followed by the world, which, as a result, suffers from dire income inequality, unemployment, poverty, and a dirty environment. This is not the Prout idea of growth and development. What are the policies needed to produce a balanced economy, which needs something more than just free enterprise? We have examined two such measures in the previous chapter—how to cleanse the environment and keep a tight leash on banks and speculation. The others are explored below.

HIGH COMPETITION

Competition among firms spurs them to produce high-quality goods at affordable prices. In the extreme example of a pure monopoly, the result is low-quality, overpriced goods accompanied by underpaid workers and irritated customers.

Such was the case with industry in the Soviet Union and until recently with some industries in Britain, where public utilities were pure monopolies. Phone service in India is among the worst in the world for the same reason. The opposite of monopoly is high competition, which occurs when a large number of companies populate an industry. In this case, firms vie with each other for workers and buyers, creating high wages, quality output, bargain prices, and happy customers. High competition, therefore, sparks a prosperous economy.

The main source of inequality in the world is high level of profits arising in industries with minimal competition. In general, the fewer the companies in a given industry, the lower the competition and the higher the prices and profits. Inequality is also high. High competition should be encouraged in most industries either through antimerger laws or through temporary subsidies to create new firms or both. Mergers among giant firms should never be permitted, especially where a company seeks to acquire another through borrowed funds. Even in a shrinking industry, behemoths should not be allowed, as they will stifle competition and eventually hurt consumers and workers. Sometimes a faltering company tries to find a partner in order to survive, which is reasonable and permissible if plenty of competition still remains. As a last resort, the government may aid the limping businesses temporarily with low-interest loans, to be paid back later after the borrower becomes profitable. In every industry there should be at least ten companies, which is the minimum number of firms needed to create high competition.

Although few pure monopolies exist today, there are many regional monopolies, each controlling about a third of an industry. Economic policy should ensure that no firm has more than 20 percent of an industry's market share; otherwise the government should help set up new firms or break up the regional monopolies into two or more companies. In Japan manufacturing and construction firms face tough rivals, but many service industries, such as retailing and airlines, have very little competition. Such regional monopolies should be split up or new private companies be created with official help. In the United States auto, computer, and pharmaceutical giants ought to be broken up into smaller companies.

FREE FOREIGN INVESTMENT, NOT FREE TRADE

Competition is perhaps the most vital force for lifting a country's living standard and eliminating poverty. But domestic and foreign competition have very different effects on the economy. In both cases, businesses have to respond to the challenge of rivals to survive, but the source of this challenge is as important as its incentives. Foreign competition springs from imported goods, whereas domestic competition signifies a rivalry among firms producing in your own country.

Within limits, the foreign challenge is salubrious, but it can also be predatory, especially if it comes from manufacturing concerns in low-wage countries. The best form of international competition springs from foreign companies located on your own soil. When transnational firms produce goods in your country, not only do they bring capital and new technology with them, they also create new jobs and increase the demand for local workers, raising wages in the process. However, such external investment should not be confused with the speculative inflow of capital into stock and bond markets. All types of speculation, domestic or foreign, are toxic and should be tightly controlled to prevent bubbles and the waste of capital. The best form of foreign challenge thus takes the form of direct international investment in productive firms.

By contrast, competition coming from imports or free trade can cripple an economy if it hurts manufacturing or any high-wage industry. If trade ignites deindustrialization, then foreign competition becomes destructive. One reason U.S. workers have lost out since the early seventies is the virtual annihilation of some of their old industries. The average manufacturing wage in America is almost twice that in service companies. The assault from international competitors has eliminated millions of manufacturing positions, whereas rising exports of service goods have created many service jobs. Unemployment is, of course, miniscule, but the net effect on real wages has been devastating because high-paying work has given way to low-wage occupations.

Domestic competition, however, poses no dangers. Foreign competition (i.e., free trade) can cripple a local industry, but domestic challenge will never do that. Take the case of television manufacturing, now extinct in the United States. When cheap imports flooded the American market, TV producers went bankrupt. Unemployed TV industry workers could not find similar jobs with another TV firm, because all domestic firms were shrinking. These workers had to move to service jobs at puny salaries.

But suppose domestic competition had increased in the industry because another company, regardless of nationality, had decided to produce televisions on U.S. soil. Some existing firms would have still lost ground, but laid-off workers would have found work with the new producer. The industry as a whole would not have been crippled. When manufactured imports flood a nation, high-wage jobs are created abroad, not in your own country. However, domestic competition spurs jobs, wages, and production in your own heartland.

Prout favors free foreign investment, not free foreign trade. Instead of unrestrained international commerce, Prout supports competitive protectionism or domestic competition. The idea is that a nation should diversify and produce a large output of high-wage goods so that at least a third of its workforce is employed in construction and manufacturing. High wages in these industries spark high salaries in other areas as well, because the goods-producing industry is the most dynamic and innovative sector of the economy. When manufacturing shrinks, the economy as a whole begins to stagnate, as shown by the post-1970 experience of the United States, Canada, Australia, and Great Britain. Japan does not have this problem yet, although it has other problems created by the bursting of the bubble economy. However, the deindustrializing process has started, and if it continues, Japan could also become a service economy. This could be prevented through proper policy, which is competitive protectionism.

If employment in the secondary sector shrinks below 33 percent of the labor force, then foreign competition should be restrained. Similarly, if manufacturing employment falls below 25 percent of the workforce, then manufacturing should be protected from imports. Competitive protectionism means shielding home industry from imports while maintaining high competition at home. Industries may be protected through tariffs or nontariff regulations, although tariffs are preferable because they also generate revenue for the government. It is noteworthy that the secret of postwar success in Japan, South Korea, and Taiwan is the policy of competitive protectionism.

What is the siren song of free trade that Prout opposes? Free-trade supporters underwrite the principle of comparative advantage, the idea that each country should specialize in those industries in which it has the highest labor productivity and meet its needs for other goods from imports. Thus countries like Australia and Canada should concentrate on the primary sector that includes agriculture, mining and fisheries. The United States should emphasize agriculture and services. Germany, Japan, and others should focus on manufacturing. This way, each country maximizes its productivity and the world as a whole is better off.

The weakness of this argument lies in its assumption that wages are the same in all occupations, so if an import-competing sector shrinks because of freer trade, it does not matter, because the workers so laid off will find equally lucrative jobs in an expanding export sector; with higher national productivity everyone will benefit, at least in the long run. In reality, wages differ from industry to industry. If the shrinking area generates higher wages than the expanding sector, then the country will suffer, since high-wage jobs will be replaced by low-wage jobs. This is the problem that has afflicted North America, Australia, and Britain.

Another problem with the free-trade logic stems from the self-serving behavior of the multinational corporations. When a country is inundated with cheap imports, domestic factories, unable to compete with Third World exporters, migrate abroad in search of low wages, bringing back even more of those cheap imports. Production and manufacturing jobs move overseas, while wages shrink at home. Thus one way to keep the multinational companies from moving out is to keep out imports from low-wage countries.

The acolytes of free trade respond that protectionism hurts consumers by raising the prices of imports and of the home goods competing with them. This is a bogus argument, because everyone is a worker first and a consumer second. If the real wage falls because of deindustrialization, then every consumer suffers, because the real wage by definition is already adjusted for any change in prices.

Normally wages and salaries increase every year. The fall in the real wage in modern economies usually means that wage growth falls short of price growth, so the purchasing power of salaries declines. History shows that when manufacturing employment shrinks because of cheap imports, then wages grow slower than inflation. Although free trade subdues the price surge, it subdues wage growth even more. Thus the consumer is worse off because his real wage has fallen. Any price benefit from free trade is more than offset by the negative effect on salaries.

The free-trade dogma is fragile, because it is divorced from reality. In the models of free traders, the government either lives on air that comes free or is a low-cost item. Indeed, many governments in the past managed their affairs with revenues collected from taxes on imports. For instance, prior to 1913 in the United States, the tariff revenue was as high as 70 percent of the total tax collection. Free traders, seeking to reduce or remove these tariffs, argued that an income tax not exceeding 7 percent should be enacted to replace the lost revenue.

Freer trade was introduced in America in 1913, and the income tax, as promised, was initially set below 7 percent. But by 1919 the tax rate had shot up to the level of 66 percent. However, not a single free-trade model even mentions the income levy. Tariffs are eliminated in these models, making consumers cheerful. And why not? Everybody is happy with zero taxes if the government can survive on air. But when income tax replaces tariffs, the cheer evaporates.

There are three arguments in favor of tariffs. One is that they should be introduced to shield high-wage industries from cheap imports. The second is that they can be used to replace other levies, such as the Social Security fees and income tax. The third argument was elaborated in the previous chapter. Namely, tariffs trim global commerce and transportation, and hence pollution, without hurting world production. If tariffs replace Social Security levies, then the consumer will face the same or lower tax bill. In addition, if foreign investment is unrestrained, then quality foreign goods will be produced on home soil. Consumers will not even miss the extensive choice of goods they now have. For instance, if high tariffs were imposed on car imports by all countries, then Lexus would be built in America rather than brought here from Japan. In fact, with tariffs, global production of goods will rise as resources are freed by the transportation industry for use in other sectors.

Perhaps a numerical example will illustrate the point clearly. Suppose a Lexus costs $40,000 if imported from abroad. If there is a tariff of 50 percent, then the U.S. price for the car will be $60,000, and the government collects $20,000 for each unit imported. Now suppose this tariff is removed. The U.S. price drops to $40,000, and the free trader celebrates it as a victory for the consumer. But he forgets that the government has lost its revenue and must collect it from the same consumer through another tax. How then does the tariff removal benefit the buyer? Of course, if the government can live on air, as it does in the economic models of free traders, then it is a different matter. But I have yet to find such a government.

In the real world, the tariff does not hurt the consumer, but it keeps the producer of import-competing goods happy. Removing the tariff does not benefit the consumer, but it hurts the high-wage worker. So why not keep the tariff?

The policy of competitive protectionism is thus far superior to free trade. History shows that all the advanced countries used it to get where they are today. Without protective tariffs, some of them, including the United States, would have remained agrarian economies. As suggested by the free-trade dogma, they would have concentrated on farming, because that is what they did best in the past. If the United States had followed this sermon, today it would be a superb farm economy. Imagine America's agricultural know-how placing men on the moon! Where would the country, and the free world, be today if American leaders of the nineteenth century had heeded the cries of free traders?

Prout suggests that tariffs should be used to generate a diversified economy and protect high-wage industries at home. If tariffs are not permissible because of global trade agreements, then such agreements should be replaced by accords on the taxation of foreign investment. But we have to break up industrial behemoths and make sure that there is plenty of domestic competition; otherwise the benefits of tariffs will be lost to regional monopolies.

BALANCED TRADE

If a country suffers from trade imbalance for a long time, there is something wrong with its economy. A persistent trade deficit, as we see in the United States, means that year after year the nation produces less than it consumes. A part of its total demand is then squandered on foreign products, and its potential GDP is lower than total spending by the amount of the deficit. In 1998 the United States had a trade deficit of nearly $170 billion, meaning the country imported goods and services that exceeded exports by this amount. If U.S. trade were in balance, American production would have been higher by $170 billion. Now higher production means higher demand for workers, which in turn means higher wages. Thus, with such a large trade deficit, U.S. wages were lower than they would have been if trade were balanced. Balanced trade clearly outshines deficit trade.

Balanced trade is also an improvement on surplus trade, where the country's demand is not enough to absorb its production. If exports match imports, production equals demand at home; with an export surplus, the GDP exceeds spending. Stated another way, national demand is limited relative to national supply in a trade surplus economy, or the consumers are not able to enjoy the full fruit of their labor, because the country does not have enough consumption opportunities. Something is amiss in the economy.

The living standard of a country at any moment is determined by production, but for the people it is determined by consumption. If consumption opportunities are limited, then the public is poorer to that extent. Some economists suggest that trade deficits are caused by high budget deficits. This is the well-known hypothesis of twin deficits that is supposed to highlight the U.S. experience. At present, Japan has a huge budget deficit, whereas the United States has a small surplus. Yet Japan has a trade surplus and the United States a trade deficit. Thus high budget deficits do not necessarily create trade deficits.

Countries where manufacturing has shrunk because of the deluge of cheap imports are the same countries that suffer from chronic deficits in trade. America, Canada, Australia, and Britain come to mind. These nations mostly export low-value products, such as food, raw materials, and services, and import high-priced items, such as cars, TVs, cameras, appliances, electrical machinery, and so on. This way, the value of their exports rarely covers the cost of imports.

Such is the importance of manufacturing that trade-surplus nations—Japan, Taiwan, Singapore, and Germany—are mostly exporters of manufactured goods. Protectionist policies, such as tariffs and import regulations, that diversify an economy also reduce trade deficits, because the country does not need to import high-priced manufactures. Similarly, a trade surplus can be eliminated by taxes on its exports. Of course, this policy will have to be combined with other measures to create domestic demand and thus an overall balance in the economy. In combating trade surplus, however, export taxes are superior to a revaluation of one's own currency. Similarly, in eliminating the trade deficit, tariffs work better than currency devaluation. In both cases, a country can raise large amounts of revenue that can be used to balance the government budget or cut other taxes.

BALANCED BUDGET

As far as possible, the government should not spend more than it earns in tax revenue. In other words, Prout favors a balanced budget policy. Budget deficits should be adopted only during emergencies, such as wars, depressions, or natural disasters. A Proutist system, being diversified, is a stable economy. It can absorb much greater shocks than modern specialized, and therefore unbalanced, economies, which constantly need red ink to maintain high employment. Almost all governments in the world today have high budget deficits and debts that will be paid by posterity. I have yet to find another generation in the history of civilization that imposed a crippling burden on its children in order to enjoy the good life for itself.

As I indicated earlier, recessions or depressions are created by a growing wage gap and speculative manias, which are unlikely to plague a balanced economy. Therefore budget deficits, which countries normally use to fight economic slumps, are unnecessary in balanced economies.

Canada and the United States are two countries that used large deficits to combat unemployment in the 1980s. Their actions have now caught up with them, as they find themselves burdened by a huge interest expense to service their debt. Money that used to invigorate education and health care now goes to the government's lenders. Prout's motto is simple: A balanced economy has a balanced budget.

AFFORDABLE HOUSING

In a balanced economy, national production and consumption are roughly equal, resulting in trade equilibrium. In advanced countries, where most people already own modern gadgets and appliances, home ownership is a major source of new consumption. When people own homes, they normally buy many other things, such as furniture, refrigerators, dishwashers, carpets, paintings, and other household items as well. Home ownership is a tonic that multiplies consumption and raises the level of national demand. For this reason, the government should make housing affordable. Home ownership, an end in itself, has wonderful tributaries, creating responsible citizens and easing life after retirement.

To make housing affordable, the long-term interest rate should be kept low, enabling people to get low-cost mortgages. Another helpful measure is the grant of tax benefits for home ownership, as we have seen in the United States since the war. Home owners may deduct their mortgage expenses, property taxes, and a percentage of mortgage interest from their taxable income. This policy effectively subsidizes the interest expense of buying a house. At other times, the government has offered an income-tax credit to induce people to buy new houses. These are all salutary policies.

In order to create an environment for low long-term interest rates, inflation must be kept under leash. This can be easily accomplished in a balanced economy, where no deficit financing is needed to meet a budget shortfall. Inflation is usually a monetary phenomenon. Therefore, if the central bank keeps a tight lid on the money mint, prices remain in check. Prout favors anti-inflationary monetary policies.

To keep housing affordable, people's credit needs have to be met. Such needs should not be financed by excessive creation of money, instead, the mortgage funds should come from savings deposited with banks. Thus bank funds should be used only for productive purposes, such as the purchase of homes and other durable goods, like cars, and appliances. Banks should not be permitted to finance speculative activities, including the purchase of stocks, bonds, gold, giant companies, and so on. At the same time, their interest costs should be kept low, enabling them to lend money at affordable rates. For this purpose, banks should not have to pay interest rates on checking accounts from which the depositor can withdraw funds at any time. Of course, savings accounts and CDs should pay market rates.

History shows that whenever financial deregulation induced banks to pay interest on checking accounts, speculative bubbles in stock and real estate markets soon followed. As their costs climbed, banks were forced into risky ventures to earn a higher return. The strategy succeeded for a while but ended in disaster since speculative bubbles always burst in the end. This is what transpired in the 1920s in the United States and in Japan between 1985 and 1990, when the bubble economy imploded into an enduring slump.

In order to create a healthy economy, the behavior of banks should be tightly controlled, but at the same time their interest expense should be kept low. The result will be a noninflationary, full-employment economy, with long-term mortgage rates no higher than 5 or 6 percent. Such low rates are a great boon to housing. For affordable housing, it is also important that the property market is in balance so that land prices are stable. If banks are not permitted to make speculative loans for real estate, then land prices remain under control. Speculation here means purchasing vast tracts of land solely for resale, not for housing or farming.

ECONOMIC DEMOCRACY

Modern factories are usually run by shareholders who own a large percentage of a company's shares. Such a shareholder is usually appointed CEO. The CEO hires a group of executives who in turn hire professional and other workers. There are two groups of employees in a company—management and laborers.

These groups can have diametrically opposite interests. Management wants maximum effort from employees and pays the going wage dictated by the labor market. If the market is tight—that is, if qualified workers are not easily available—then they receive a salary commensurate with their qualifications and productivity. However, if unemployment is high and/or workers are easily available, productivity considerations are set aside, and the employee is usually paid less than his contribution to the company.

When it comes to managerial salaries, labor market tightness usually does not matter. CEOs are normally in a position to determine their own pay, which they want to be as high as possible without upsetting the corporate directors. To justify high self-remuneration, company chiefs normally pay high wages to other managers. The CEO also determines the salary of directors, who in turn approve the CEO's salary. Management incomes tend to be so high, then, because each party sets a lucrative salary for the other in mutual self-interest. No wonder then, the maximum wage in the United States is more than two thousand times the minimum wage. According to the *New York Times,* the financial services giant Citigroup paid over $25 million in salary, bonus, and stock options to each of its two top executives in 1999, after the company showed a decline in its profits from the previous year.[55] Since the annual minimum annual wage is about $10,000, the executives' pay was more than twenty-five hundred times the minimum wage. Who knows what the top officers would have been paid if the company profits had actually risen?

Outlandish corporate salaries in America used to raise people's eyebrows in the early 1990s, when employee downsizing was at its zenith. Since then the practice has become commonplace. CEOs now make more even when their companies lose money, or when they are fired, they receive a hefty severance package. Nowhere else in the world are the wage differentials so extreme. In Japan, the income disparity is much smaller. There the average CEO earns about twenty-five times the minimum salary. As we have seen, it is possible for national productivity to rise while wages decline or remain constant. Workers in the United States have lost 25 percent of their purchasing power since 1972, while average CEO pay and perks have more than tripled—all this in spite of rising labor productivity. Such pervasive inequalities lead to insufficient product demand, forcing the government to resort to budget deficits that raise total spending and waste resources.

In order to create an efficient and fair system, Prout proposes that economic democracy supplement the free-enterprise framework resulting from high competition. In this system, company workers own the majority of shares. Management is still in the hands of experts and professionals, but the board of directors is answerable to employees, not outside shareholders. In fact, the board consists mainly of representatives elected by the workers. Such a board is not likely to approve of any policies that increase the chasm between labor productivity and wages.

Because of the democratic nature of this structure, the gap between worker and management salaries is likely to be small. Inherent in democracy is the presumption that inequalities are low. In the United States the president earns $200,000 a year. He has perks similar to those of CEOs, but he earns ten to a hundred times less than what some company officers make. This is because there is democracy in politics, but autocracy in the corporations. Why else would top executives earn huge bonuses even when their company's profitability plunges?

Not only is economic democracy fair, it is also far more productive. When workers own the factory, they are loyal to it and work very hard, knowing that their effort will be rewarded. Wages would also be higher, although management salaries would be lower. Each employee would be paid a certain wage and a year-end bonus, depending on his efficiency and company profits. The same formula would apply to management salaries as well.

In this scenario, note that companies are still run by experts, so productive efficiency will be at least as high as before. In reality, with employee ownership of the majority shares, productivity will be higher. Another advantage of economic democracy is that unemployment is likely to be low. It is normal for all economies to go through ups and downs, but the ups and downs of capitalism occasionally get out of control and produce major inflation or depressions, culminating in high unemployment and despair.

When people are laid off today, official spending rises to feed the unemployed. The government in turn raises taxes to finance unemployment compensation, so the employed end up supporting the unemployed. Under economic democracy, no hardworking person would be laid off, because all employees jointly own the company or at least its majority shares. If business slows down, then working hours and wages would be reduced for all. This way, everybody would share the pain, and no one would have to suffer the psychological trauma of being unemployed.

The current system is wasteful and debilitating for the jobless. In an economic downturn, even today, the employed assist the unemployed through higher taxes. The pain is shared even in the current system, although not equally, but there is a middleman collecting taxes to aid the jobless. This function will be unnecessary under economic democracy. There will be neither wasted resources nor the stigma of being unemployed.

Economic democracies require no deficit financing by the government to maintain high production, which in turn needs high demand or consumption. When inequality is low, consumption tends to be large, and when inequality rises, consumer spending falls, because the rich are able to save a lot more than the poor. Once a person's major needs are satisfied, a further rise in income goes mostly into savings. Hence, when a few become affluent and income disparity grows, consumer spending falls. Production then suffers, because companies lose money if they can't sell their goods. To boost spending, the government steps in, borrowing money from the wealthy and spending it on goods and services. This is an artificial prop to the economy, and its cumulative effect is a mountain of government debt. That is why whenever inequality is high, or asset markets for land and stocks are in imbalance, government debt soars. Such is the case in Italy, Canada, America, Japan, Australia, and elsewhere.

With economic democracy, inequality is automatically low, so consumption and national demand are large. The government has no need to introduce its own consumption spending to support high output and employment. The system is inherently stable. In the United States, with one of the highest levels of inequality in the world, the government debt is now so high that the official interest expense alone exceeds federal borrowing from the affluent. The wealthy receive more in interest from their Treasury bonds than the government borrows from them. As a result, the state has to reduce its spending on pivotal programs like education and law enforcement. The overall effect on demand, production, and wages is negative, while debt continues to be high. Such is the ultimate curse of inequality.

When wages rise in sync with productivity, both the GDP and real wages grow apace, because consumer demand then keeps up with supply. With producers assured of a growing market, business investment also expands rapidly; so does new technology, as well as counter technology, which in turn ignites high productivity growth and real wages without defiling the environment. In economic democracy, workers and hence consumers are in a win-win position, and stock markets and speculative euphorias are mercifully subdued. A democratic economy is innately a high-growth and low-inequality economy.

Economic democracy is practical only in large companies, such as Microsoft, AT&T, Toyota, Sony, IBM, Mercedes-Benz, and so on. In big firms, at least 51 percent of the shares should be in the hands of employees, while the rest may be owned by outsiders. The majority of the board of directors will then consist of employees or their representatives. Medium-sized firms may also operate in this way.

In small companies, though, this system may or may not be practical. Businesses with less than a thousand employees may be individually owned or run as cooperatives, where shares may or may not belong to the employees. There are many consumer co-ops in Japan, especially in Tokyo and Osaka. Members join them by investing in them, whereas in large companies employees need not invest money to become part owners. Once a worker has finished a period of probation of, say, three to five years, he or she should automatically become a part owner of a large company. In a consumer co-op, on the other hand, some investment is necessary. Otherwise, co-ops are run on the same democratic principles as medium and large companies.

Governments must be committed to creating economic democracy, just as they once had to change to bring about political democracy. The federal government could do this by targeting a major firm in any industry, buying 51 percent of its shares in the stock market, and then selling them at subsidized rates to the firm's employees.

The workers could buy the shares in installments; that is, a small fraction of their salary could be deducted every month to pay for their shares. A model is then created in each industry. Once the model firm reveals its natural superiority in terms of efficiency, employee morale, and wages, other companies in that industry will follow suit and sell out to the employees. Alternatively, the government could use its tax revenue to buy shares from many firms and convert the entire industry into a democratic setup. This way, one by one economic democracy will spread to all the large and medium corporations.

There is no need for unions in democratic companies because workers are majority owners themselves. Every employee would be paid a need-based minimum wage plus a premium, depending on education, experience, and skill, as well as a year-end bonus in proportion to profit. Hard work, innovation, and intelligence would be rewarded with extra bonuses, whereas laziness, dishonesty, and inefficiency would be penalized through the loss of bonus, and, as a last resort, the loss of job. In the rare case of job loss, the company would buy back the worker's shares at the market price.

Some people confuse worker management and ownership with socialism. The system is more like mass capitalism, because shares of Fortune 500 corporations would be majority owned by a vast number of people. Unlike socialism, in an economic democracy the state is not engaged in the production of goods and services. Once the new system is established, government intervention in the economy would be minimal.

Some prototypes of employee-managed enterprises already exist today. Among the most successful worker-owned or -managed firms is United Airlines, with ninety-one thousand employees worldwide. It is the largest airline in the world. Hundreds and thousands of companies have downsized their workforces during the 1990s—not United Airlines. Another employee-owned enterprise with no history of downsizing is Science Applications International Corporation. With thirty-five thousand employees, it is among the largest of environmental concerns in the United States. Other notable firms are Wardell Braiding Machine Company, Colburn Insurance Service, Bookpeople, and TIC. In Canada TEUCU is a fast-growing employee-owned credit union. In the coming inflationary depression, such companies will survive better than traditional companies and pave the way for the formation of others like them. Nothing succeeds like success.

THE MINIMUM WAGE

Prout asserts that everyone's wage rate should be such that he or she can at least afford the basic needs of life—food, clothing, housing, education, and health care. This means the government should set a minimum wage high enough to make necessities affordable to every employee with an average family of three, including the earner and two dependents.

Take, for instance, the United States, where the minimum wage is $5.15 per hour. At this rate, for full-time work of forty hours per week, or two thousand hours per year, with a two-week vacation, the annual salary comes to $10,300. About ten million people in America earn a minimum wage or have their pay tied to it. Their families are minimum-wage households. The official poverty line for a three-person family begins at about $12,900. That is to say, the basic needs of life, as defined by the government, require an annual income of $13,000 in rounded figures. According to Prout, the minimum wage should then be $6.50 per hour, about where it was in the mid-1960s. Prout recommends a need-based minimum wage, rather than an arbitrary one.

Once workers are paid at least the need-based wage, the government would not have to spend much to alleviate poverty. Welfare spending would then plummet and be needed only for the unemployed and those who are physically or mentally unable to work. Of course, the economic system should be able to provide jobs to all those willing and able to work. Economists today suggest that if the minimum wage is set at a high level, there will be a lot of unemployment, especially among teenagers and unskilled workers. There is no empirical support for this view. Economic data, both from the United States and Japan, suggest that when income inequality is low, growth and employment are high. In addition, the system is more efficient because the government does not have to collect taxes to subsidize the poor and eliminate poverty. The public sector is smaller to that extent. By contrast, a low minimum wage contributes to high income inequality, which in turn contributes to joblessness. For example, the 1960s had the highest minimum wage in U.S. history, yet the decade ended at one of the lowest rates of unemployment, 3.5 percent. During the 1990s, the minimum wage has been raised periodically, but job losses have steadily dwindled. A need-based minimum salary is thus the lifeblood of a stable and balanced economy.

Throughout history, the ax of exploitation has fallen the hardest on the physical worker. This was true in all civilizations in the past and is true today. The reason is that of all workers, physical laborers have the least marketable skills. Yet their toil is indispensable to the survival of society. They perform jobs considered menial and hazardous by others. They truly need and deserve a helping hand from the state. The government should fix a minimum-wage rate high enough to enable the relatively unskilled workers to satisfy their minimum requirements. There are minimum-wage laws in many democratic countries. But many such wages are too low to make much of a dent in the poverty of physical workers. Prout's minimum wage, however, would be high enough to ensure that everyone can meet their basic needs.

Prout's need-based minimum wage will ensure that poverty is eliminated today. But what about tomorrow? What if prices go up sharply or if national productivity rises due to advanced technology?

In order to ensure that inequality and the resulting devastation remain under control over time Prout favors a linkage between the minimum wage and per-capita GDP at current prices. The idea is that if prices rise or national productivity climbs so that the GDP per person goes up, then basic pay should also increase to that extent. When the purchasing power of minimum wage falls, real wages tumble for millions of people, since minimum pay serves as a floor for the salaries of most production workers. This is why it is not surprising that as the inflation-adjusted basic wage sank in the 1980s, so did the average real wage for as many as a hundred million Americans. During the eighties, the minimum wage remained stuck at $3.35 per hour, while prices jumped 40 percent. The economy grew year after year, the stock market soared, Congressional salaries doubled, but the government could not bring itself to raise the minimum pay. Thus the purchasing power of the lowest salary in America plummeted by the increase in the cost of living, that is, by 40 percent. This is ultimately self-destructive. If the minimum wage were to keep pace with inflation and productivity growth, then real wages for all workers would likely rise in sync with national productivity, thereby generating a balanced economy. Need-based minimum pay is central to the Proutist economy.

A SMALL PUBLIC SECTOR

The public sector should be as small as possible, because big government means heavy taxation and a large bureaucracy. When the state utilizes capital and labor to manage society, it takes resources away from the private sector. Private production declines with the expansion of the bureaucracy. Therefore, big government normally means a lower real GDP, unless the economy is in recession and there are unemployed resources that can be absorbed by the state without lowering private production.

Large bureaucracies are also associated with heavy corruption. Prout favors a small government and, hence, light taxation. In an economic democracy, there is minimal risk of layoffs, so the government does not need to collect taxes for unemployment compensation. Nor does it need to boost spending to raise demand, because in a low-inequality economy with affordable housing there is no shortage of consumer spending.

The government's main functions should be the provision of defense, internal security through police, care for the elderly and the handicapped, free education, and, if possible, free basic health care. Economic functions of the government should be limited to maintaining high domestic competition and low inequality, for high disparity means an unhealthy economy with high budget deficits and public debt.

In an economy with a need-based minimum wage, welfare spending is likely to be low. People are usually attracted to the government dole when the private sector offers a low wage, but if the basic wage is sufficient to buy life's necessities, then living on welfare has little charm. For this reason, welfare benefits should be kept much lower than the minimum wage, except for those who are incapable of working. Those who cannot work should be paid the basic wage in addition to any help they may receive from private charities and their relatives.

The government should offer a social insurance program for the elderly, but the revenue so collected should never be used to finance other projects. Social Security taxes should be deposited in a trust fund that is managed by a government agency in the interest of the taxpayer. A real problem has arisen in the United States and Japan whereby hefty Social Security taxes have been imposed supposedly to pay for future benefits. In reality, these revenues have been used up for financing budget deficits, so little is left in the Social Security fund. Bluntly stated, there has been a massive fraud in the United States and Japan. Politicians promised that high taxes would be used to create a social insurance surplus; instead this revenue has been squandered on government consumption to fight unemployment. Such are the woes of unbalanced economies.

The government should provide free education up to the Bachelor of Arts degree, ensuring an equality of opportunity for everybody. In today's world, learning is the key to success and should not be denied to the needy. Lack of education breeds crime and wastes human potential. To harness society's intellectual resources, education should be free to all in public schools, colleges, and universities. Private education should be welcomed as a supplement for individuals who wish to use their own resources. Free education was the real key to the miracle economies of Germany, Japan, and Korea. In the United States, although education is heavily subsidized by state and federal governments, a large number of students must go into debt to finish college. College tuition has been soaring in recent years, placing a real burden on finances of the middle class. This can be changed by substantially increasing federal funding. Whatever money is now spent annually on student loans should be disbursed to needy and deserving pupils as scholarships. Government spending will rise slightly, but in a balanced economy, it could be easily financed by growing revenues.

If at all possible, basic health care should also be free to the public, as it is in Britain, Canada, and France. At the very least, health insurance should be managed by the government, not by private corporations, which operate for their own profits and not in the best interests of patients, doctors, and hospitals. Since health care is a necessity, the profit motive should be reined as far as possible when managing its provision.

Private health insurance has created a crisis in the United States. Doctors, medicines, and hospitals are so expensive that almost 14 percent of the GDP goes into health care alone, compared to 6 percent in Japan and 10 percent in Canada. Of $1.3 trillion spent annually on the health needs in America, more than $100 billion goes to insurance companies, whose CEOs earn millions in salaries. At the same time, nearly forty million Americans have no health insurance at all. If the middleman were eliminated, the government could manage the medicare industry and offer free insurance to the poor with no addition to medical costs. Thus, there are five main tasks for the government—defense, law and order, education, health care, and supervision of the economy. Other tasks performed by modern governments, including unemployment compensation and welfare, are likely to be minimal in a Proutist economy. Therefore the overall tax burden and resource wastage will also be minimal.

REFORMS IN JAPAN AND THE ASIAN TIGERS

The policies and reforms suggested here and before apply to all nations and regions. For Japan and the Asian Tigers, some other initiatives are also desirable. Asian woes stem mostly from insufficient demand, which forces them to send their production to foreign countries, which in turn have to accept huge trade deficits. Trade imbalances eventually cause havoc in all economies.

Rising domestic demand in Asia will solve many problems in the world. One of the best ways to stimulate the demand is to promote housing and construction. The U.S. government has occasionally offered housing tax credits to fight recessions with great success, and high consumption in America results chiefly from the availability of affordable housing. According to the Housing Loan Corporation of Japan, home owners spend five times as much money on appliances in the first year of home purchase as the average worker. Even though house prices continue to fall in Japan, they are still too high for most people, especially when they lack confidence in the economy.

If the government were to offer an income-tax credit of 10 percent on the purchase of a new home only for the three years between 2000 to 2003, this could serve as a healthy stimulus. Let us say the cost of a new home is $50,000. Ten percent of this figure is $5,000, which is then the tax savings to a new home owner against his income-tax bill. At the end of the year, the proud buyer of a new house can present his receipt to the government and claim his tax refund. All the Asian economies should adopt the housing tax credit to stimulate home demand.

There is an additional problem in Japan that may not affect others. Home ownership in the country is high, but the average home size is very small. The typical Japanese housewife has little space left at home to buy and store any more products. The government can drastically lower interest rates and taxes, even give large handouts to the public, but it won't have much impact on domestic demand because of the space constraint. Where are the people going to store new products in their already stuffed residences?

It is because of such small homes that all the government policies to stimulate the economy have been abortive so far. The state has funneled more than $1 trillion into public works projects to jump-start the economy, but with no success. Instead of building roads, bridges, and airports, the government should build high apartment towers with large suites in accordance with Hong Kong and Singapore. Once the space constraint in Japanese housing is lifted, the public will quickly respond by expanding its consumption—filling the additional space with new furniture, rugs, and appliances. The reason the Japanese have copious savings is that because of their restricted space, they are unable to buy bulky items or durable goods. The prescription is very simple. Let the government and private construction companies build large high-rise apartments, and the people will buy plenty of goods, raising national demand in the process. This solution has already proven effective in Hong Kong and Singapore.

Some economists, such as Paul Krugman of MIT, John Makin of the American Enterprise Institute, and Nouriel Roubini of New York University, have carefully explored Japan's continuing dilemma, and offered a variety of remedies. Krugman and Makin blame the Japanese malaise on what is technically known as a liquidity trap, where a country's monetary policy becomes totally ineffective, but fiscal expansion is supposed to be very effective.[56] They suggest that the Bank of Japan create expectations of future inflation by printing oodles of money. The idea is that when people expect prices to rise they will rush to buy goods today rather than in the future, raising current domestic demand. However, this prescription has two problems. First, the Bank of Japan has been pumping vast quantities of money into the banking system since 1997, but prices continue to fall, thus perpetuating a deflationary rather than an inflationary environment. Second, even if inflationary expectations can be generated, a very big if, where are the Japanese going to store their extra purchases? Their homes, already stuffed to the hilt, are extremely small.

The liquidity trap argument is also somewhat misleading, because the conventional remedy associated with it, namely fiscal expansion through massive budget deficits, has miserably failed in Japan. The country is caught not in a depression-style liquidity trap but in a housing trap, and only fiscal expansion designed to ease this bottleneck can now help. Once the housing constraint is lifted, monetary stimulus or policy will also start working.

By contrast, Roubini, as well as Makin, recommend structural reforms such as bank bailouts, deregulation of industry and finance, changing corporate accounting practices, labor downsizing, and so on. It is hard to understand how such remedies will generate additional demand; they are designed to work from the side of supply, and if they succeed in their avowed objective of improving productive efficiency, they will exacerbate the problem of excess supply or over production. Only demand-oriented reforms and Proutist policies offered here will do the job.

CONCLUSION

Crony capitalism is about to go the way of Soviet communism, producing a few years of turmoil in its wake. Unfortunately, the giddy optimism of today will soon give way to the agony of despair. It will seem to be endless, but you should remember that nothing, not even a nightmare, lasts forever. Greatness in society springs from the abyss of human spirit. It is for us to call on our congressmen and senators to push through the above-mentioned reforms, thereby turning adversity into a blessing.

Among the intensely dark clouds on the horizon, there is at least one silver lining—and that is Prout. Once Prout comes into being, there will be a worldwide golden age, and few will mourn the demise of the age of acquisitors in vogue today. Natural evolution ensures that every new system dwarfs the one it replaces. Prout will surpass everything the world has seen so far, starting a new era of peace, harmony, and prosperity for all. Let's hope the freshness of the new system will outlast the new millennium. The words of Prout's author Prabhat Ranjan Sarkar brim with supreme optimism:

> Just as the advent of the purple dawn is inevitable at the end of the cimmerian darkness of the interlunar light, exactly the same way I know that a gloriously brilliant chapter will also come after the endless reproach and humiliation of the neglected humanity of today.
>
> Those who love humanity, those who desire the welfare of the living beings should be vigorously active from this very moment after shaking off all lethargy and sloth so that the most auspicious hour arrives at the earliest.[57]

As Sarkar promises us, the advent of Prout in the near future, and an effulgent new epoch in the coming millennium, are simply inevitable.

NOTES

1. See, for instance, Ravi Batra, *The Great American Deception* (New York: John Wiley and Sons, 1996), chap. 1.
2. There are several books about the Great Depression. One of the best is from James West Davidson, W. Gienapp, C. Heyrman, M. Lytle, and M. Stoff, *Nation of Nations: A Narrative History of the American Republic* (New York: McGraw-Hill, 1990).
3. Edward M. Burns and L. Ralph, *World Civilizations* (New York: W. W. Norton, 1974), 1219.
4. Norman A. Graebner, G. Fite, and P. White, *A History of the American People* (New York: McGraw-Hill, 1975), 835.
5. Louis A. Perez, *Cuba: Between Reform and Revolution* (New York: Oxford University Press, 1995).
6. *Time,* "The Mystic Who Lit the Fires of Hatred," 7 January, 1980, 12.
7. The money growth data can be obtained from Ravi Batra, *The Great Depression of 1990* (New York: Simon & Schuster, 1987), and *Economic Report of the President* (Washington D.C.: U.S. Council of Economic Advisers, February 1999). Look for the figures on M2, a measure of money supply, in the *Economic Report of the President,* 407.
8. The inflation data sources are the same as those in note 7 above.
9. Cf. John Galbraith, *The World Economy since the Wars: A Personal View* (Boston: Houghton Mifflin, 1994), 210; David Levy, "1990s: A Contained Depression," *Challenge,* July–August 1991, 35–42; Lawrence Hunter, "The Never-Ending Recession," *Wall Street Journal,* 14 September, 1991,

A14; as quoted in the *New York Times,* on April 16, 1996, Senator Kennedy said to the Senate, "The 'quiet depression' facing American workers is the central economic, social and political issue of 1996. When the economy is wrong, nothing else is right" (A10).

10. *Time,* "Why Are We so Gloomy," 13 January 1992, 34.

11. The *Economic Report of the President,* February 1998, 320.

12. Jason DeParle, "Class Is No Longer a Four-Letter Word," *New York Times Magazine,* 17 March 1996, 41.

13. Cf. Bob Herbert, "Bogeyman Economics," *New York Times,* 4 April 1997, A15.

14. A company has other costs as well, especially the expense of raw materials and offices. But raw materials and offices are also produced with the help of labor and capital. Therefore, for the economy as a whole, only two groups, capitalists and workers, mostly share in the national pie. Landowners and farmers also contribute to the GDP, but their share is just 3 percent of U.S. output, and can be ignored for the sake of simplicity.

15. For expressing this view see economists Takafoshi Ito, *The Japanese Economy* (Cambridge, Mass.: MIT Press, 1992); and Takafusa Nakamura, *The Postwar Japanese Economy,* 2d (Tokyo: Tokyo University Press, 1995).

16. See Associated Press as reported in the *Dallas Morning News,* 25 February 1999, H1.

17. Michael E. Porter, *Competitive Advantage of Nations* (New York: The Free Press, 1990), 401.

18. Walter Russell Mead, *The Low-Wage Challenge to Global Growth* (Washington D.C.: Economic Policy Institute, 1990), 16.

19. John Moroney, "What do you mean you haven't made millennial plans yet?" *Forbes FYI,* Winter 1998, 93.

20. Chris Taylor, "Y2K: The History and the Hype," *Time,* 18 January 1999, 72.

21. Jim Lord, *A Survival Guide for the Year 2000 Problem* (Phoenix: J. Marion, 1997).

22. Barnaby Feder and Andrew Pollack, "Computers and 2000: Race for Security," *New York Times,* 27 December 1998, 1.

23. Richard Lacoyo, "The End of the World As We Know It," *Time,* 18 January 1999, 60.

24. Jane Quinn, "Help! Y2K Is on the Way," *Newsweek,* 18 January 1999, 46.

25. Quoted in Barnaby Feder and Andrew Pollack, "Computers and 2000: Race for Security," *New York Times,* 27 December 1998, 19.

26. Richard Lacoyo, "The End of the World As We Know It," *Time,* 18 January 1999, 62–64.

27. Quoted in Charles Kindleberger, *Manias, Panics and Crashes* (New York: Basic Books, 1978), 34.

28. James Cramer and Michael Serrill, "Catching Asian Flu," *Time,* 3 November 1997, 44.

29. Ravi Batra, *Stock Market Crashes of 1998 and 1999: The Asian Crisis and Your Future* (Dallas: Liberty Press, 1997), 155–58.

30. Joshua Cooper Ramo, "The Three Marketeers," *Time,* 15 February 1999, 35–36.

31. Kenneth Klee and Rich Thomas, "The Party Rolls On," *Newsweek,* 28 December 1998, 74.

32. Paul Krugman, "Should the Fed Care about Stock Bubbles?" *Fortune,* 1 March 1999, 36.

33. Louis Uchitelle, "Sky-High Stocks Breed Debt, Sowing the Seeds of a Slump," *New York Times,* 14 February 1999, BU4.

34. David Sanger, "From Trust Busters to Trust Trusters," *New York Times,* 6 December 1998, 18.

35. Nicholas Kristof and David Sanger, "How U.S. Wooed Asia to Let Cash Flow In," *New York Times,* 16 February 1999, 1.

36. Ravi Batra, *The Great American Deception,* 262.

37. P. R. Sarkar, *Human Society, Part 2* (Calcutta: A. M. Press, 1967).

38. Ravi Batra, *The Downfall of Capitalism and Communism;* see also Ravi Batra, *Stock Market Crashes of 1998 and 1999,* chaps. 1 and 6.

39. Louis Uchitelle, "A Surplus Built on Bricks of Income Inequality," *New York Times,* 28 February 1999, 3, 4.

40. Suze Orman, *The Nine Steps to Financial Freedom* (New York: Crown, 1998), 133.

41. Ibid., 135.

42. Douglas Franz and Peter Truell, "Long-Term Capital: A Case of Markets over Minds," *New York Times,* 11 October 1998.

43. *Business Week,* "Fighting to Survive," 8 February 1999, 72.

44. Charles Schwab, *Guide to Financial Independence* (New York: Three Rivers Press, 1998); Jordan Goodman, *Everyone's Money Guide* (Chicago: Dearborn Financial Publishing, 1998).

45. James Cook, *The Start-up Entrepreneur* (New York: Harper and Row, 1986), 236.

46. Leon Wortman, *Small Business Management* (New York: American Management Association, 1970), 24.

47. P. R. Sarkar, *Prout in a Nutshell: 1–20* (Calcutta: Orient Press, 1988).

48. Jane Gross, "Missing Lesson in Computer Class: Avoiding Injury," *New York Times,* 15 March 1999, 1.

49. Ibid.

50. For further discussion of these issues, see Ravi Batra, *The Myth of Free Trade* (New York: Macmillan, 1993), chap. 11; Batra, *The Great American Depression,* chap. 12; and Batra, *Stock Market Crashes of 1998 and 1999,* chap. 7.

51. See Jerzy Osiatynski, *Collected Works of Michael Kalecki,* Vol. 1 (New York: Oxford University Press, 1990), 37.

52. Ibid.

53. *New York Times,* "Global Market's Lethal Magic," 21 February 1999, 14; *The Economist,* "Could it Happen Again," 20 February 1999, 19; Paul Krugman, "Can Deflation be Prevented," web.mit.edu, 21 February 1999, 1.

54. See Louis Uchitelle, "The Stronger It Gets, the Sweatier the Palms," *New York Times,* 21 March 1999, 4, 1, for views by Solow and Buffett.

55. Timothy O'Brien, "Handsome Pay for the Co-Chairmen of Citigroup," *New York Times,* 9 March 1999, C 1.

56. Paul Krugman, "Japan's Trap," web.mit.edu; the articles by Nouriel Roubini, "Japan's Economic Crisis," and John Makin, "Japan's Disastrous Keynesian Experiment," can also be accessed from Krugman's article on his web site.

57. P. R. Sarkar, *Ananda Vanii* (Quotes of Joy) (Mexico City: ERU Press, 1991), 60.

INDEX